GW01019140

Enhance Your Thinking Skills

MINDPOWER
JOURNEY THROUGH THE MIND AND BODY
COOKERY AROUND THE WORLD
LOST CIVILIZATIONS
THE ILLUSTRATED LIBRARY OF THE EARTH
SYSTEM EARTH
LIBRARY OF CURIOUS AND UNUSUAL FACTS
BUILDING BLOCKS
A CHILD'S FIRST LIBRARY OF LEARNING
VOYAGE THROUGH THE UNIVERSE
THE THIRD REICH
MYSTERIES OF THE UNKNOWN
TIME-LIFE HISTORY OF THE WORLD
FITNESS, HEALTH & NUTRITION
HEALTHY HOME COOKING
UNDERSTANDING COMPUTERS
THE ENCHANTED WORLD
LIBRARY OF NATIONS
PLANET EARTH
THE GOOD COOK
THE WORLD'S WILD PLACES

M Í N D P O W E R

Enhance Your Thinking Skills

TIME-LIFE BOOKS
Amsterdam

MINDPOWER

Created, edited, and designed by DK Direct Limited,
62-65 Chandos Place, London WC2N 4HS

A DORLING KINDERSLEY BOOK

DK DIRECT LIMITED

Series Editor Luci Collings
Deputy Series Editor Sue Leonard
Senior Editor Lee Stacy
Project Editor Sue George
Editors Francesca Baines, Ann Kay

Managing Art Editor Ruth Shane
Designers Luke Herriott, Becky Willis
Additional Design Tanya Mukherjee

Publisher Jonathan Reed
Editorial Director Reg Grant
Design Director Tony Foo
Production Manager Ian Paton

Editorial Consultants Keren Smedley and Denis Sartain
Contributors Vida Adamoli, Terry Burrows, Luci Collings,
Tim Cooke, Ann Kay, Christine Murdock,
Margaret Popper, Kate Swainson

Editorial Researcher L. Brooke
Indexer Ella Skene

TIME-LIFE BOOKS EUROPEAN EDITION
Staff for Enhance Your Thinking Skills
Editorial Manager Christine Noble
Editorial Assistant Mark Stephenson
Design Director Mary Staples
Designer Dawn McGinn
Editorial Production Justina Cox
European edition edited by Tim Cooke

First Time-Life European English language edition 1996
ISBN 0 7054 1636 4
TIME-LIFE is a trademark of Time-Warner Inc., U.S.A.

Printed by GEA, Milan, and bound by GEP, Cremona, Italy

30 29 28 27 26 25 24 23 22 21 20 19 18 17 16 15 14 13 12 11 10 9 8 7 6 5 4 3 2 1

CONTENTS

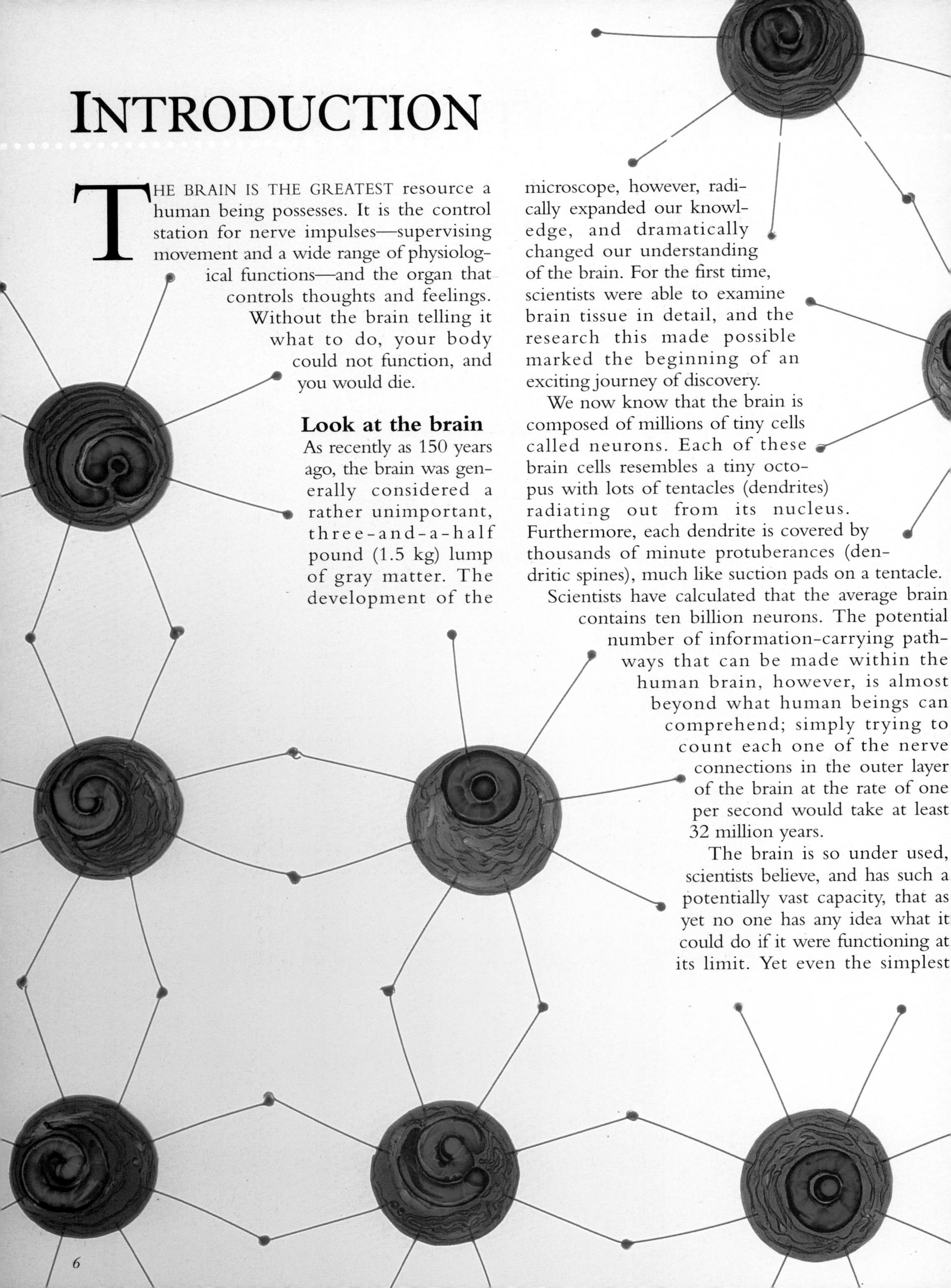

INTRODUCTION

THE BRAIN IS THE GREATEST resource a human being possesses. It is the control station for nerve impulses—supervising movement and a wide range of physiological functions—and the organ that controls thoughts and feelings. Without the brain telling it what to do, your body could not function, and you would die.

Look at the brain

As recently as 150 years ago, the brain was generally considered a rather unimportant, three-and-a-half pound (1.5 kg) lump of gray matter. The development of the microscope, however, radically expanded our knowledge, and dramatically changed our understanding of the brain. For the first time, scientists were able to examine brain tissue in detail, and the research this made possible marked the beginning of an exciting journey of discovery.

We now know that the brain is composed of millions of tiny cells called neurons. Each of these brain cells resembles a tiny octopus with lots of tentacles (dendrites) radiating out from its nucleus. Furthermore, each dendrite is covered by thousands of minute protuberances (dendritic spines), much like suction pads on a tentacle. Scientists have calculated that the average brain contains ten billion neurons. The potential number of information-carrying pathways that can be made within the human brain, however, is almost beyond what human beings can comprehend; simply trying to count each one of the nerve connections in the outer layer of the brain at the rate of one per second would take at least 32 million years.

The brain is so under used, scientists believe, and has such a potentially vast capacity, that as yet no one has any idea what it could do if it were functioning at its limit. Yet even the simplest things it does are truly miraculous. For instance, the brain allows us to convert minute perturbations in air pressure into language and then instantly decipher the meaning of the words. It translates the wavelengths of light received by the retina into colored, three-dimensional, moving pictures.

Thinking and learning

Apart from its role in controlling the purely physiological aspects of the body, the brain controls all of our thoughts and feelings. These thoughts include ideas, judgments, speculation, dreams, memories, and the conceptualization of emotion. They help you reason, reflect, speculate, theorize, deduce, concentrate, deliberate, believe, imagine, and invent. Each word implies a subtly different method of approach, suited to solving a certain type of problem.

The brain that reasons well and learns well, that can solve problems and think creatively, is judged to be intelligent. Intelligence is generally accepted as something you either have or don't have, and there is nothing much you can do to enhance it. It is widely held that once the brain reaches maturity, it loses much of its ability to assimilate the complex or the unfamiliar. Intelligence, however, is more complicated than that, and the belief that you cannot improve your mental abilities is incorrect.

Boost your brain power

In order to boost your cerebral power it is important to use your brain every day, and make active thinking an important part of your life. As with everything else, practice makes perfect, and if you regularly stretch your mind, your thought processes will run more smoothly. Reading is good brain food, as are discussing issues with others, keeping your mind open to fresh ideas, and studying new subjects. Research indicates that mental activity may actually increase the number of connecting pathways in the brain, thereby helping you to process facts and absorb ideas more effectively.

This volume looks at how the brain works. It investigates thinking skills, reasoning, and the imaginative leapfrogging that is at the heart of creative thinking. As you will learn, thinking is a skill that can be taught and developed. Through games, puzzles, logical posers, and clearly set-out information, we show you how to enhance your thinking skills—and unleash your problem-solving ability.

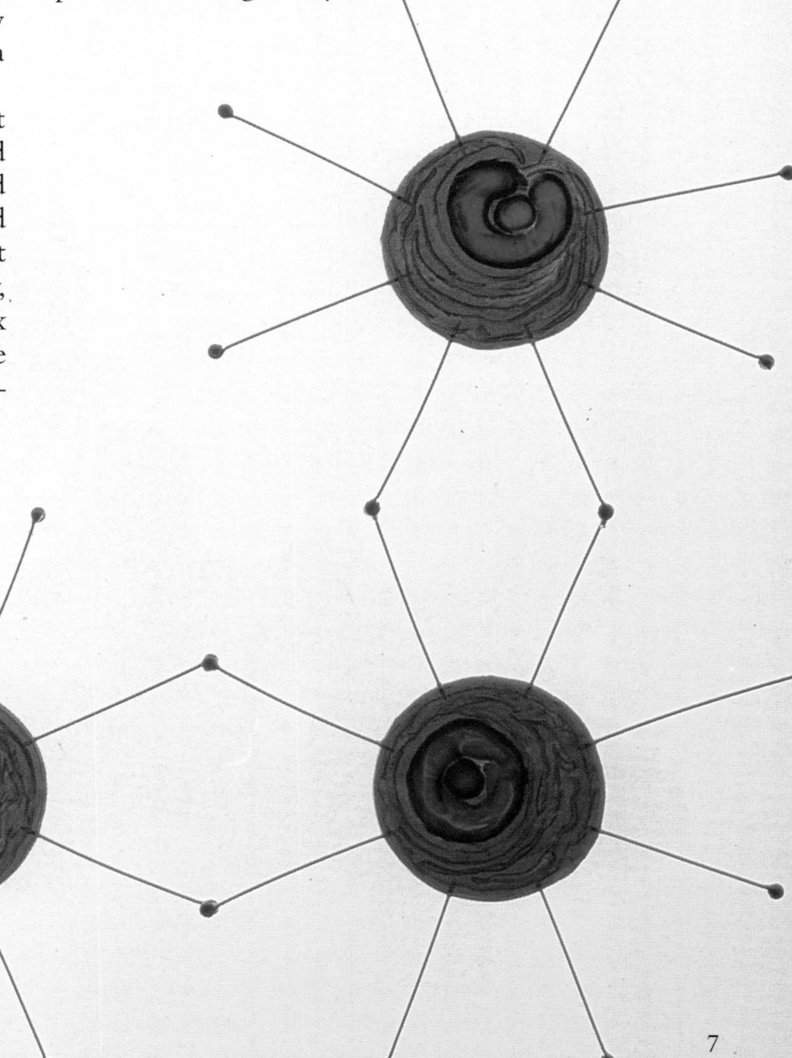

Make connections
The nerve cells in your brain are joined together by information-carrying dendrites.

THE POWER OF HUMAN THOUGHT

Human beings have an instinctive desire to understand the workings of the brain, because knowing how it works helps us to understand ourselves. However, people have often misunderstood what the brain is capable of, and even now, most of us drastically underestimate its power.

The mind in history

The function and capacity of the brain are now widely recognized, but in the past there were many mistaken beliefs about the nature of the brain. In ancient times, the human mind was thought to exist separately from the body in the form of vapor, gas, or an intangible spirit. The Greek philosopher Aristotle believed that the heart was the source of memory and sensation. Even during the Renaissance, the brain itself was still not understood, although it was realized that the center of thought and consciousness was found there. The nineteenth century saw a huge rise in the popularity of a so-called science called phrenology. This technique was developed by a Viennese anatomist called Franz Josef Gell, who believed that reading the bumps on a person's head was the key to revealing his or her character.

Although the brain was still thought to be a relatively simple mechanism in the 1930s and 40s, great strides in unravelling its mysteries have been made more recently. The expansion of the neurosciences into more than 20 disciplines concerned with each and every aspect of the brain is a scientific breakthrough that many observers consider as significant as the Darwinian revolution in biology. Despite this, we are still only on the threshold of discovering the brain's real capabilities.

At various times, the brain has been compared to clockwork, machinery, and electrical systems; today the most frequent comparison is with the computer. But even such powerful and complicated machines offer an inadequate parallel with the human brain. While computers can perform a wide range of thinking tasks, from completing complex mathematical equations to monitoring safety in nuclear power plants, they are light years away from being able to rival the

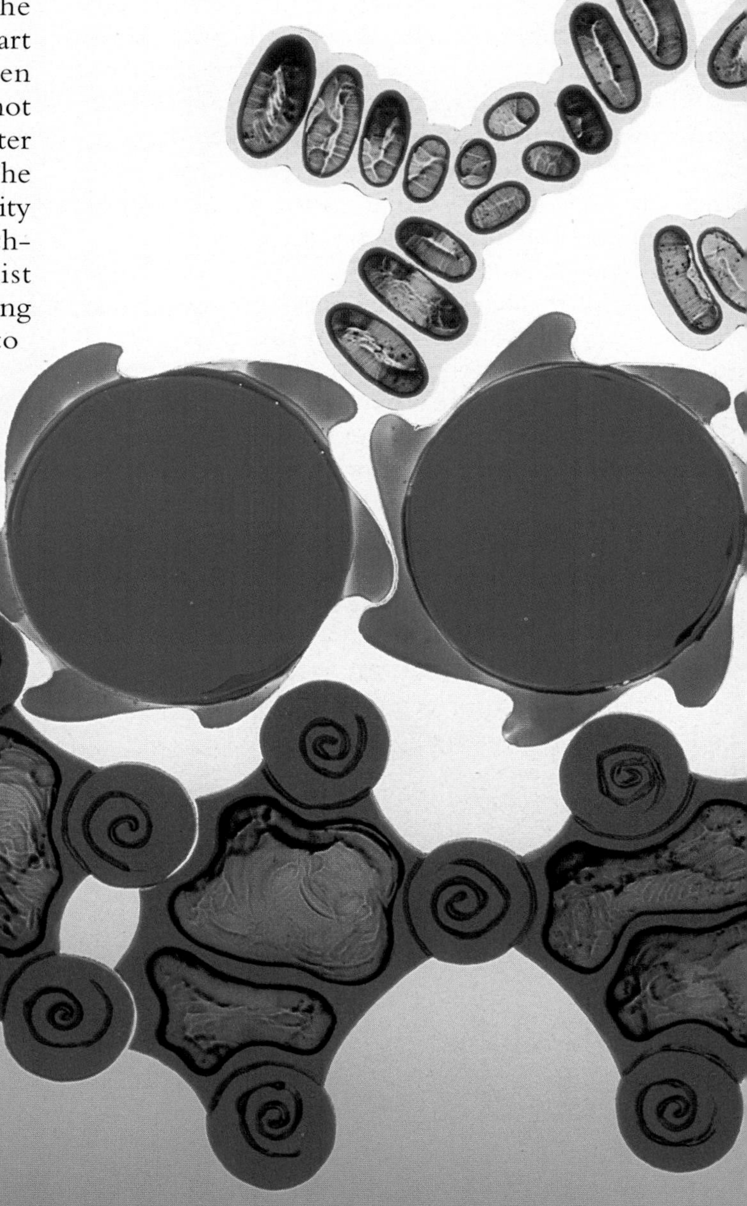

human brain. In particular, the human mind is unparalleled in its mastery of subtle functions such as interpretation, intuition, instinct, and creativity.

The areas where computers are dominant, and where they have made the most dramatic advances during the last 50 years, are those that involve memory, logic, and communication. Some fields—education, mathematics, scientific and sociological research, data processing, information storage and retrieval, and telecommunications, for example—have been completely transformed by computer technology, and have, in their turn, altered our culture and our everyday lives accordingly.

Ageing and Ability

The body reaches its physical peak between the ages of 18 and 24. After that, the assumption is that physical and mental power steadily declines. However, this need not be true. Most of us can expect to retain our mental abilities well into old age, and the fact that this is assumed not to be the case is a manifestation of ageism. Research has shown that even if you lose 10,000 brain cells over a lifetime, by the time you are 80 that would amount to a tiny three percent of the total.

Mental activity

Like any other part of your body, your brain responds to exercise, and if you keep using it, it will keep working. When it feels as if your brain has become sluggish, and your memory dim, make use of memory techniques to keep you mentally alert. Research has shown that if you keep your brain stimulated, it will grow more dendritic spines on the tentacles of each cell, and these will increase the total number of connections within your brain along which information can travel.

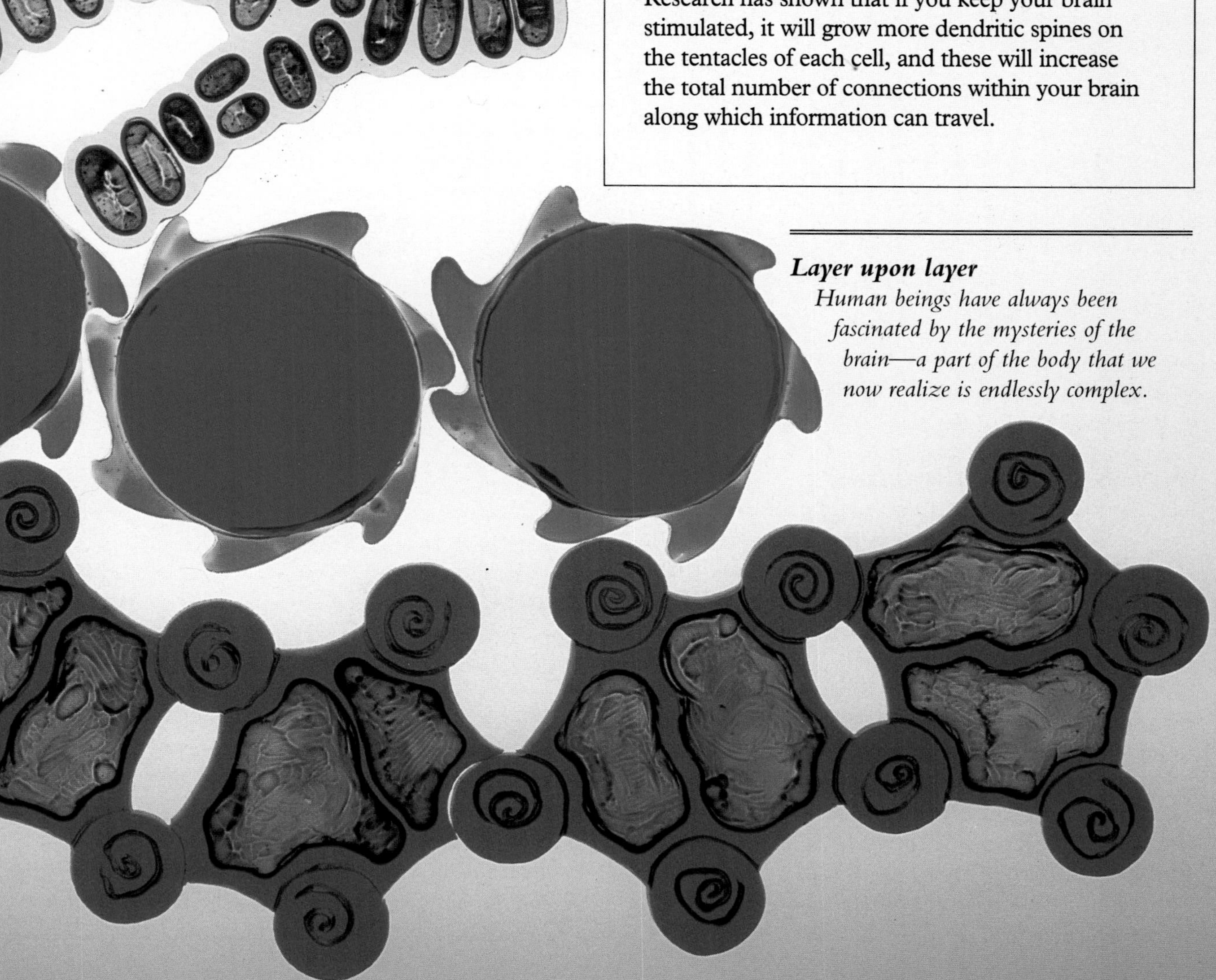

Layer upon layer

Human beings have always been fascinated by the mysteries of the brain—a part of the body that we now realize is endlessly complex.

You Are What You Think

The way we think, and what we think about, are the essence of who we are. An old Buddhist saying sums this up succinctly: "All that we are is the result of what we have thought." The nature of our thinking is a product of everything we have felt, heard, and experienced from babyhood onward. Yet for much of the time, these thoughts run through our heads like background noise, and we are barely aware of them. However, although we may not be fully aware of all the messages we send to ourselves, the power they have over us is immense.

How you use your mind

Once you grasp the impact of these messages, you can understand how crucial it is to develop good thinking skills. It's vital to learn how to focus your thoughts, as well as to examine and challenge those that hold you back or are making you into something you don't want to be.

The French existentialist philosopher and writer Jean-Paul Sartre compared human beings to playwrights who, with their thoughts, and the actions arising from them, write the script of their lives. Viewed in this way, whether a life is boring or exciting, meaningful or devoid of purpose, successful or unsuccessful, ultimately depends on the person who is living it.

What's in your thoughts?

The way in which you use your mind is as important as the content of your thoughts; each affects the other. For instance, what would go through your mind if you were contemplating whether to leave one job for another? If the question is one that provokes panic, you will overload the issue with fear and a sense of doom, preventing you from evaluating the problem clearly. On the other hand, if you apply your mind rationally, you will be able to arrive at a well-considered solution.

Similarly, if you are anticipating that the party you have been invited to is going to be an ordeal, you will approach the prospect with no sense of pleasure. If you decide that the occasion will be enjoyable, however, you will frame it in a different context. In both these cases, the thought processes you apply are the same—even though the situations themselves are very different.

Positive-on-positive

Because your thinking shapes the person you are, the more positive your thoughts, the more dynamic and fulfilling your life will be. Indeed, the technique of making your brain work for you rather than against you is an advanced form of positive thinking. In his book *Make the Most of Your Mind*, Tony Buzan stresses the importance

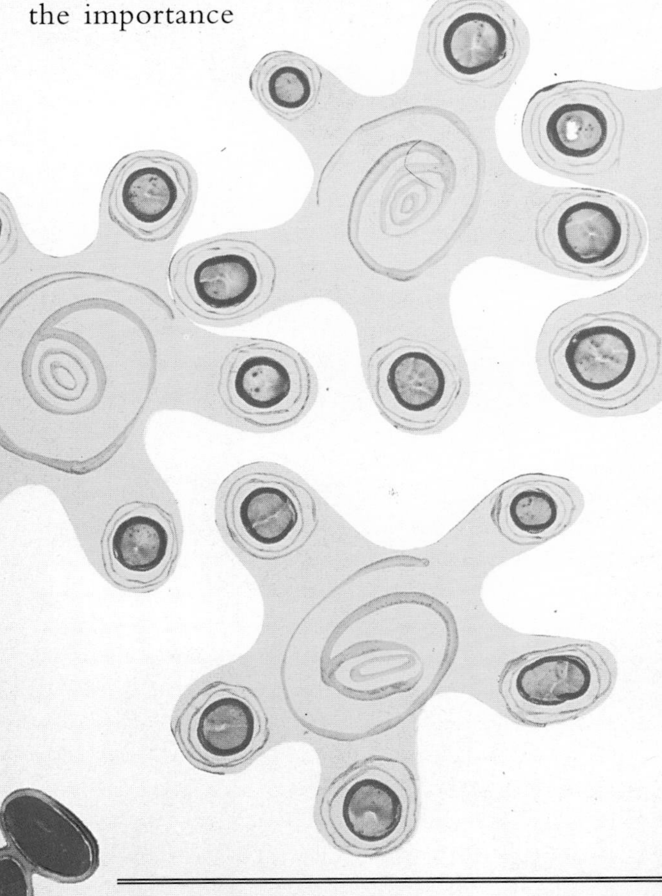

Positive and negative

The human brain is made up of about ten thousand million nerve cells. The connections between all these cells form the most complex communication circuit in existence.

of programming a positive on to a positive. Therefore, he suggests that instead of programming yourself not to get ill, you should program yourself to get even fitter, visualizing yourself in glowing health. Similarly, instead of programming yourself never to fail, you should visualize your goal and program yourself to succeed. Instead of programming yourself to be stupid, program yourself to become increasingly quick minded and attentive.

Buzan also gives an example of how misdirected positive thinking can bring about a negative result. On the fifth tee of a particular course, a golfer drives into a waterhole. As this has happened on three consecutive occasions, he wants to program himself not to go into the same waterhole again. He spends considerable time on this programming and yet, on his fourth visit to the waterhole, the same thing happens. As Buzan points out, the error lies in the fact that the golfer was programming his brain—and therefore also his body—to concentrate on the waterhole. Instead of putting a positive on to a negative (the waterhole), he should have put a positive on to a positive and focused on his ultimate goal, the far green.

Clarify your goals

Tony Buzan's positive-on-positive approach can be applied to all areas of your life. He suggests visualization as a powerful auto-suggestive technique. This is a method of focusing your imagination toward "seeing" a future in which you are achieving your ambitions. Clarifying your goals, then repeating positive-on-positive instructions, will help your brain to imprint a new way of thinking. It is best to try visualization when you are relaxed, for example, lying quietly on the sofa.

DIRECTED THINKING

The verb "to think" has a great variety of meanings. It has become a blanket term to describe a whole range of psychological processes that go on within our heads and which may or may not be translated into action. For example, it is used as a synonym for remembering (as in "I can't think where I put that letter"), or for belief (as in "I think she is insecure about her abilities"). "Think" is also used to denote guesswork ("I think there are 700 jellybeans in the bowl") or choice ("I think I'll have the leek and potato soup").

Focus your thoughts

The sort of thinking that most interests psychologists, however, is called directed thinking. Directed thinking, the outward appearance of which is powerfully portrayed in Auguste Rodin's famous statue *The Thinker*, is the mental process of reasoning or pondering or reflecting. In directed thinking, a set of cerebral activities are directed at the solution of a specific problem. This could be learning a new computer program, hammering out a holiday compromise with your partner, or formulating a workable household budget.

People often find difficulties in carrying out directed thinking efficiently. In this book, you will find ways of improving how you focus on problems, and discover tricks and short-cuts that will help you to improve the way you organize your thoughts. Work your way through the information given, and test yourself with the quizzes and problem-solving exercises; your thinking will become more effective as a result.

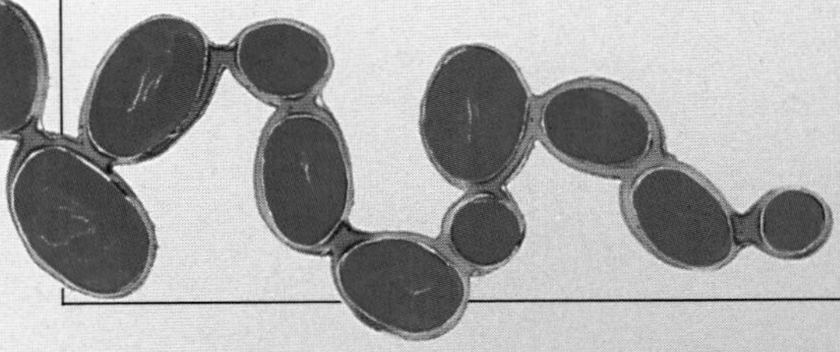

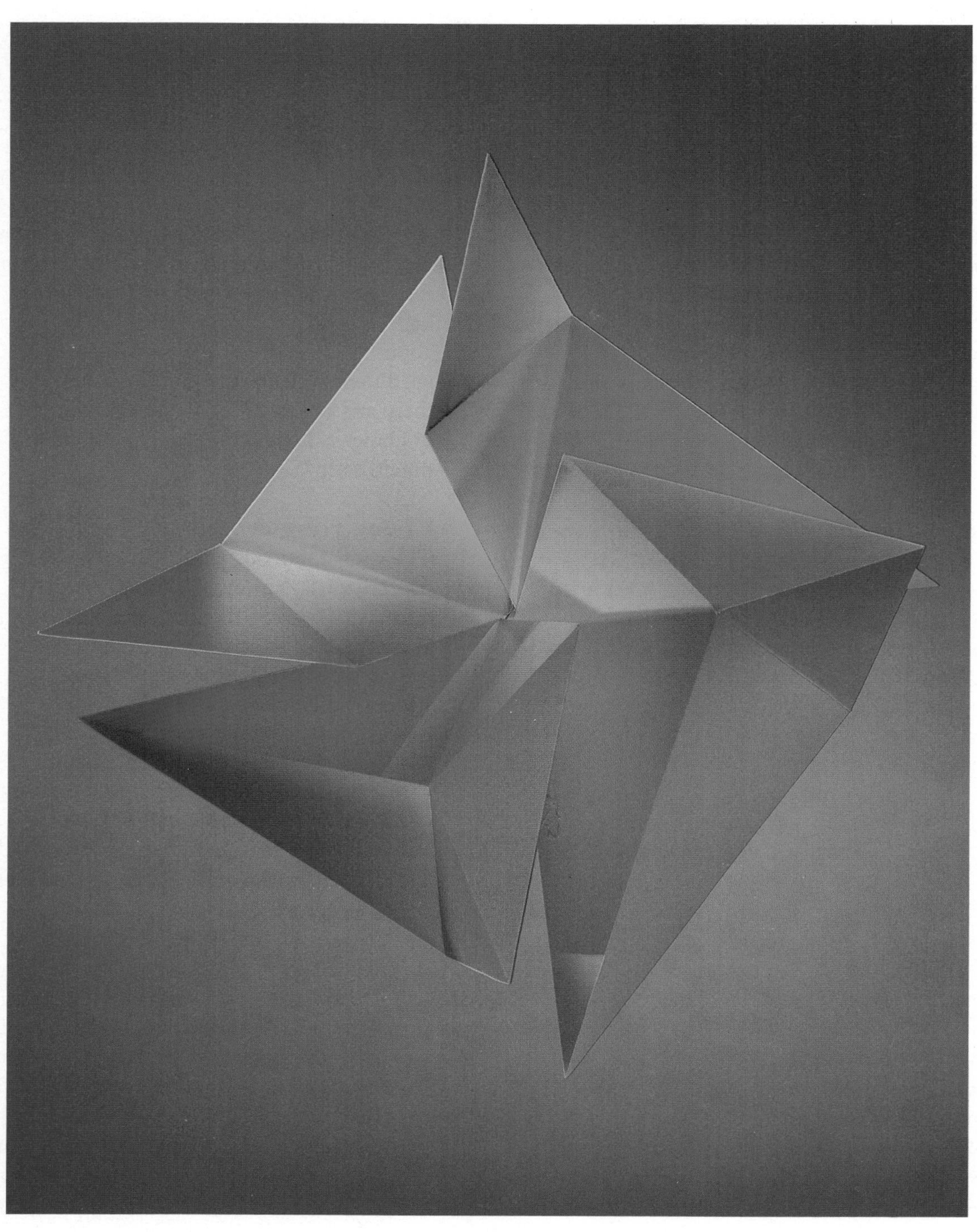

CHAPTER ONE

MIND MATTERS

IN ORDER TO IMPROVE your thinking skills, it is helpful to understand a little about how your brain works—how it actually thinks. This chapter begins by explaining, in simple terms, the functions of different parts of the brain and how they contribute to the thinking process. First, we look at one of the key functions of the brain—memory. Memory means much more than just remembering events. The brain refers to memories in order to make sense of the present, enabling you to understand and learn from your experiences. This chapter has practical exercises to test different areas of your memory, and tips to improve your memory skills.

Then, we look at logic and creativity. The brain is divided in half, each side being responsible for a different type of activity—the left for logic, the right for creativity. Although logic tends to be valued over intuition, there is growing awareness that more intuitive thinking leads to more creative solutions (see "Left or Right?" on pages 20-21). Scientists have also observed structural differences between male and female brains, characterized by different abilities. Neither brain is superior—just different. For example, men tend to have faster reaction times, but women process information faster.

People make bad decisions for many reasons. This chapter looks at those that result from flaws in thinking, and suggests ways to overcome them. One common problem is the tendency to stick to set patterns of thinking. "Generating Creative Solutions" on pages 26-27 sets out techniques for encouraging you to break out of these patterns, such as lateral thinking and brainstorming. On other occasions you may be aware that you went wrong because you failed to see the flaw in your reasoning. In "Where Thinking Skills Let You Down" on pages 30-31, there is a checklist to help you avoid making such mistakes. You may also be persuaded by others to act against your better judgment. It is often difficult to remain true to yourself, but again there are techniques (see "How to Think for Yourself" on pages 32-33) to help you.

Bad decisions are often made when people are unable to analyze large amounts of information properly, and so fall back on mental shortcuts. Remember, however, that these shortcuts can become generalizations, stereotypes, or prejudices. Whatever traps you tend to fall into, the purpose of this chapter is to make you aware that thinking is simply a skill—one that can be improved just like any other.

UNDERSTANDING THE WAY YOU THINK WILL HELP YOU TO IMPROVE YOUR THINKING TECHNIQUES, AND ENABLE YOU TO MAKE BETTER AND MORE CREATIVE DECISIONS.

HOW THE BRAIN WORKS

YOUR BRAIN IS NOT ONLY the most important organ in your body, it is also the most complicated structure in the universe. One eminent researcher, Sir Charles Sherrington, alluding to the intricate workings of the brain, described it as an "enchanted loom, where millions of flashing shuttles weave a dissolving (but meaningful) pattern, as if the Milky Way had entered upon some cosmic dance."

The brain map

The brain is made up of several distinct parts. The lower part of the brain, called the brain stem, controls the functions that keep you alive, such as heartbeat, respiration, and digestion.

The biggest part of your brain is the cerebrum. The heavily folded surface is known as the cortex, a layer about 1/16 to 1/4 inch (2 to 6 mm) thick, which is the brain's "gray matter." All the nerve cells (neurons) here form a complex network that controls higher intellectual functions, such as memory and learning, interpreting signals received by your senses, and guiding voluntary movement.

Among the mental and bodily functions controlled by the brain are:

- mathematical calculations
- writing, speech, and language comprehension
- the creation of symbolic ideas
- emotions, from anxiety to optimism
- skilled and intricate movements
- vision
- the recognition of sounds
- registering sensation and processing and integrating information from one or more senses

Specific parts of the brain may be involved in different types of learning, but it seems that no single area controls all learning. The brain has many convergence zones that act as "relay stations" to transmit messages from one part of the brain to another.

Miracle machine

The fabric of our lives is woven in a magic loom—the brain.

BRAIN FACTS

- Your brain constitutes only two percent of your body weight—but consumes 20 percent of its energy.
- The cortex of your brain has ten billion neurons, which develop about three months after conception. You have approximately the same number when you are 80 years old. These neurons are nourished and protected by 100 billion cells called glial cells.
- Your senses are already well developed at birth: newborn babies respond to sound and can recognize smells, objects, and faces.
- Each central body of a neuron has delicate fibers called dendrites. There are about 100,000 miles (160,930 km) of dendrites in your brain.
- The folding surface of your brain consists of six cellular layers. If it was spread flat, it would cover about 400 sq in (2,580 sq cm). The pattern of the folding is unique: no one else has your brain!
- Each second, there are about 100,000 different chemical reactions occurring in your brain. Certain chemicals you take into your body—alcohol, morphine, even caffeine and nicotine—affect thinking adversely by depressing the central nervous system.
- Intelligence is a function of the connections between the neurons, not the number of neurons.
- Each neuron may make about 10,000-15,000 connections with other neurons. The total number of connections, called synapses, is probably ten trillion.
- Scientists have discovered the existence of "pleasure centers" and "punishment centers" in the brain. When stimulated, a pleasure center gives such satisfaction that it feels more important than other drives—even if the person's life is threatened.
- Brain cells suffer permanent damage if they are deprived of oxygen for more than two minutes.

How thinking works

Most people automatically associate the brain with a process commonly known as thinking, although a better term might be "awareness." Brain activity occurs when neurons send messages to one another in the form of chemical and electrical signals. These messages are received by branches from the cell body, known as dendrites, and transmitted along an extension of a cell—the axon. Chemicals known as neurotransmitters, released when a neuron is stimulated or "excited," speed information to other neurons.

What people think of as "knowledge" is the memory of having made these patterns (or connections) in the past. So babies start off with no previous knowledge, but gradually they are able to recall the quickest pathway to access information—and the better memory they have for this, the more information they can access.

There are several levels of brain activity, depending on what is needed at a particular time:

Ticking over. In order to maintain the life-sustaining balance of all of the body functions, your brain is always responding to signals from nerves throughout your body, and sending out corrective instructions if an imbalance occurs. Because your brain is always active, even when you are asleep or unconscious, this activity is constant. It is also beyond your conscious control.

Attention. At this level, you are, to varying degrees, awake and alert. Attention can be quite diffuse (during sleep or daydreams, for example), but suppose you are awake and feel a sudden, burning pain, such as when you touch a hot object. You don't think about your response: alerted by pain, an involuntary reflex action controlled by the brain takes over, and your hand jerks away. In other circumstances, you may not even be aware of your mental processes, but you're taking in and responding to many signals. You're watching and listening to traffic, attempting to figure out whether you're hungry, trying not to bump into other people, and perhaps planning your work—all at the same time!

Directed thinking. This is generally what people believe the brain is for: we reason, ponder, and reflect. At its best, directed thinking can help you to "figure out" problems. This infinitely complex level of activity also occurs when you learn, when you remember, and when you plan for the future. It is why you can apply yourself to anything from a recipe to mathematics, and why people have been able to harness fire and create works of art.

Memories Are Made of This

The French writer Marcel Proust begins his series of novels, *Remembrance of Things Past*, with the narrator biting into a madeleine cake, the taste of which triggers a long chain of intense memories. Most of us have experienced this close link between sensory impressions and memory: how frequently has a long-forgotten event sprung vividly to mind as the result of something apparently trivial such as the distant pealing of bells or the smell of a certain flower?

The what and the where

Your memory is inextricably intertwined with all of your thinking processes. In essence, your brain would not be able to function without it because memory is actually the process by which your brain learns—memories are the building blocks of thought. Without memory, you would be incapable of understanding your experiences; you would be without language or learning skills, with no sense of the past and no way of planning for the future.

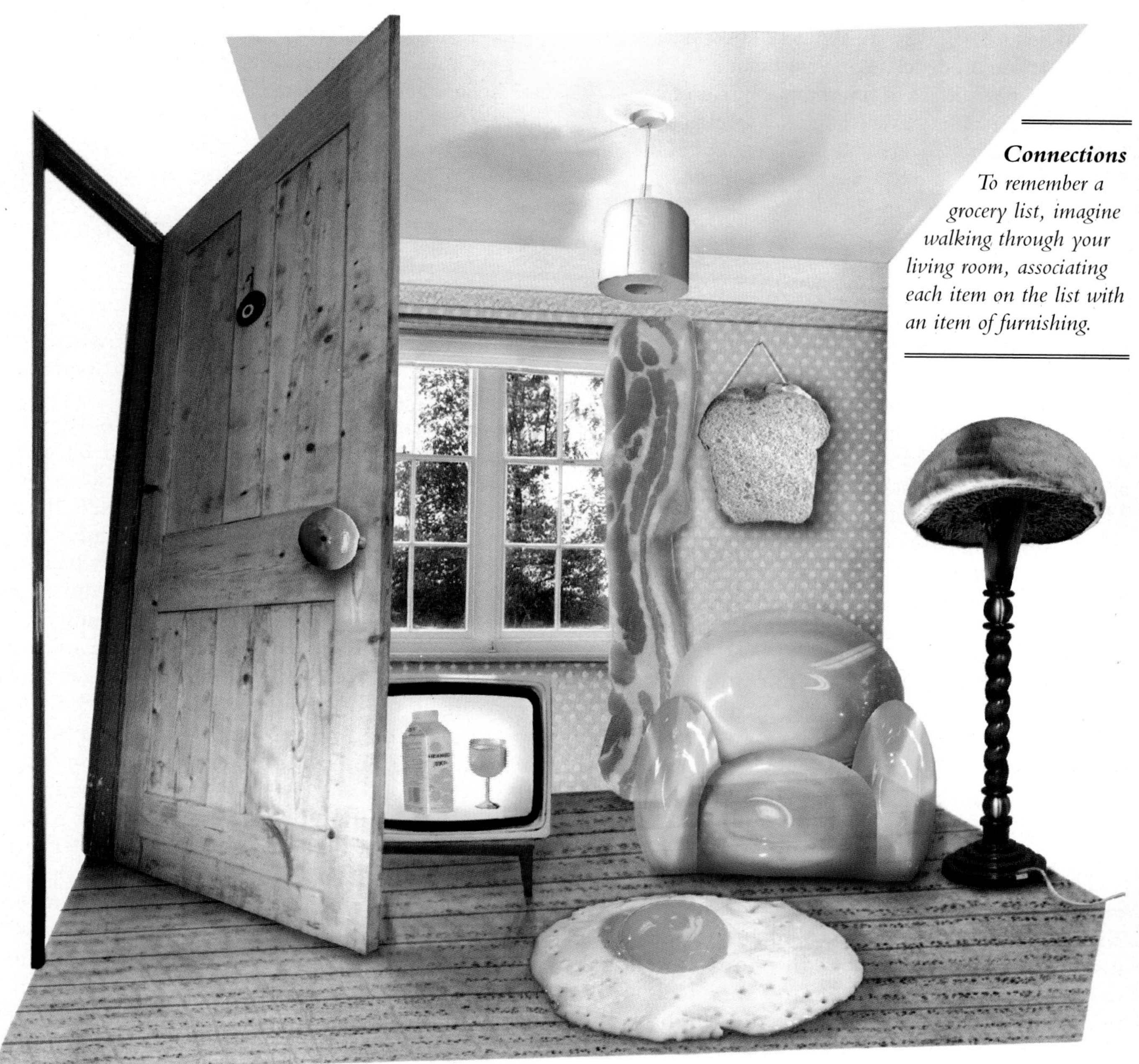

Connections

To remember a grocery list, imagine walking through your living room, associating each item on the list with an item of furnishing.

Memories consist of messages that are constantly traveling down the billions of interconnected neuron cells packed into the brain. Just how closely linked memory is with other mental functions is shown by the fact that information seems to be stored in many different areas of the brain—there isn't one particular place that acts only as a memory store.

Whenever you are faced with a new piece of information, your brain makes sense of it by rapidly comparing and contrasting it with what has gone before. When you simply add two small numbers together, you have to keep them in your short-term memory while you work with them, and—from memory—recognize them as numbers.

Different memories

The senses play a major role in memory because it is through them that we take in our impressions of everything that is going on around us. This input is really the first step in the three-stage memory process that consists of:

1. Intake—how we register information when our various senses are stimulated.

2. Storage—how we retain information.

3. Retrieval—how we "remember" information.

The way that we store information can also be broken down into three stages: sensory memory, short-term memory, and long-term memory. Many psychologists believe that our senses act as a kind of buffer. So, for example, when our eyes take in information initially, this is stored very briefly by our sensory systems—that is, it is stored in the parts of the brain responsible for the senses.

Some of this sensory information will be lost. The rest will pass into our short-term memory bank. From here, too, it may be lost, or processed further and lodged in our long-term memory. Some information passes directly from sensory memory to long-term memory.

Some people seem to have a better long-term memory than others—they retain information easily, and can access it readily. This can make all kinds of thought much easier because it enables them to draw on a range of information much faster. To learn how to use your long-term memory more efficiently, you need to start by ceasing to view memory as something that occurs after the fact, and see it as centering on how you absorb information in the first place.

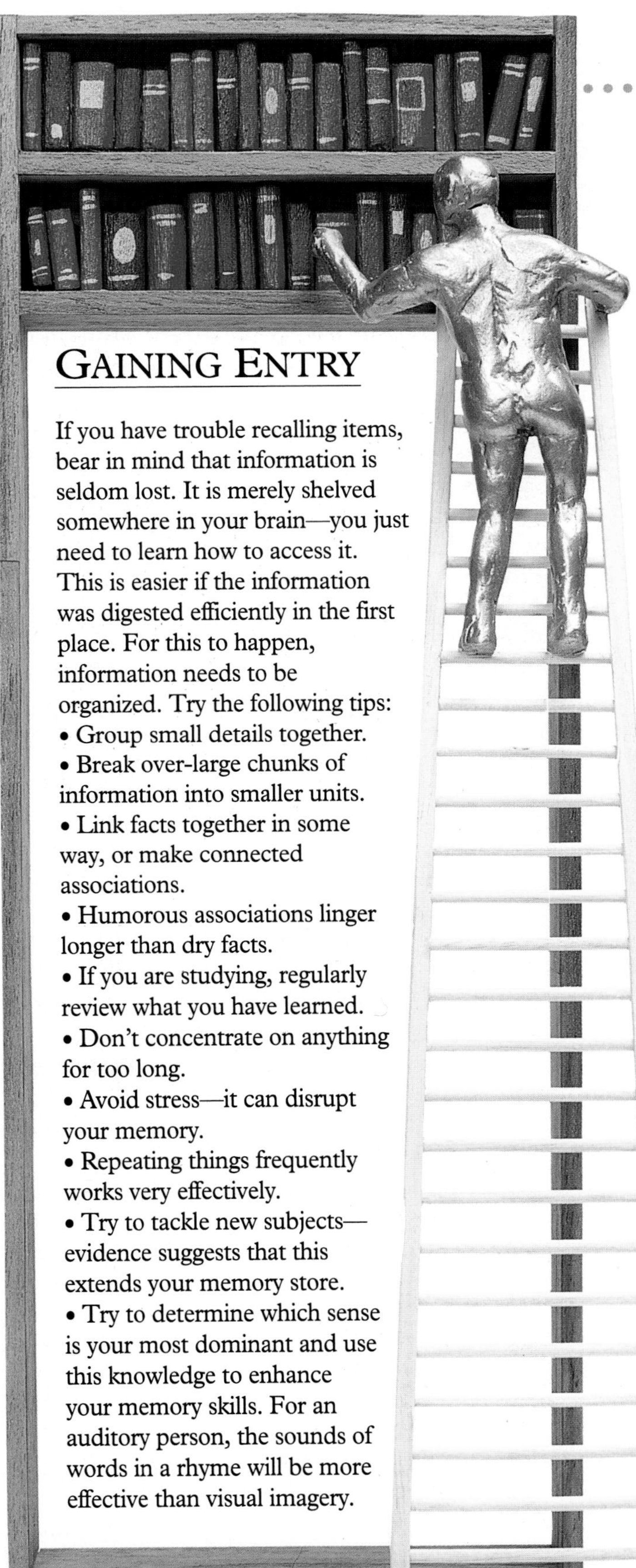

Gaining Entry

If you have trouble recalling items, bear in mind that information is seldom lost. It is merely shelved somewhere in your brain—you just need to learn how to access it. This is easier if the information was digested efficiently in the first place. For this to happen, information needs to be organized. Try the following tips:

- Group small details together.
- Break over-large chunks of information into smaller units.
- Link facts together in some way, or make connected associations.
- Humorous associations linger longer than dry facts.
- If you are studying, regularly review what you have learned.
- Don't concentrate on anything for too long.
- Avoid stress—it can disrupt your memory.
- Repeating things frequently works very effectively.
- Try to tackle new subjects—evidence suggests that this extends your memory store.
- Try to determine which sense is your most dominant and use this knowledge to enhance your memory skills. For an auditory person, the sounds of words in a rhyme will be more effective than visual imagery.

TEST YOUR MEMORY

Short-term memory is important for everyday activities. Often called "working memory," it seems to last for around 15 to 30 seconds, or up to a few minutes if a conscious effort is made—perhaps by repeating something out loud several times, as you do when you are unable to write down a phone number you have been given. Short-term memory can hold only a limited amount of information, although this too can be extended by grouping like items together.

To test your short-term memory, look very carefully at the painting on this page for one minute. Then cover it up and read the explanatory text below. Read at your normal speed, concentrating properly, but avoid straining over every word or you will not gain an accurate impression of your everyday memory skills.

Now cover the text, read the questions, and jot down your answers. Work through these questions swiftly, and then uncover the picture and text and add up how many answers you got right. This kind of test is both effective and entertaining, and, if you practice it with other passages of text or images you have to hand, you will soon find your memory becoming sharper. Turn to "Solutions," on page 130, for an analysis of your score.

Read on...

The painting shown here, called *The Countess's Morning Levée*, is one of a series of six, collectively entitled *Marriage à la Mode*. This series, painted around 1743, is the work of the English satirical artist William Hogarth (1697–1764). Here, he turns his attention to the impoverished aristocrats who married into the prosperous middle class. The young couple involved in this ill-fated marriage are a viscount, whose father has squandered the family wealth, and a rich merchant's daughter.

In *The Countess's Morning Levée*, the lady in question is shown "holding court" one morning in her lavish boudoir, surrounded by fawning and decadent hangers-on. The vain lawyer known as Silvertongue lolls in a familiar fashion on a sofa by her side; he is inviting the countess to a masked ball. Silvertongue's portrait also hangs on the wall in the upper left of the painting. An Italian opera singer performs, much to the admiration of a woman seated nearby, while a French hairdresser styles the countess's hair. The horned figure held by the young boy-servant in the foreground shows that Silvertongue will have his way—horns symbolized a man whose wife committed adultery.

In the complete series of paintings, the mismatched couple fall into separate lives of ruinous extravagance and debauchery, and the viscount has to be treated for venereal disease. His wife surrounds herself with a sycophantic entourage, while Silvertongue becomes her lover. The young husband discovers them and is killed by Silvertongue. When the countess discovers that Silvertongue has been hanged, she commits suicide.

William Hogarth began as an engraver, training as a painter in his spare time. By the 1730s, he was working as a portrait painter, and was also establishing a new art-form that found instant success. This popular fashion took the form of a series of pictures with an improving moral; mini-melodramas about what Hogarth considered to be the social and political ills of the day. He became a master at exposing deceit, debauchery, pretentiousness, and hypocrisy, and he also attacked "foreign" influences—French and Italian fashions were all the rage, but Hogarth supported what he saw as the down-to-earth qualities of the English citizen.

How much do you remember?

1. How many paintings are there on the walls?

2. What happens to the countess at the end of this moral tale?

3. What can be seen in the bottom left of the painting, in the foreground?

4. In what century was Hogarth born?

5. Roughly how many people are there in the painting (accuracy to the nearest two will do)?

6. As he unpacks his basket, what is the boy holding?

7. What is the name of this series of paintings?

8. What color are the drapes around the bed?

9. How did Hogarth start his career?

10. What is the man reclining on the couch holding?

11. How many other paintings are in this series?

12. What instrument is the standing figure on the left of the picture playing?

13. What is happening to the countess?

14. What is this series of pictures criticizing?

15. How many women are there in the painting (excluding those in paintings on the walls)?

16. Why does the husband have to seek treatment?

17. What is the figure on the far left doing?

18. What is the name of the countess's lover?

19. What is the theme of the paintings on the walls?

20. What sort of outside influences was William Hogarth strongly opposed to?

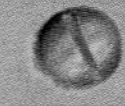

LEFT OR RIGHT?

Viewed from above, the brain has two distinct halves, or hemispheres; between them, these are thought to govern everything from keeping your internal organs functioning to contemplating the meaning of life. They are connected in the center of the brain through millions of nerve fibers known as the corpus callosum, but they also act independently. For instance, injuries to the left-hand side of the brain can cause paralysis to the opposite side of the body, and vice versa.

Experiments during the 1960s explored how this "split brain" works. Some mental activities, notably language and sequential thinking (the ability to analyze information one bit after another), which you need for mathematical calculations, appear to be controlled from one cerebral hemisphere. Seen to be the "logical" side, this hemisphere is also known as the "dominant" one, so-called not because it is intrinsically superior, but because it is more efficient at performing the activities that tend to be valued in Western culture.

Logic and creativity

In people who are naturally right handed, the dominant hemisphere is almost always the left. Curiously, in about two-thirds of left handers, the left side of the brain is also dominant. This may be because in over half of newborn babies, the left temporal lobe—which contains the specific part of the brain primarily responsible for language—is already slightly larger than the right. So what goes on in what is known as the non-dominant side? It appears that this hemisphere—usually, but not always, the right—is important for visual recognition of images or patterns, spatial orientation, and the kind of thinking that grasps things all at once or "intuitively," rather than bit by bit. For example, because it influences how you recognize faces, the right side of the brain helps you understand nonverbal communication, such as body language and facial expressions, that

Divided in two?
Although one side of your brain is more concerned with logic, and the other with creativity, you function best when both sides work together.

contribute to "intuitive" insights. One American researcher, Robert Ornstein, compared the electrical activity in the two spheres during different mental activities. In many people, he found that the right side showed less activity when a mathematical problem was worked on, but greater activity when colored patterns had to be matched. Other clues came from people who had suffered damage to part of their brain. If the left side was damaged, there was often loss of speech, poor reading, and less-logical thinking. Damage to the right affected their ability to recognize faces or dress themselves.

So, as far as medical research has been able to ascertain, the right side of the brain is involved in parallel, rather than sequential, thinking. Parallel thinking seems to be the mechanism that pulls everything together when you experience a sudden flash of insight or understanding. For this reason, it tends to be associated with artistic appreciation and creative thought.

Bridging the gap

The two sides of the healthy brain do not function in isolation; they communicate with each other via the corpus callosum, a bridge of 200 million nerve fibers that relays nerve impulses from one hemisphere to the other. This structure appears to be slightly different in men and women (see "Sex Differences," pp. 22-23).

Most everyday tasks involve both left- and right-brain skills. Reading, for example, involves analysis (left brain), but also the recognition of letters (right brain) and frequently the production of imaginative images (right brain). Musical ability also seems to involve both hemispheres: Untrained musicians may use only the right, "intuitive" mode, but a professional uses the left hemisphere as well to analyze how the music is constructed.

However, because so much education gives precedence to verbal and analytical abilities, many people tend to let their "logical" judgments run roughshod over their intuition, ignoring what they "feel" to be true or useful in favor of what they can figure out. But the right-brain facility for allowing your attention to become wide-ranging and diffuse, instead of sharply focused, is most definitely worth cultivating, since it can help you learn many new skills and tap your hidden wells of talent and creativity.

RIGHT-BRAIN REFUGE

In their book *Right-Brain Learning in 30 Days,* Dr. Keith Harary and Pamela Weintraub suggest that nonlinear and nonverbal ways of learning can enhance overall mental skills by creating a right-brain refuge. This is a special learning environment—a place to master anything. To create it, ensure that:

- your room is quiet and peaceful.
- there is a couch or a comfortable easy chair.
- you have paper for drawing and writing, and all the equipment you need to learn a particular subject. For example, if you want to improve your golf game, make sure that you have your clubs and shoes there with you, as well as photographs, books and instructional video tapes.
- you use appropriate objects to enhance your receptiveness and create the right mood. The authors suggest, for example, that if you are studying Spanish, you surround yourself with that country's music and artifacts.

When you are in your right-brain refuge, use creative visualization to see yourself in your mind's eye successfully achieving a task, such as the golf score you want or having a fluent conversation in another language.

These right-brain techniques are most effective if supplemented by left-brain techniques of analysis and repetition. In this way, your learning will soon become faster and more enjoyable.

Absorbing information
Put yourself in a state of "alert relaxation," by lying down and playing tapes describing the goals you want to accomplish.

SEX DIFFERENCES

Are there really differences between the way men and women think? Much of what is considered to be male and female behavior is decided by society's cultural mores, and therefore changes over time—but that does not mean there are no biologically based differences between men and women. However, the precise nature and significance of these differences remains the subject of much debate.

When you're born

Even before the discovery of new ways to investigate the workings of the brain, many people noticed that boys and girls think and behave differently, almost from birth. Newborn girls, for instance, utter sounds and speak sooner than newborn boys, so that by the time they are two years old, girls have larger vocabularies. Boys make less eye contact with their friends, and prefer to play not just with toys but with all the other objects in their environment—such as a screwdriver or nails—for which they may find novel and dangerous uses. So can there be any biological explanations to account for these differences?

What's in your genes?

Your gender—whether you are born male or female—is determined by the genes you inherit from your parents. Genes are located in chromosomes, which carry the genetic information that together governs the stages of fetal development and makes up the whole of an individual. Hormones influence both body development—including brain structure—and behavior. For example, men generally perform better in spatial tests in which distances must be judged or objects recognized when they are viewed from different angles. One study found that women with high levels of the male hormones called androgens performed these tasks as well as men.

During the fifth week of embryonic life, the human brain develops rapidly. For one more week, the sexual structures are neither male nor female, but around the sixth week after fertilization, sexual development begins. This new stage includes the production of hormones from cell structures. These structures will become either the female ovaries or the male testes. Each of us has both the male hormones, androgens, and the female hormones, estrogens. After six weeks of embryonic development, one or other type will predominate.

Versatile or specialized?

Until recently, most medical and psychological investigations of the brain have focused almost exclusively on the male brain, and what was true of the male brain was thought to be true of the female brain. However, it has now been discovered that the female brain has its own unique organization. For example, there is more overlap between the hemispheres; that is, the specific functions thought to be performed in either the left brain or

X or Y chromosomes?

Everyone inherits some sexual characteristics through the genetic material found in chromosomes—but what you do with your own unique set of characteristics is up to you.

the right brain are not as clearly localized as in men. Because of this, some researchers describe the female brain as more versatile in that when one part is damaged, its function is compensated for fairly easily; male brains, however, cannot recover so well.

One reason for this versatility may be that the corpus callosum—the relay station composed of nerve fibers that links the two halves of the brain—is thicker in women. This difference suggests that more information is being exchanged in the female brain, while the male brain is more specialized. The female brain is especially suited to the highly specialized skill of language—speech production, and a mastery of grammar and spelling—which for women is located almost exclusively in the front left-hand side of the brain. In men, however, this area covers both the front and back of the same hemisphere. It is not entirely clear to what extent this positional difference enhances women's language skills, but present technological advancements in research promise a better understanding of the human brain in the near future.

Your brain is unique

Whether there is an advantage in having a specialized brain that is good at concentration, or a more versatile brain that is predisposed to intuitive thinking, is not clear. What is true is that a different type of intelligence—that is, a different mode of thinking—does not imply a "better" way to think: It does not mean that men are more intelligent than women, or that surgeons are smarter than composers. In fact, intelligence is determined only partly by genes: environment, opportunity, talent, and motivation all play vital roles. The quality we call intelligence knows no gender boundaries; everyone has a unique way of figuring out his or her own world.

WHO'S GOOD AT WHAT?

Women tend to be better than men at some things—and vice versa. This list compares the different skills at which the sexes tend to excel.

Men

- better day vision
- faster physical reaction times
- more interest in objects
- superior spatial skills (eye-to-brain coordination)
- greater physical strength (faster at things like running and swimming and more effective at lifting weights)
- superior skill in geometry and trigonometry
- greater capacity for risk taking and exploration

Women

- better night vision
- faster information processing
- more interest in people and environment
- better language skills
- greater manual dexterity and movements involving deftness and precision
- better grasp of algebra and general arithmetical calculations
- greater responsiveness to all stimuli such as taste, hearing, smell, and especially touch

ARE YOU SET IN YOUR WAYS?

EVERY DAY YOU ARE FACED with all kinds of problem-solving situations—from conjuring up a meal with limited ingredients, to maximizing working space in an office. How you approach these problems reveals a great deal about the nature of your thinking skills.

Do you always adopt the same approach, simply because it's worked before in similar situations? Or do you find that a particular problem is going round and round in your head with no solution in sight? If both of these are true, then that is probably because they are closely linked. Most people fail to realize that the problems aren't imposing the difficulties—it is their personal limitations and rigid thinking patterns that are creating the problem.

There are many kinds of problem-solving strategies, and the most important lesson we can learn is that we should tailor our strategy to the nature of the problem at hand. To discover whether you have a flexible approach or are locking away your potential without realizing it, try these puzzles. Then, turn to "Solutions," on pages 130-131, for the answers.

1. Number-crunching

a) Which number continues this series: 5, 7, 9, 14, 19, 24, 26, 28, 33, 38, 43, 45 __?

b) What is the missing number in this sequence: 12, 6, 24, 12, 48, __ 96, 48?

c) Answer this as fast as possible, without using a calculator. What is the sum of 115.5 + 72.25 – 43.25? Is it: 144.25, 144.5, 143.75, or 142.25?

d) If 185 (140) 95, then what is the missing figure inside the brackets here: 89 (__) 103?

2. The right words

a) Of the animals appearing in the list below, which is the odd one out?
horse snake elephant tortoise

b) Find a word with the same meaning as both of these:
candid *and* mark letter

c) Which fruit is the odd one out?
apple plum cherry lemon raspberry

d) Which words are missing in the following?
fish is to ___ as cars are to roads
porcupines are to spines as tortoise is to ___
woodpeckers are to insects as sheep are to ___

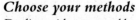

Choose your methods
Dealing with every problem in the same way will not always give the required results.

3. Seeing for yourself

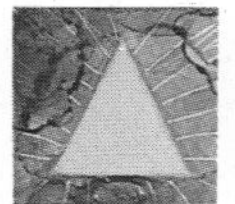  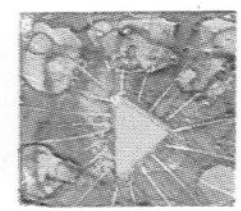 

a) In the above sequence, which is the odd one out?

b) The square counters in the above image form an arrow pointing to the left. Your task is to make the arrow point to the right, by moving as few counters as possible.

c) Four golf balls can be placed so that each touches the other three. Five coins can be arranged so that each coin touches the other four. Is it possible to place six matches so that each touches the other five? The matches should not be bent or broken.

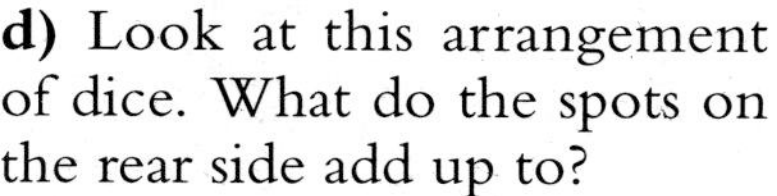

d) Look at this arrangement of dice. What do the spots on the rear side add up to?

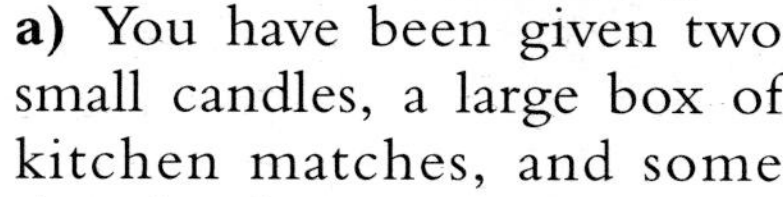

4. The final challenge

a) You have been given two small candles, a large box of kitchen matches, and some thumbtacks. Your task now is to mount the candles on the wall. How would you go about doing it?

b) Look at this pattern of nine dots. What you have to do, without lifting your pencil from the paper, is draw no more than four straight lines so that they pass through all the dots.

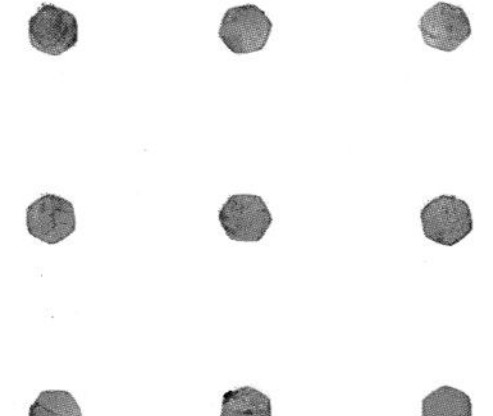

c) A man was driving a truck with a roof exactly 15 feet (4.5 m) from the ground. Approaching a bridge, he failed to see a sign reading "Low bridge. Vehicles of 15 feet or more follow alternative route," and got his truck stuck fast under the bridge. Despite revving his engine as hard as he possibly could, he was still unable to move the vehicle. Finally, he had an idea that enabled him to dislodge his truck. What did he do?

d) It is noon, and a terrible hailstorm is raging. The weather forecaster predicts that the ferocious hail will soon turn to rain, and once it has done so it will continue to pour down all day. Given this information, how do you know whether or not it is going to be sunny in 36 hours time?

GENERATING CREATIVE SOLUTIONS

The ideas machine
Vary your problem-solving techniques and you may discover a number of innovative solutions.

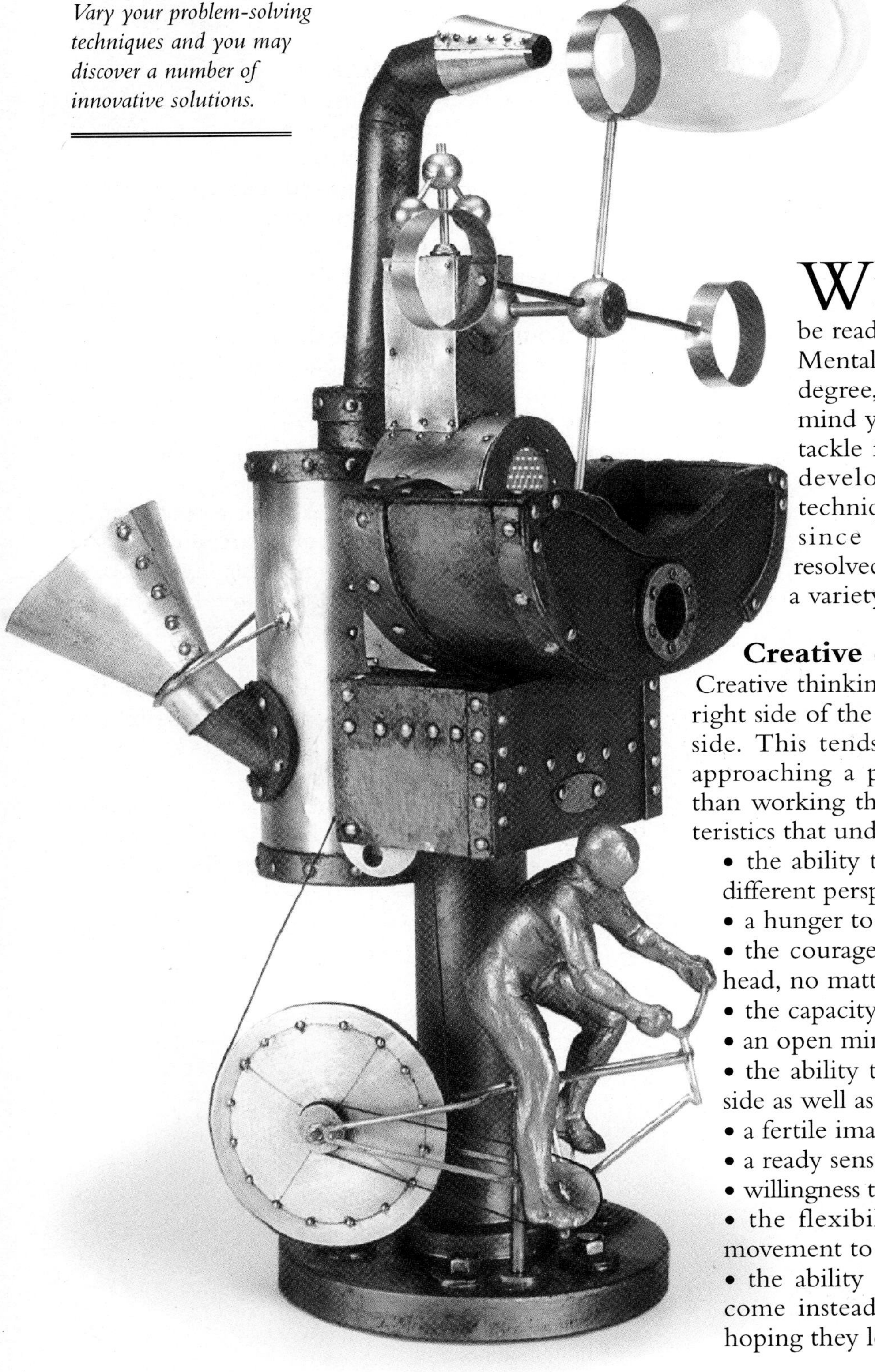

When you have completed the quiz on the previous pages, you should be ready for some more creative thinking. Mental blindness affects all of us to some degree, but once you learn to free your mind you'll see any problems you have to tackle in a whole new light. In addition, developing a wide range of thinking techniques will benefit you almost daily, since most everyday problems are resolved far more efficiently if you can use a variety of approaches.

Creative checklist

Creative thinking often involves using the intuitive right side of the brain as opposed to the logical left side. This tends to encourage lateral thinking—approaching a problem from a fresh angle rather than working through it step by step. The characteristics that underlie creative thinking include:

- the ability to look at a problem from as many different perspectives as possible
- a hunger to find original solutions
- the courage to turn accepted notions on their head, no matter what other people think
- the capacity to dismantle a problem
- an open mind
- the ability to respond readily to your intuitive side as well as your emotions
- a fertile imagination
- a ready sense of humor
- willingness to draw on a wide range of subjects
- the flexibility to allow images, sound, and movement to assist in the creative process
- the ability to work back from a desired outcome instead of following "logical" steps, and hoping they lead you to the best solution

Thinking strategies

Once you get into the habit of finding creative answers to things, you will have no desire to return to your former way of thinking. Ascertaining what approach works best, and being willing to change direction until you find a solution, is the way to succeed. There are various creative problem-solving techniques you can use:

Brainstorming. This can be done alone or in groups, and involves expressing every idea that comes to mind. Don't hold back from considering things that seem silly, or unconnected. As a starting point, think of an outlandish answer to your problem. Say your task was to design a new car (see below). You could say: "What if the car had no wheels?" One way of maneuvering such a car might be to have it move on a hovercraft skirt. This may not lead to a viable idea, but because it could make parking easier, it might get you to look at the parking problem differently and guide you toward an alternative and innovative solution.

Analogies and metaphors. From time to time, you can get bogged down in the finer details of a dilemma; you may be able to overcome this mental block if you find a parallel way of expressing the problem. For example, if you have been asked to think of a new system for filing information on your computer system, you could imagine this as a series of interconnected rabbits' burrows. This scene would perhaps lift your spirits and free your problem-solving abilities.

Sleeping on it. It can be very easy to believe that you are achieving nothing if you are not actively engaged in thinking about a problem. But the brain continues to pick over ideas, even when you are not concentrating. How often have you remembered a name while concentrating on something else? If you've generated possible solutions to a problem, and still seem to be getting nowhere, leave it and do something relaxing. You'll probably find the ideal solution will come when you least expect it.

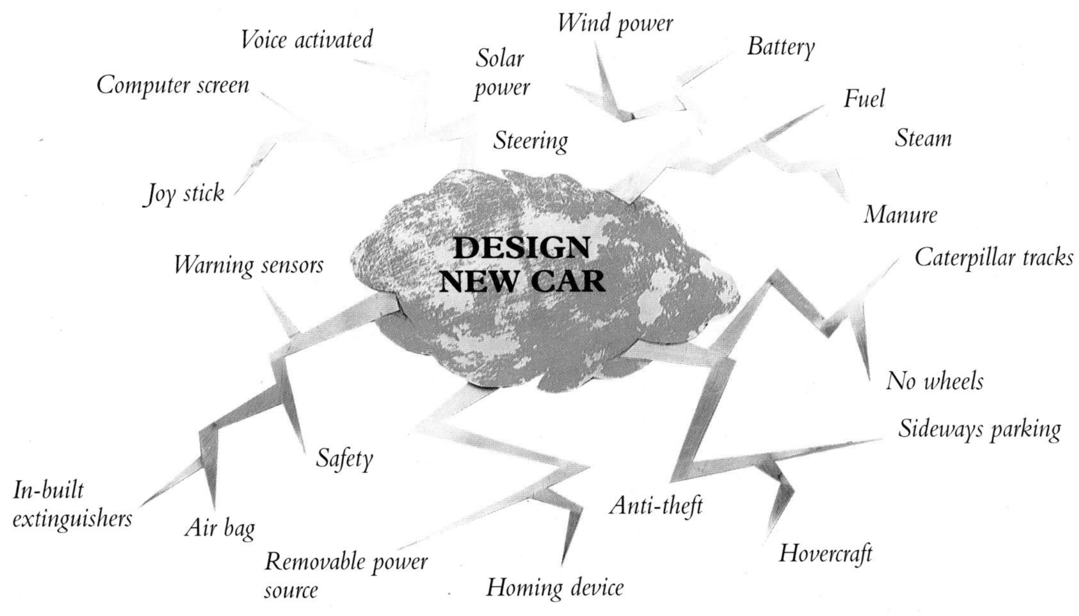

THINK CREATIVELY

Now that you've explored what creativity might mean to you, it is time to look at how creative you are already—and how creative you could be if you developed this facility. Few people can aspire to creative genius on the scale of Leonardo da Vinci or Albert Einstein, but most can improve the quality of their thinking enormously, simply by allowing their creative impulses to come to the fore. The setting of limitations will stifle creative thought time and time again—so just relax and let your creative juices flow! To get a picture of how creative you are already, try out the following exercises.

How creative is your thinking?

To find out whether you are already thinking creatively—and how far you still have to go—read questions 1-12, answering "often," "sometimes," or "never."

1. Do you tend to have strong feelings when you look at certain views or paintings, listen to particular pieces of music, or see a shape or color that appeals to you?

2. Do you take notice of your dreams, and use their content to help solve problems or provide insight into your personality?

3. Are you able to argue from a different point of view from your own?

4. Do you draw plans and sketches, listen to music, recite words out loud, and make up rhymes, ditties, and stories to help the thinking process along?

5. Are you able to think about several different things at once?

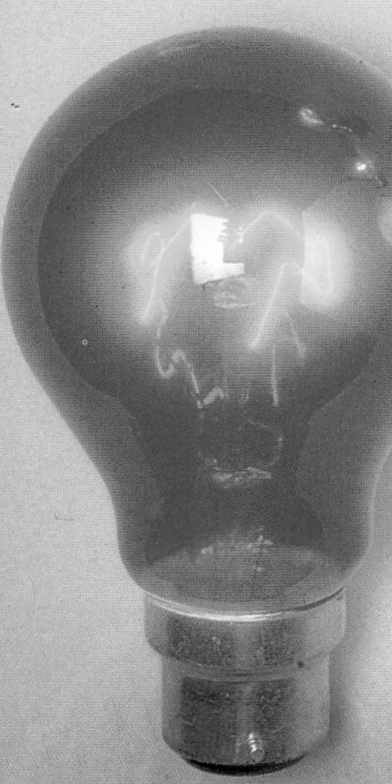

Seeing the light

Inspiration will come more often if you practice creative thinking.

6. How often do you consciously make use of your imagination, both at work and home? Do you avoid censoring your daydreams just because they are implausible?

7. Do you enjoy expanding your mental abilities through tricks, puzzles, and games?

8. Are you able to maintain your beliefs and opinions, whether or not people around you, or current opinion, agrees with you?

9. Does sensory stimulation tend to have a more powerful effect on you than intellectual challenge?

10. After thinking about a problem for some time, does the solution often come to you when you are doing something completely different, or after a dream?

11. How often do you express yourself artistically, for instance by cooking, singing in a choir, dancing, or writing a journal?

12. Do you enjoy finding alternative ways of solving problems long after you have come up with workable solutions to them?

What's your score?

Score 3 for each time you answered "often," 1 for every time you answered "sometimes," and 0 for each "never." Then, add up the figures to see how you scored.

A score between 0-12 indicates poor use of your creative skills. If you would like to change this aspect of yourself, use the ideas in this book to kick-start your creative-thinking potential.

Those people who scored between 13-24 are already thinking creatively a lot of the time. However, you will find your life much richer and more enjoyable if you are able to use your thinking skills even more widely.

If you scored between 25-36, then your creative thinking skills are already finely tuned and seem to be in constant and productive use. To develop them even more, make use of the exercises that you read in this book.

Don't worry if you scored much less than you would like: Practice makes perfect, and whatever your score, you can improve your creativity by working at it. There are many ways of doing this. One is by deciding to increase your involvement in creative activities, perhaps by introducing a bit of change into your routine. There are surprisingly easy ways to do this: Try taking a different route home from work, for instance, listening to the types of music you do not normally play, or visiting museums and art galleries.

You also need to exercise your problem-solving skills through attempting puzzles like those that appear on this page. Try your best to solve these problems and, although solving them can seem difficult, don't be tempted to give up on the puzzles before you have really tried hard. Exercising your problem-solving abilities in this way will help you to keep your general thinking skills sharp and well tuned.

The string problem

This is a classic problem-solving exercise, one that will really stretch your creative muscles. You are standing in a room that has two lengths of string hanging down from the ceiling. Your job is to tie the two strings together. However, they are fixed so far apart that, if you hold one of them, you cannot reach the other. The room is completely bare and all that you have with you is what is conventionally contained in a pocket or handbag. So what do you do now? How will you manage to complete the task?

When you think you've figured it out, or are completely stumped, turn to "Solutions," on page 131.

Pin Them Together

One of the most common blocks to creativity is "functional blindness"—the inability to think of any other uses for a given object apart from its conventional one. To see how seriously you suffer from this, try listing as many uses as possible for an ordinary pin.

However, as Tony Buzan shows in his book *Make the Most of Your Mind*, a far more searching test is trying to link a pin with a list of random words. You don't always have to make the pin and the object work together in any way—you just have to link them. So, if the words were "orange" and "clock," you might say a pin could make a hole through the skin of an orange so you could start to peel it, and a pin might also be linked to a clock because clocks are often made of metal, like pins. Try linking a pin to each of the following items: cup, geography, space shuttle, washing machine, flower, happiness, drapes, computer, Spain, window, cloud, automobile, birthday, yellow, vacation, chair, brick, rain.

How Thinking Goes Wrong

DO YOU KNOW WHY the way you are thinking does not always bring you the results you want? Maybe you feel dissatisfied with the effectiveness of your decision-making. You can improve your ability to make sound decisions if you know where you're likely to go wrong.

Rule number one about your thinking skills, regardless of how you rate them yourself, is that there is unlikely to be anything fundamentally wrong with your brain. The only thing at fault is probably the way you use, or fail to use, the dazzling brainpower you were born with. There are all kinds of specific techniques you can use to help your decision-making along, but first it is well worth checking whether you are falling into any common traps.

Thinking problems

You can sabotage the effectiveness of your mental powers in many ways, which can roughly be grouped into the following areas:

Choose the right route

There are many precautions you can take to help you avoid traps and dead ends.

1. Faulty data
- acting on false information
- acting on incomplete information
- misinterpreting available data

2. Flawed perceptions
- being swayed by your own set of prejudices, and making false assumptions
- lacking confidence in your own mental abilities
- allowing yourself to be persuaded by another's forceful argument
- being too easily impressed by facts and figures or technical jargon
- being unclear about what you really think as an individual
- failing to take personal responsibility and leaning heavily on established patterns of thought and action

3. Unfavorable circumstances
- lack of planning short-cuts
- not giving matters your full attention
- failing to see the whole problem
- trying to tackle tasks when you are over tired or too busy
- carrying out tasks too hurriedly

Spotting the pitfalls

Many situations involve more than one of the traps listed above. At their heart will be the recurrent problem of acting on false or incomplete information—an obstacle to good decision-making.

Say, for example, that you wanted to buy a certain financial policy. You may well go to a broker, allow him or her to explain the choice of policies to you, and make your decision based on this.

You are probably quite happy with this procedure, and feel that you have come away with the best policy, but what are the hidden traps? Firstly, it is unlikely that either you, or the broker, could possibly know every single policy in existence, and so you have incomplete information at your disposal. Your decision might also be based on totally false information—the broker could be lying to you. You may have gone to the broker because you, as an individual, tend to lack confidence in yourself where financial matters are concerned.

Like many people nowadays, you are encouraged to respect "experts," and might assume that, because the broker is smartly dressed and has an impressive office, he or she is giving you the best advice. A combination of technical jargon from the broker, along with a lack of time to make enquiries yourself, could make you very vulnerable to being persuaded that a certain policy is the one for you.

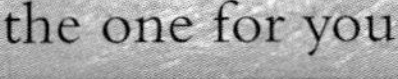

Giving yourself a chance

This example is not designed to make you think that you must spend your life investigating everything you purchase and the credentials of everybody who offers you professional advice. We all have to rely on others to a certain extent to help us through complex issues, and we are all limited by time—we may also choose to do better things with our time than examine endless policies without any prior knowledge.

Making your escape

No one can escape mental traps entirely, but it is possible to avoid them to a large degree in certain aspects of a situation. As ever, greater awareness is the key. For example, if you are tired or are being distracted in some way, then try to watch what you are doing especially carefully, and don't tackle anything too ambitious.

Believe in your own judgment, and beware of jargon. Question your prejudices and

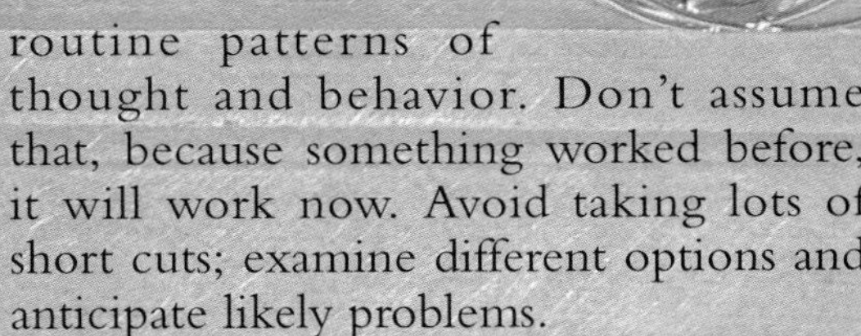

routine patterns of thought and behavior. Don't assume that, because something worked before, it will work now. Avoid taking lots of short cuts; examine different options and anticipate likely problems.

Having said all of this, don't be too hard on yourself when your mental powers let you down—learn to distinguish between slips and mistakes. Slips, such as dropping your door keys down a hole in the road, may have disastrous consequences, but are hard to avoid.

Mistakes, on the other hand, often spring from lack of proper reasoning—like setting out on a very long journey without doing a full set of basic checks on your automobile. It's up to you to be aware and learn to respond appropriately to different situations—to take responsibility for the way you think.

How to Think for Yourself

Have you ever bought something you didn't really want or need, simply because the salesman or woman persuaded you to do so? Many people find that they are unable to counteract the determined efforts of others, but with the right attitude, you can fight against them.

If you are aware of the tactics salespeople employ, you can be on guard and protect yourself. You are much more likely to find yourself ensnared in mental traps if you allow others to do the thinking for you. Life is now an increasingly complex affair, and the numbers of choices facing individuals can seem daunting. Don't allow yourself to be swamped. Learn to spot the signs of approaching persuasion and resist them, and you will soon be reclaiming your life and feeling much more satisfied.

The enemy within... and all around

Take yourself on a mental walk through your average day. You are bombarded with a constant barrage of persuasive messages—from the radio, TV, newspapers, magazines, billboards, and so on. Some are trying to sell you a new washing machine, others are persuading you to adopt a new political outlook. Most of us would consider ourselves to be wary and critical in the face of any kind of advertising, but the art of persuasion has easily kept pace with us and has become ever more subtle and sophisticated.

It's not just the advertisers that you have to contend with. Most of your relatives and friends are probably only too happy to give their advice on what you should do in any given situation, whether you asked for it or not. And all kinds of professionals will eagerly beat a path to your door to perform a range of tasks from managing your financial affairs to decorating your home.

Artful persuasion

Whether it's a sales assistant luring you into buying a new, sophisticated car, or someone at your door trying to recruit you into a religious group, the effective techniques of persuasion remain the same:

- using data, statistics, or jargon to impress you
- skating over contentious areas of the discussion
- playing to your real desires
- playing to your innermost prejudices and fears
- making an issue relevant to you personally
- using the soft-sell approach to win your confidence

Research has shown that certain conditions make us more receptive to changing our attitudes. For example, if the persuader appears to have expert knowledge, and especially if he or she has an attractive personality and is well presented, then he or she will stand a far greater chance of getting us to do what they want.

What can you do to push back the tide of other people's thoughts and opinions, and at the same time assert yourself? The main way is by asking questions... and more questions.

Questions to ask yourself

1. In every situation, ask yourself exactly what you want at the outset, and keep reviewing this over and over again throughout the process.

Is it really you?
Nowadays it is impossible to escape the ubiquitous advertisements claiming that they know what's best for you. The reality is that only you know what it is you really want—the trick is believing enough in yourself to say "no."

2. In all areas of your life, check that your fixed beliefs and routines remain right for you. Then your reaction to the persuasion of others will be more solid and take less effort to maintain. The information or goods that other people attempt to "sell" you may be what you want, but first you need to be sure they fit in with a set of long-term beliefs to which you are committed.

Questions to ask other people
1. Ask people for as much information about the object or notion that they are "selling" as possible. Don't be satisfied with vague answers on their part.
2. Ask others questions about themselves—so that you can begin to understand their role in the situation, and just why they are trying to win you over. Try to establish whether it is wise to trust others' judgment by asking yourself if they have your best interests at heart, and whether they can possibly know anything about you.

Believe in yourself

Even if you have decided to let someone manage one aspect of your home or work life, let that decision be a conscious one, and don't be persuaded to take on any services when you are tired and stressed. In fact, if you are not at your best in some way, try to put off major decisions until you are feeling confident and can digest all the facts and possible options—don't let others railroad you into making the decision they would have chosen. It is you who will be dealing with the consequences.

FALSE ASSUMPTIONS

How many legs does a table have? "Four" was probably your first response, yet pedestal tables have one leg, tripod tables have three legs, and some large tables have six legs or even more. What you did was conjure an image of the most common type of table, and automatically assume that all others are constructed in the same way.

This logic constitutes a kind of mental shortcut that can be useful: in daily life, we are bombarded with so much information that analyzing it all would be impossible. What your brain does, therefore, is fit each new piece of information into an existing framework. Say, for example, you are late for work because a heavy snowfall has delayed your train; the next time it snows, you might reasonably assume the same thing will happen, and allow extra time for your journey.

Mental laziness

Problems arise, however, when you use a similar thought process to construct erroneous conclusions based on false, irrelevant, or inadequate information. If, for instance, you take a day off work and decide to travel into town to do some shopping, you might set off for home in the middle of the afternoon, reasoning that, until the end of the working day, the trains will be empty. Unfortunately, the trains are almost as packed with children on their way home from school as they are with adults during rush hour, so, loaded with packages, you have to stand all the way. The misleading assumption here is that, during the times when you have no need to travel by train, nobody else does either.

While recognizing that there are some assumptions that may be necessary in order for you to get on in life, you shouldn't depend on them, allowing your thoughts, beliefs, and behavior to be narrow and inflexible. If you feel that your first impressions are always right, then you may begin to absorb and interpret only those facts that back up your existing opinions: If you see a shabbily dressed, scruffy-looking young man running after a frail elderly woman on her own, for example, would you assume that he was about to mug her? Or would you consider the possibility that he was trying to return something to the woman that she had dropped accidentally?

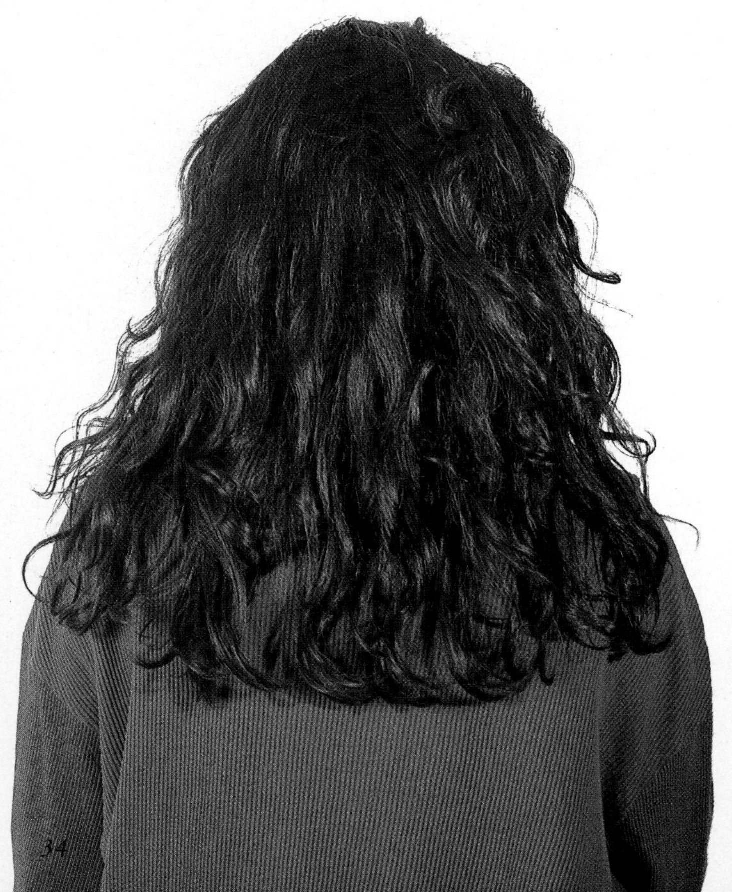

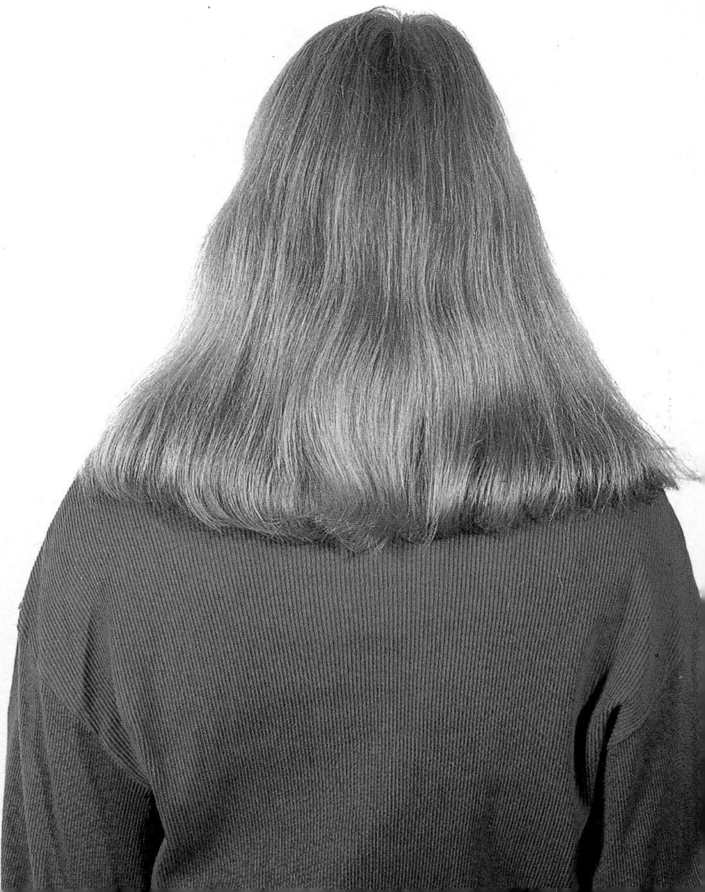

Now read on...

To test how readily you rely on your own assumptions and prejudices, read the following story, then consider the questions at the end:

One wet Friday night, the vice-president of Dabco Corporation hailed a taxicab outside the Carlton Tower and directed the driver to the Blue Moon bar. "At last," the vice-president thought, "the end of a nightmare week, and all I want is a relaxing night and a few drinks." This evening, however, relaxation was not on the cards. David, a Blue Moon regular, had brought a friend who was trying to move into management and wanted some advice. For the vice-president, there were too many social occasions that had been spoiled by people wanting free information—why couldn't they simply make an appointment, like everybody else? Late in the evening, the telephone on the bar rang and the bartender hollered out wearily, "Is there a Vice-President Bukowski in the bar? Someone by the name of Vivien wants to speak to you." "Freshening up as usual—I'll see what I can do," replied another regular, setting off drunkenly to knock on the door of the ladies' restroom.

1. What relationship do you think the person on the phone has to the main character?
2. What image do you have of the bartender?
3. What image do you have of the main character?
4. What image do you have of the drunk?
5. Why does the drunk head for the ladies' room?

Drawing conclusions

You may have assumed that this story is about a businessman's night out—it seems full of stereotypes such as the jaded bartender and the drunk.

In fact, the vice-president is in the ladies' room because she is female. The caller is her aunt (it could have been a partner or friend), and the bartender and the drunk are also female; there is nothing to suggest otherwise, yet even female readers may assume that a top executive with an aggressive manner ("Why can't they make an appointment...") is male.

Of course, you might have guessed correctly because the subject of this article made you aware. If so, remember this is the sort of awareness you should always exercise: questioning your assumptions, exercising your creative thinking, and constantly trying to keep your mind the way it should be—open.

Judging by appearances
Are these individuals male or female? If you're tempted to make snap judgments, *turn to page 131 to find out if you are right.*

The Right Decision?

Decision-making is at the very center of our lives—from whether to have a cup of tea or coffee to whether we should open up a business. Some decisions primarily affect just ourselves or our immediate circle; others can affect much larger numbers of people. Of course, we want to make the right decision as often as possible. Everyone makes wrong decisions sometimes, but your margin of error can be narrowed if you take a closer look at the thinking practices underlying your decision-making. There are four major areas where poor mental practices could seriously disrupt your ability to make the right decision:

1. Falling for false logic, by not taking full account of all aspects of a problem.

2. Making assumptions and jumping to conclusions, not taking time to consider what's happening.

3. Failing to either consider or review all the viable options available to you.

4. Failing to anticipate what might go wrong and preparing for this.

Look at the following four scenarios illustrating the above points, and judge whether you would make the same thinking mistakes as the people involved:

False logic

A corner delicatessen was failing to reach the turnover that its owners had hoped for, and so they decided to increase the range of goods stocked. They believed that they would pull in more customers, including those popping out for sudden purchases when they didn't have the time or the inclination to go further afield. Much to their puzzlement, turnover actually fell, but why did it do so? Although it seems logical to assume that a diversification of goods will lead to more customers, who will buy a wider range of products, this does not allow for human nature; the regulars had come to perceive the shop as specializing in delicatessen goods. When other products appeared, they seemed to "water down" the store's character, and the customers forgot what its strength had been in the first place. It would almost certainly have been wiser to build on what the business was known and valued for—the customers could even have been asked for their views on what they wanted from the shop.

Overlooking your options

Sally was a freelance writer, always conscientious about seeing that her vital computer was properly insured. When she moved into a new rented office and wanted to change the details on her policy, the company increased the premiums considerably—partly because of the rising incidence of computer theft. They also required her to pay a larger proportion of any replacement cost herself.

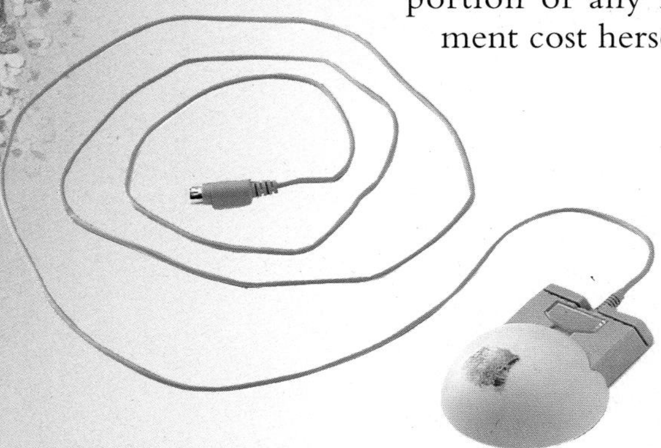

Then disaster struck—her computer was stolen. Because Sally couldn't prove the thief had forced entry, she received very little money, and was considerably out of pocket. The option she had overlooked was investing in a system to secure the computer to her desk and alarm it. This would certainly have made her computer less of a target, and she could have saved the amount of her premium in a high-interest account in case of theft. Sally ignored this option because she was locked into a blind alley of thinking that the only way to safeguard valuables is to insure them.

Jumping to conclusions

Jerry and Diana's relationship had been having problems for some time, and the spark seemed to be fading fast. One day, Diana announced that she was thinking of going back to school. Jerry assumed this was another sign that she found him intellectually unchallenging and was growing away from him. He decided they should call it a day.

Diana was horrified, and further discussion revealed that she had made her move in order to broaden her horizons and lift her out of the rut she found herself in. This in turn, she hoped, might breathe some fresh air into their relationship. Jerry, unfortunately, had made the fatal mistake of drawing his conclusion in isolation, without taking the trouble to investigate the possible reasons behind Diana's decision.

What could go wrong?

Ben had been feeling out of sorts, and decided that a good way to cheer himself up would be to organize a huge party for his birthday. He spent a considerable amount of time and effort investigating various possible venues and catering companies, and eventually chose the most elaborate arrangements available before sending out his invitations.

When the night of his birthday arrived, a large group of his friends were unable to join him because they got a last-minute chance to go on an exotic holiday together; this in turn deterred a few others from attending, so the small number of guests who did show up felt uncomfortable rattling around in the grand room Ben had hired. He found the whole experience very distressing since he had counted on a large turnout. If he had considered what might go wrong, he might have arranged a more informal gathering at home, or booked a more adaptable venue—perhaps one with two intimate, adjoining rooms rather than one huge one.

Breaking out

Being wise on behalf of other people is easy, but in fact everyone can improve their decision-making with more directed thinking. If you consistently limit yourself through habit, assumption, and restricted options while you are in the process of making decisions, you only have a limited chance of ensuring those decisions are successful. Instead, make sure you look closely at all your options.

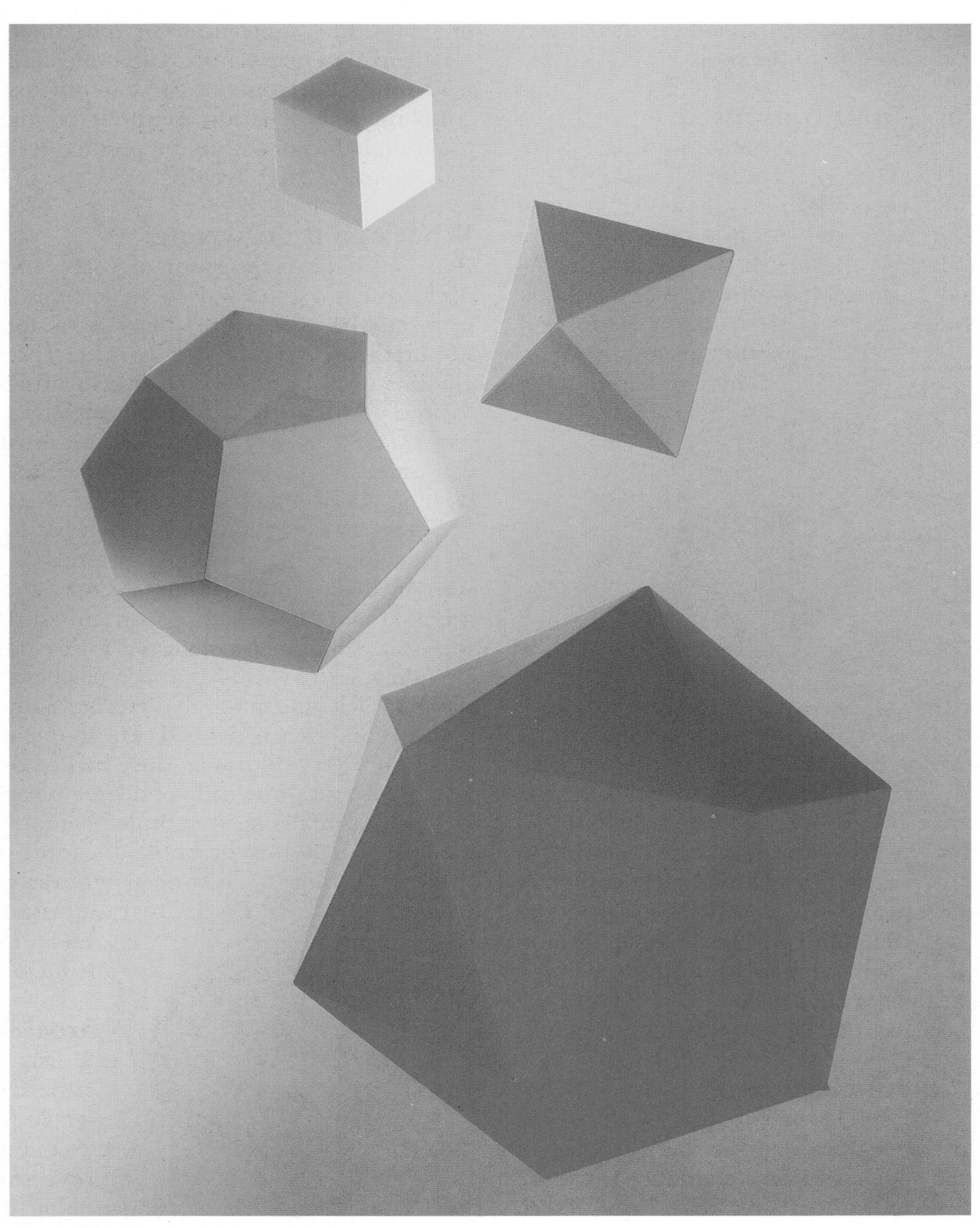

CHAPTER TWO

THINKING IT THROUGH

WHEN YOU ARE wondering how to tackle a tricky subject, do you ever pause to consider if the style of thinking you are using is the best and the most effective for the task? Some people approach all problem solving in exactly the same way, but by identifying and implementing an appropriate type of thinking for the situation at hand, you'll make it much easier to deal with productively.

This chapter opens with a collection of simple and intriguing quizzes, such as "What's Your Thinking Style?" on pages 40-41, that will help you to identify the strengths and weaknesses in your own thinking habits. Working through these puzzles will give you a head start toward channeling all your abilities in a more efficient way.

Following on from this, the chapter takes a close look at various aspects of logic. The science of logic—the process of reasoning in a step-by-step way—is a precise and rigorous discipline with its own rules. Thinking logically is an important ingredient in thinking successfully. By learning, for example, how not to make false assumptions, and by working through a series of ingenious games, you will find out how to employ your logical abilities to maximum effect. "Using Logic" on pages 42-43 will point you in the right direction.

This chapter then goes on to examine three broad categories of thinking style. The first of these is convergent thinking, essentially a linear, step-by-step progression toward one "correct" answer; this style is described on pages 50-51. This is contrasted with divergent thinking (pages 54-55), in which trains of thought can set you off in any number of directions, leading to a wide range of workable solutions.

In situations where you're not looking for one, obvious, answer, modes of thinking that involve making connections between seemingly unrelated subjects may be more useful. Here, radiant thinking (defined in "Branching Out" on pages 56-57) comes into its own.

To solve problems successfully, you need a sound grasp of the facts as well as a facility with several types of thinking. This chapter looks at issues such as perseverance and testing workable hypotheses, which allows you to preempt problems before they arise. Finally, it offers a chance for you to put all your problem-solving skills into practice as you play the role of detective in a brainteasing murder-mystery story.

HARNESSING YOUR THINKING POWER AND LEARNING HOW TO FOCUS IT EFFECTIVELY WILL ENHANCE YOUR ABILITY TO COPE IN A WIDE VARIETY OF SITUATIONS.

WHAT'S YOUR THINKING STYLE?

MENTAL CAPACITY CAN VARY greatly from one person to another, and while most mental skills can to a large degree be worked at and improved upon, the truth is that some people are naturally better at a wider array of tasks than others. This varying aptitude, the component responsible for a person performing well or less well across the range of abilities, is known as intelligence.

Comparing the intelligence of individuals by valuing it numerically dates from 1905, when the French government commissioned psychologist Alfred Binet to devise a test that would identify slow-developing children. His work inspired many others, including American psychologist Lewis Terman, who in 1916 coined the phrase IQ, or "Intelligence Quotient."

Today, the most familiar IQ scale is the Stanford-Binet intelligence score. Firstly, the subject takes a series of tests designed to ascertain a mental age in years and months. To calculate IQ, the mental age is divided by the chronological age and the result is multiplied by 100. For example, if a 9-year-old has a mental age of 12, the calculation is 144 (mental age in months) ÷ 108 (chronological age in months) x 100 = 133 (IQ rating). An IQ score of 100 indicates an average intellectual level for the subject's age.

Intelligence testing has attracted controversy over the years, especially when it is used to make crucial decisions about people's future. Criticism has stemmed from the fact that IQ tests judge only logical and verbal reasoning, whereas, academics now argue, intelligence involves more than simply being able to deal with numbers, words, and shapes. In the early 1990s, American psychologists Peter Salovey and John Mayer introduced the notion of emotional intelligence (EQ). They observed a group of four-year-old children and noted that those who exhibited the most effective self-discipline in a series of simple will-power tests went on to perform better academically and socially.

While the issue of what constitutes intelligence will continue to be debated, there is no doubt that IQ-type testing can provide insight into an individual's intellectual functioning. This can assist in the development of natural skills and talents, and play an important role in making sound life choices. Here is a simple test that will make you more aware of the way you think. The answers are on page 132.

Section 1

1. Which shape is the odd one out?

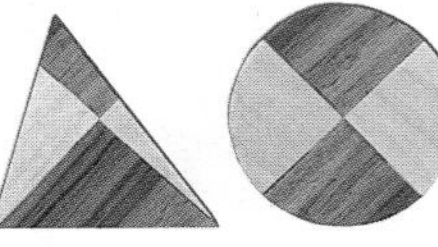
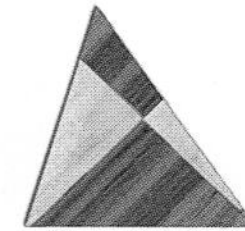
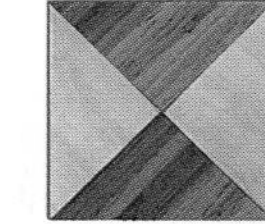

2. Which of the four small designs is a mirror image of the large one?

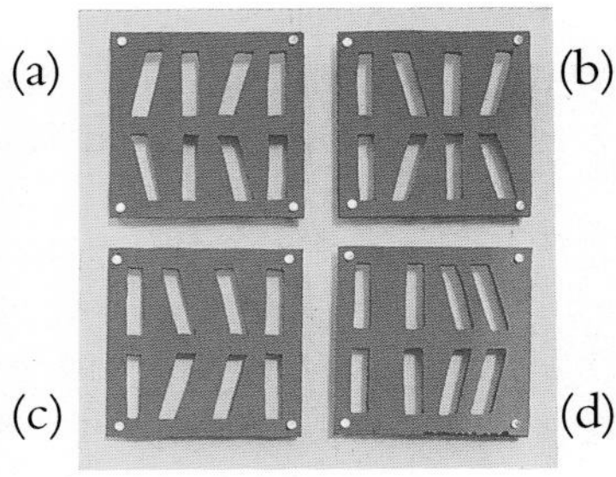

3. Identify the missing image from the choices given.

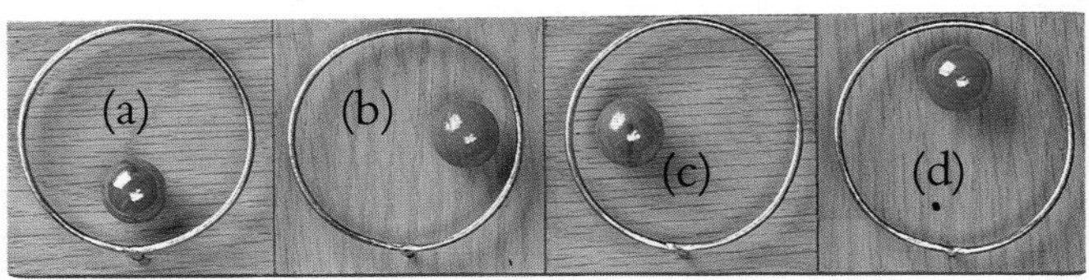

4. Fill in the appropriate image.

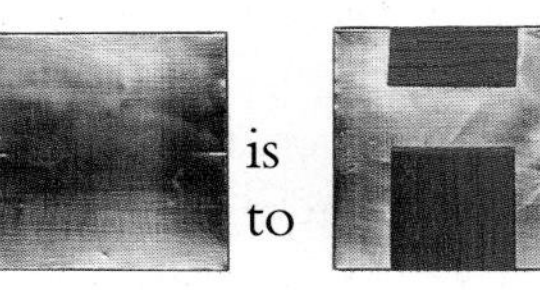
is to
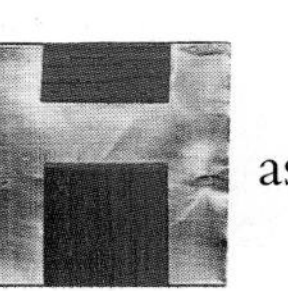
as
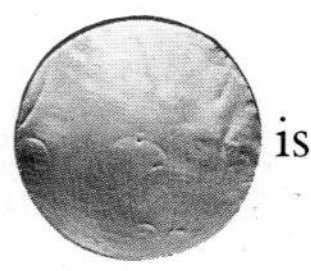
is to

5. Which design is the odd one out?

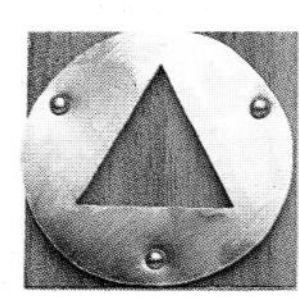

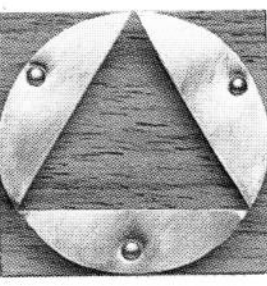

6. Is the missing image (a), (b), (c), or (d) below?

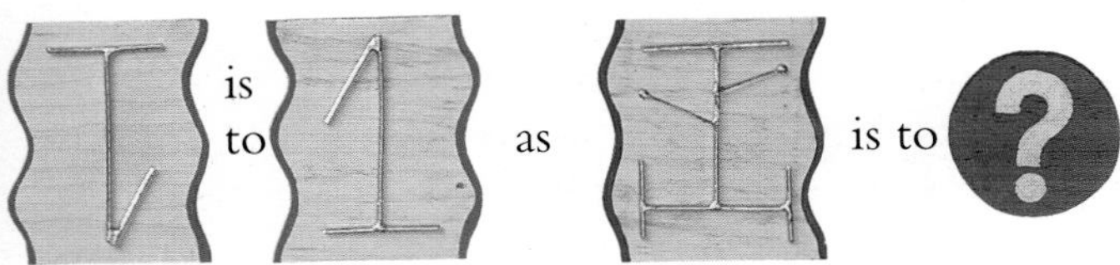

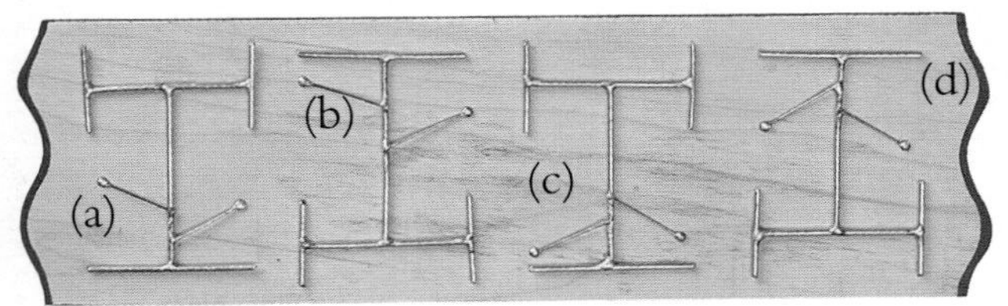

7. Pick out the missing pair of arrows.

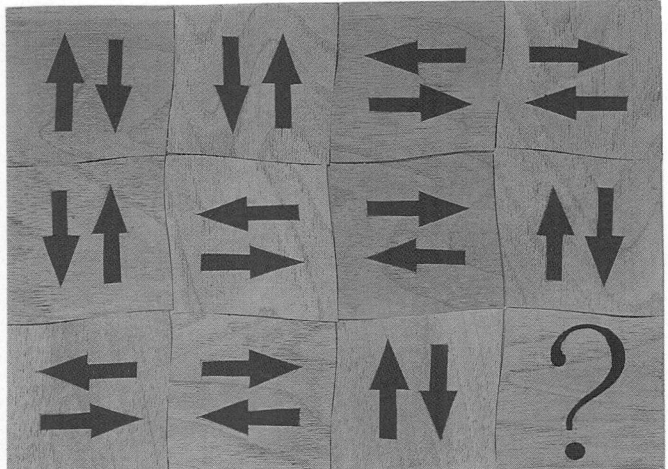

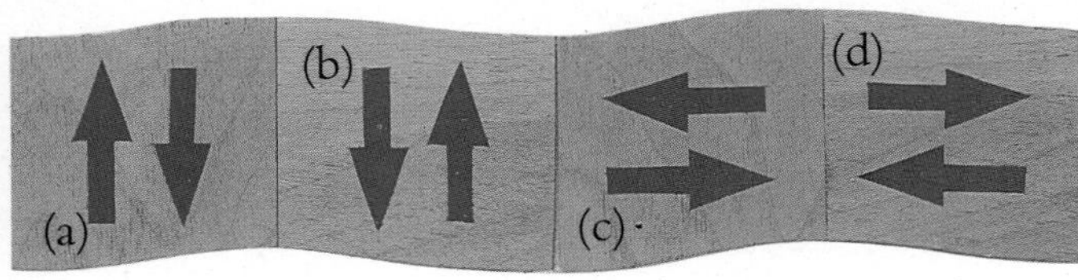

8. Which small face mirrors the large one?

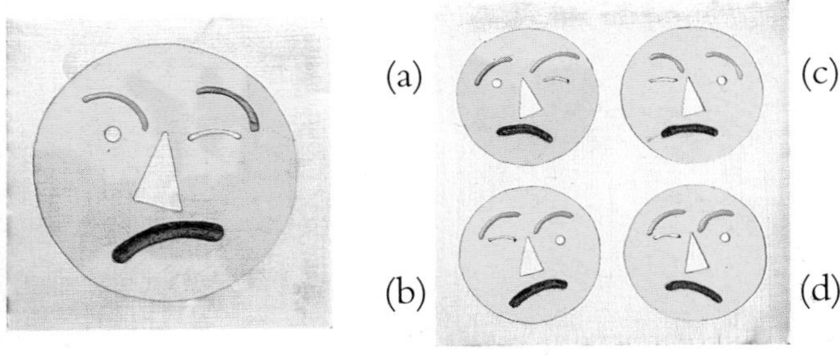

Section 2

1. In this sequence of numbers, what comes next?
4, 8, 12, 16, __

2. In this sequence of numbers, what comes next?
31, 29, 26, 22, __

3. Tom has $1.00. Mike has 9 cents less than Bob. Bob has half as much as Tom. How much money does Mike have?

4. If A + B = 3, and 2 - B = 1, what is A?

5. Which number is the odd one out?
1, 5, 9, 13, 16, 21.

6. A is 30 miles from B. If a motorist takes half an hour to complete the journey, at what speed is she traveling?

7. If 25 percent of all the eggs in a particular consignment are bad, how many good eggs are there likely to be in a carton of 80?

8. Which is the greater value, 39 percent of 429 or 40 percent of 417?

9. If it takes 4.5 m of material to make a tablecloth, how many tablecloths will you get out of 36 m?

10. 71 is as much more than 63 as it is less than what number?

Section 3

1. Dog is to fox as canary is to ___? Choose from: cat, seagull, goldfish, wolf.

2. Rearrange the following words to make a sentence, then determine whether the sentence is true or false. Legs Most Nine Have Dogs.

3. Which is the odd one out?
wheelbarrow, spade, bicycle, car.

4. Row is to boat as ___ is to car? Choose from: engine, road, drive, wheel.

5. Bat is to baseball as ___ is to ice hockey? Choose from: skate, ball, puck, hockey stick.

6. Which is the odd one out?
barber, comb, haircut, scissors, razor.

7. Rearrange the following words to make a sentence, then determine whether the sentence is true or false. In The Never Sharks Water Swim Can.

8. Janice sits in front of Janet. Tim sits in front of Janice. Janet sits behind Tim. Tom sits in front of Tim. Who sits at the back?

9. Dish is to fish as ___ is to race? Choose from: speed, pace, track, stadium.

10. Which is the odd word out?
fish, carp, bream, swim, shark?

Using Logic

Most of us think of logic as the act of thinking in a reasonable way. But logic is also a science that, according to *Webster's Dictionary*, "deals with the principles and criteria of validity of inference and demonstration." Whichever way you view it, logic is woven closely into the fabric of modern life, from the structure of legal and economic systems to many of the popular learning and teaching methods. A factual, rational view of life underlines the way society is run throughout the whole of the Western world.

But logic's methodical, step-by-step approach cannot provide all the answers. Logic alone will not yield the flashes of insight that lead to extraordinary scientific discoveries or works of art. It can, however, be used to great advantage as a tool for organizing thought. To do this, you need to understand how logic works and where its pitfalls lie.

A case in point

All zebras have four legs, a table has four legs, so my table is a zebra? Clearly false logic.

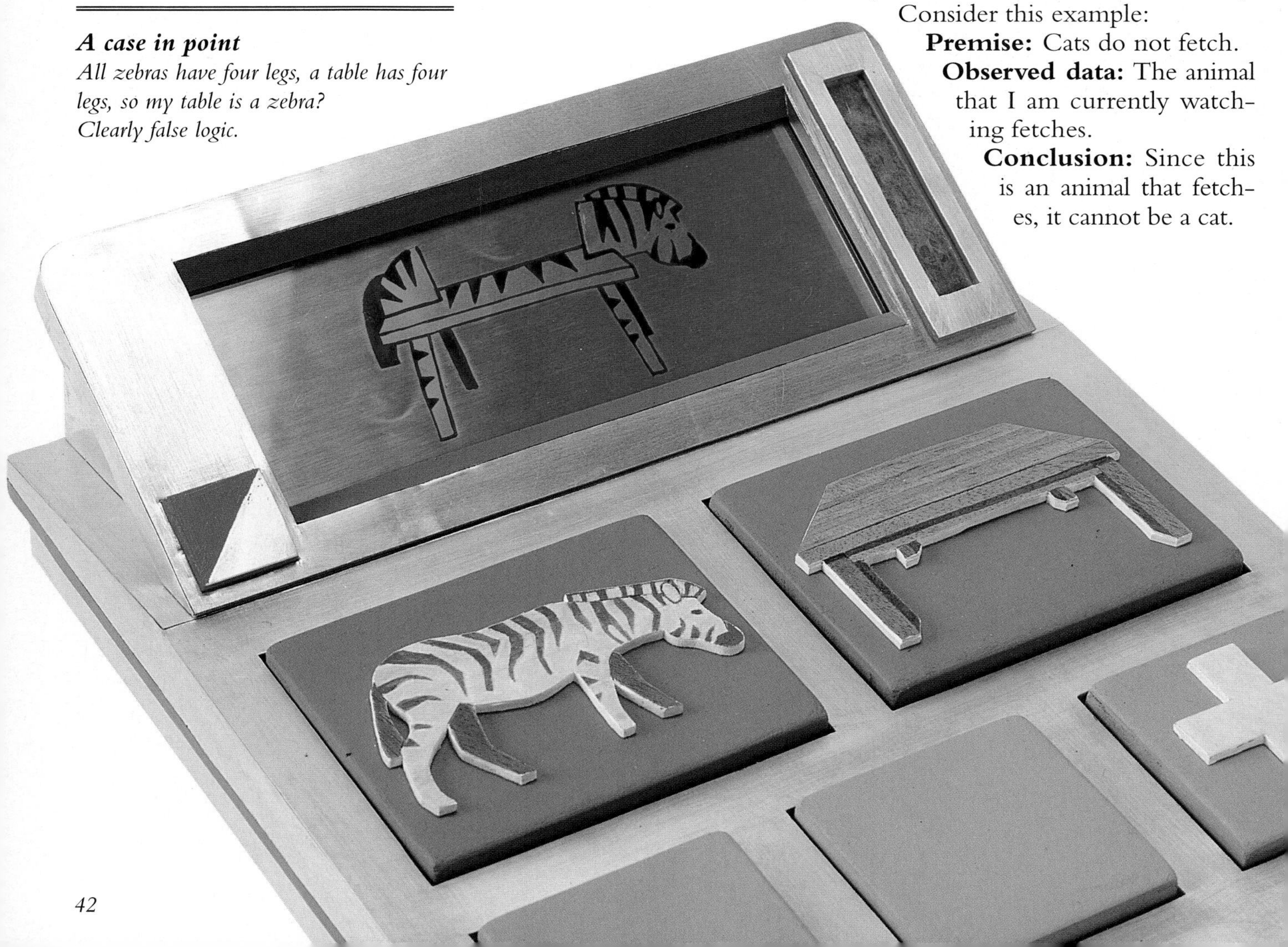

The ABC of logical argument

A logical argument can be broken down into three main elements: the premise, the evidence or observable data, and the conclusion.

The first step of a logical argument sets out at least one premise—a truth assumed to be accurate. As a second step, the premise is applied to the evidence or data—what we can see or understand ourselves. The final step involves reaching a conclusion that satisfies the premise while accounting for the observable data.

The following examples show the three elements in action and demonstrate how your choice of premises and data, and how you interpret them, is the key to building a sound, logical argument.

The premise

A watertight argument has to have an accurate premise. This may seem obvious, but a good premise can be hard to come by. Consider this example:

Premise: Cats do not fetch.

Observed data: The animal that I am currently watching fetches.

Conclusion: Since this is an animal that fetches, it cannot be a cat.

If the animal you were talking about was your friend Laura's cat, Isabella, your conclusion would be wrong. Not only does Isabella retrieve a paper ball when Laura throws it, she has also been known to appear in Laura's bed at four in the morning, carrying that same paper ball in her mouth, and poking Laura repeatedly in the nose until she sits up in bed far enough to play fetch.

The fault with this argument lies in its premise. At first glance, it seems pretty strong—dogs, not cats, are the fetching species according to popular animal lore. Nevertheless, this premise is not universally true and some cats do fetch. Too often, people anchor their arguments to premises that they just *assume* to be true.

Finding a universally true premise is not easy. We usually choose premises based on either personal experience or information that encompasses a broader range of experience. Even so, there may be exceptions to the premises we put forward. One way of reinforcing a logical argument is to choose more than one premise—say, a list of several important feline characteristics—to apply to what you observe, so that the element of chance is reduced considerably.

The data

Just as premises can be faulty, so can our perception of data, and this may seriously weaken an argument. Ensuring that the data we use is valid strengthens it. The following is a clear example of a problem where the apparently logical manner in which the facts are interpreted leads to a totally inaccurate conclusion:

Premise: We cannot eat very hard things because we are unable to bite through them.
Observed data: Coconuts are very hard.
Conclusion: Therefore, we can't eat coconuts.

The premise was correct, but we were led to a false conclusion because we were acting on false, or rather incomplete, data—obviously, the outer shell of a coconut is hard, but the inside is much softer and *is* edible.

A gap in the argument
Weak premises and data will destroy the watertight seal on your conclusions.

The conclusion

The final potential for weakness in a logical argument is the way in which the premise and the data are interpreted in order to produce a conclusion. An unassailable premise, even taken together with a set of well-observed data, can still add up to a generally inadequate conclusion.

Consider this scenario. A local community group is looking into efficient ways of dealing with the locally produced waste. While they are considering various methods of getting rid of it, one member puts forward the suggestion that it should be burned. His argument runs as follows:

Premise: To safeguard the health of the community, it is vital that all garbage be disposed of effectively.
Observed data: The quickest and easiest way to get rid of garbage is to burn it.
Conclusion: Therefore, incinerating garbage must be the most desirable way to dispose of the community's waste.

This is an excellent example of adding two and two and coming up with a number other than four. The premise and the data were without fault, but simply putting them together results in an unsatisfactory and erroneous conclusion. In fact, recycling is usually a much more efficient and ecologically sensitive way of dealing with the problem. What this, and all the other examples show is that, when employed in the correct situations, there is nothing misguided about logic—what must be avoided, however, is being misled by *false logic.*

The wider view

In order to avoid this pitfall, make sure you keep alert to the many traps you could fall into along the way. What you often need to do is look a little bit beyond the boundaries of an argument's three logical steps, and incorporate other information that you know is relevant. In this last example, yes, of course, it is both healthy and necessary to get rid of garbage, but it is well known that one of the best ways to deal with waste—and the healthiest environmentally—is to recycle it.

Do You Think Straight?

Now that you've considered the elements of logical thinking as outlined on pages 42–43, test your skill by reading the following tale and trying out the puzzles along the way. In each section, you are given a premise and a collection of evidence, or "observable data," and asked to draw your conclusions from these. For the purpose of this exercise, assume that all the premises are true. Then, turn to "Solutions" on pages 132–133 to find out if your conclusions are correct.

Episode 1: Tinseltown

In the country of Dreamland, Tinseltown is the city where film actors and their agents live. Everyone in the city of Tinseltown is either an actor or an agent. One of the really peculiar things about Tinseltown is that actors always tell the truth, while agents always lie. (*The premise.*)

A young actress coming to Tinseltown to get into the movies runs into three people sipping cocktails around a table at a sidewalk café. She goes to the one closest to the sidewalk, a woman sporting bouffant hair and glasses studded with rhinestones, and asks, "Are you an actor or an agent?"

Bouffant mumbles her response, so the young actress turns to the man sitting next to her and says, "What did she say?" The man in question wears plaid, pencil trousers. Replying to her question he says, "She said she is an agent." At this point the third person at the table, a muscular man with a dazzling smile, pipes up, "Don't believe him, he's lying." (*The observed data.*)

Question: *To what professions do Pencil Trousers and Muscle Man belong?*

Episode 2: On to Rerun Pass

Unable to figure out the answer to her question, the young actress hops into her pink Cadillac convertible and drives to the next town, Rerun Pass.

There are three types of inhabitants in Rerun Pass: actors, agents, and directors. As in Tinseltown, actors always tell the truth and agents always lie. Directors in Rerun Pass, however, are more like normal people—sometimes they lie and sometimes they tell the truth—so they are referred to as "Normals" in the local slang. The town's founders decreed that actors could only marry agents and vice versa (so, by default, directors can only marry directors). That means that in any married couple, either both people are directors, or one person is an actor while the other person is an agent. (*The premise.*)

Our heroine has heard about the famous Rerun Pass Bar & Grill, which is run in their spare time by a married couple. The wife tends the bar while her husband is the short-order cook. Unfortunately, our heroine can't remember if the couple are actors, agents, or directors when they are not in their bar.

On entering the establishment, a gloomy red and gold place rather like a Victorian boudoir, she sees that the only two people there are the short-order cook and the bartender. The short-order cook is a tall, stick-skinny man wearing a spangled jacket. Before she opens the menu, he says, "My wife is not Normal."

Having finished her burger and fries, our heroine decides to stop off at the bar for a drink. Before she can say, "Shirley Temple," the bartender says to her, "My husband is not Normal." (*The observed data.*) Question: *What professions do the short-order cook and the bartender belong to outside their bar?*

Episode 3: Stopover in San Smarto

Discouraged by her inability to engage in a straight conversation with anyone, our young hopeful jumps into her car once more and starts to drive. Just as she notices the sign welcoming her to San Smarto, she realizes that she has forgotten about a lunch date she made with an old friend who lives just outside Tinseltown. In fact, she's even lost track of what day it is, so she decides to stop off in San Smarto in order to find out.

She has heard a great deal about this wealthy town where only producers and casting directors live. She has also been warned about their curious customs. Producers, who always wear faded blue work shirts unbuttoned at the neck to reveal their deep tans and chunky gold chains, tell lies on Mondays, Tuesdays, and Wednesdays, but otherwise tell the truth. Casting directors, who wear only Armani suits, lie on Thursdays, Fridays, and Saturdays, but tell the truth on all the other days. (*The premise.*)

Our determined hopeful decides to stop off at the local country club to ascertain the day of the week. She approaches a producer who is talking to a casting director.

"I'm very sorry to interrupt," she says, "but would you be kind enough to tell me what day of the week it is?"

The producer is the first to answer. "Yesterday was one of my lying days," he says helpfully. The casting director then chimes in, "Yesterday was one of my lying days too." (*The observed data.*) Question: *What day of the week is it?*

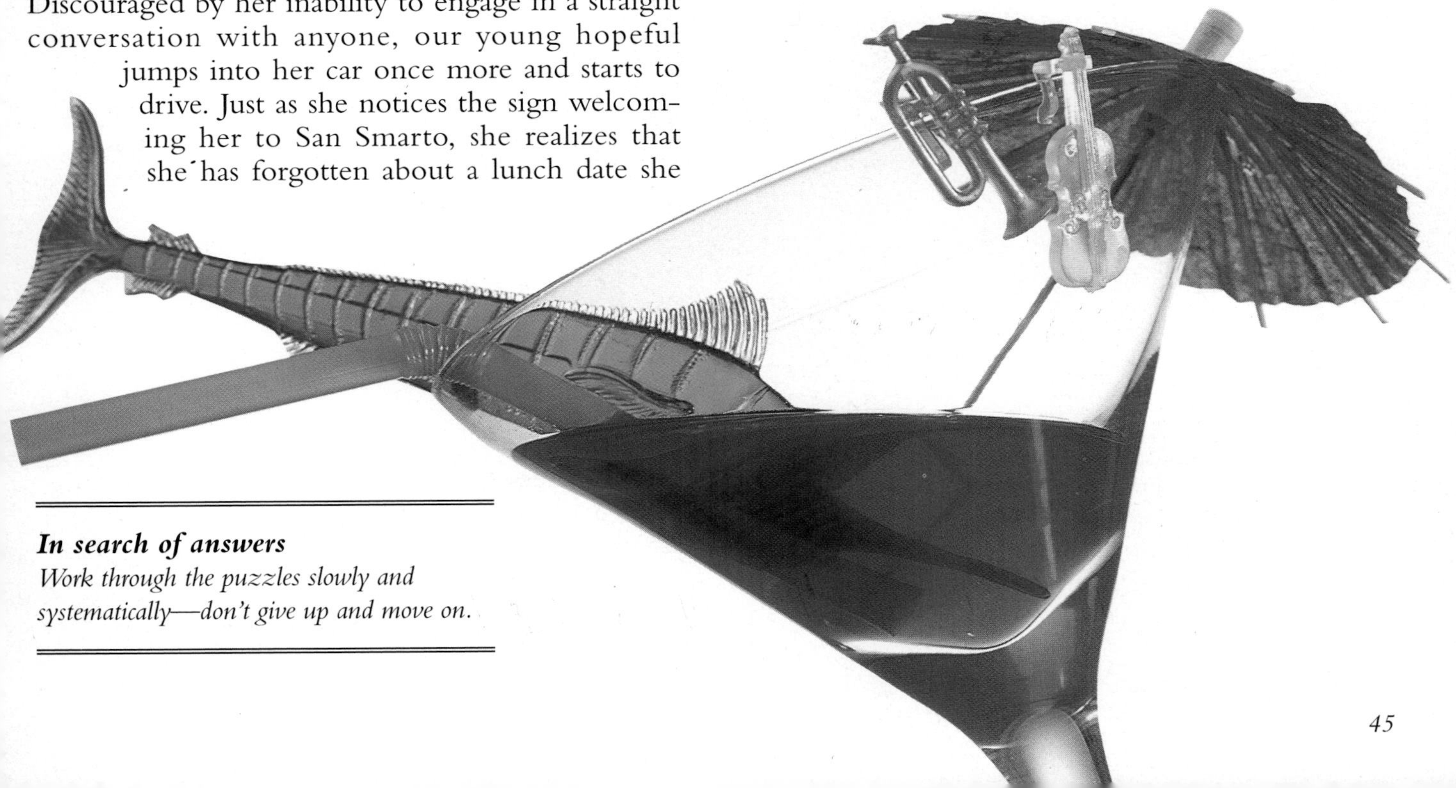

In search of answers
Work through the puzzles slowly and systematically—don't give up and move on.

Logical Moves

To win at some games you just need a certain amount of luck—a good roll of the dice, for example, or a hand of aces. Others require speed, manual dexterity, or a good memory. Many of the more complex and sophisticated games, however, involve few or none of these elements but instead demand a high level of skill that combines natural aptitude with strategic, logical thinking.

Chess is a game that lends itself particularly well to logical thinking, and is a good illustration of the premise-data-conclusion strategy set out on pages 42–43. According to this, the first step toward a logical solution is the premise. In chess, the premise consists of the moves that are allowed for each piece. Good chess players think not only about their own potential moves, but also those of their opponent; the more skillful the player, the longer the sequence of moves he or she is able to envisage in order to decide on the most advantageous one. The observed data would be the position of the pieces on the board at any one time; the conclusion, the move the player decides to make.

Experts and beginners

To consider all the possibilities of a particular chess position ten moves ahead would involve a player looking at something like a billion billion billion scenarios. Even if considering each one took only a millionth of a second, it would still take 1,000 billion years. So, just how does a grand master do it?

Advanced chess players have a great deal of experience to draw on when it comes to predicting what sort of moves are likely to come up. This experience forms part of the premise

PLAYING GAMES WITH MEMORY

Grand masters remember chess positions better and work out possible moves more efficiently than less expert players. Although memory would seem to be the dominant skill required, studies indicate a situation that is more complex. The boards above show the results of an experiment that clearly proves this point. In this test, expert and not-so-expert players were shown a board (left), with pieces in position, for five seconds. They were then asked to re-create what they had seen. As you can see, the masters (middle) achieved results that were much closer to the actual positions than the average players (right). However, when the masters were presented with bizarre or unlikely positions, their recall was no better than that of the average players. This finding shows that it is because masters can recognize game patterns from experience—and not simply because they have better visual memories—that they are able to re-create the positions with greater accuracy.

they construct about what the subsequent moves could be. They classify the possibilities in terms of broad strategic offense or defense moves—a "kingside attack with pawns," for example.

So, being a great chess player—or a player of any other type of strategic game, for that matter—isn't simply a question of being faster than anyone else at processing possibilities. What an expert chess player has, rather, is the ability to process possibilities in chunks, based on the experience that comes from hours of practice. Grand masters, therefore, tend to consider board positions in a fairly abstract way, whereas beginners to the game tend to form a mental picture of the possible positions of pieces actually in place on the chess board.

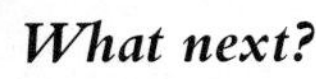

What next?

To tackle many strategic games, you simply have to learn to apply a few logical thinking rules.

Man versus computer

The development of communications technology has always been accompanied by the controversial question of whether computers could be superior to man when it comes to the type of logical thinking typified by chess. However, while successive generations of computers are processing information at increasingly high speeds, no software has yet begun to rival the complex subtleties of the human brain. Chess demands a unique combination of knowledge, experience, and intuitive flair, and in this respect a specialist computer program is still vastly inferior to the genius of a grand master.

FACT OR ASSUMPTION?

The key to constructing a sound argument is choosing a solid premise. Such premises come from information that is presented to you, then filtered through your values and experiences. Make sure, however, to assess the facts concerned carefully, rather than accept them at face value. Sometimes, for example, information is true, but gives only a partial view of the situation. Consider the following argument:

Women and wages

"According to the most recent statistics available, the average working person in the U.S. has a median weekly income of $381. The median income for men, however, is $445, whereas for women, it is only $309. Many people find it shocking that, in the present day, women still earn at a level that is less than 70 percent of that applicable for men. They claim that if the U.S. were really an unbiased culture, men and women would be on a financial par. But these defenders of women's rights are overlooking one simple biological fact: women are the people who give birth.

"The truth is that women earn less than men because they leave to have children, and are therefore not in the workforce long enough to attain the most senior, highest-paying, jobs. They are not willing to make the sacrifices necessary to get these jobs, nor do they really want the stress that goes with increased responsibility. Because women do not make the same degree of commitment to their career as men, it is logical that they should command lower salaries.

"In fact, the so-called 'glass ceiling' is a spurious justification women use to back up their demands for higher pay. By crying discrimination, they hope to obscure the fact that they are a less-reliable part of the workforce. Companies cannot be expected to invest the same amount of money in a woman who is likely to leave to raise a family, as they invest in a man with a long-term future. After all, it is a woman's choice whether or not she works. Men don't have the option of staying at home, so it is only fair that they are paid more to compensate."

Now skim through this text again, underlining the sections that are fact and those that are subjective opinion or guesswork. How much do you think is opinion, or interpretation? Actually, aside from the broad assertions that women drop out of the workforce, have babies, and are paid less than men, the preceding text is nearly all opinion. The

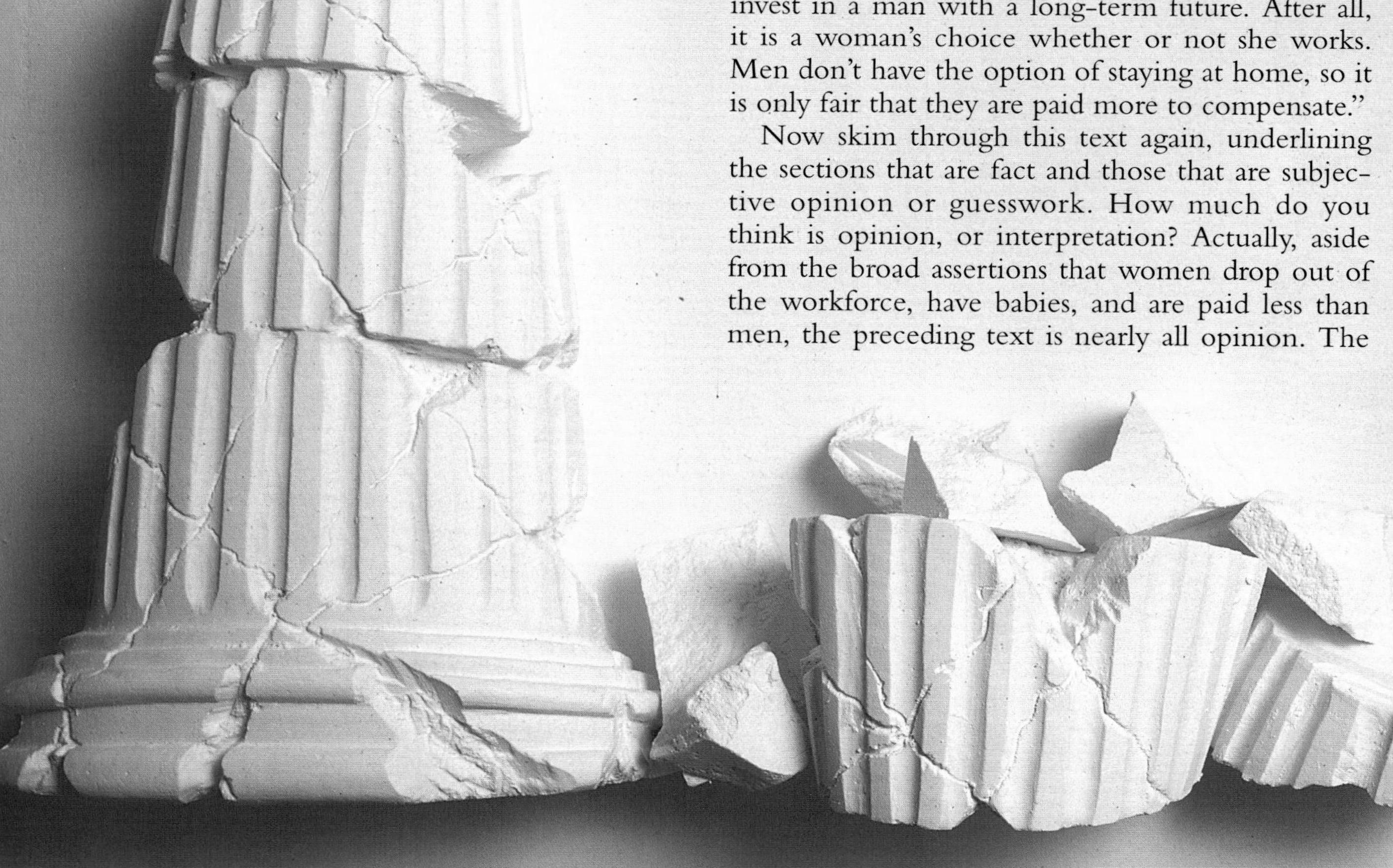

few facts are sprinkled through a rambling, illogical, prejudiced argument to give an impression of veracity.

In truth, while some women leave work to have children, by no means all do; the recent U.S. census shows that new mothers have actually increased their labor participation. In 1988, 51 percent of mothers between 18 and 44 with children under one were working, compared to 31 percent in 1976. Note that these statistics do not include working mothers with older children. So, while women undeniably give birth, they do not necessarily stop working afterward.

The explanation offered as to why women are paid less is only one possible interpretation of the situation, and has no factual basis. It is just as likely that women are paid less because of discrimination, or the existence of an ingrained conservatism—the so-called glass ceiling—as it is that they earn lower wages because they are less reliable.

The whole picture

Note that the argument contains no objective criteria for the value of men and women's work in terms of productivity, company loyalty, efficiency, or any other measure of their worth to a profit-making enterprise.

The statistics in the original argument, while accurate, are very selective, since they were plucked from a large body of research to back up a specific opinion. The following figures, also relating to average weekly wages, were gathered in the same way, by the same organization:

Male managers, administrators	$667
Female managers, administrators	$421
Male professionals, technicians	$565
Female professionals, technicians	$475

This very different picture reveals a large discrepancy in pay between women and men in the same job strata. What's more, it illustrates the difference between a logical argument, and one based on a flawed premise.

Firm foundations
No matter how persuasive an argument may be, it is worthless without first having a solid factual base.

Convergent Thinking

ONE OF THE MOST important first steps in enhancing your thinking skills is to realize that different kinds of problems demand different kinds of thought processes. For instance, you wouldn't want to use a group problem-solving strategy, such as brainstorming, when trying to find the answer to a simple mathematical problem. Psychologists, recognizing the different problem-solving approaches, often divide thinking processes into two main categories:

- **Convergent thinking.** This tends to be a linear, logical, step-by-step process. If you were to represent convergent thinking as a simple drawing, it might look like a straight line through several points or stages, leading to one "right" answer.

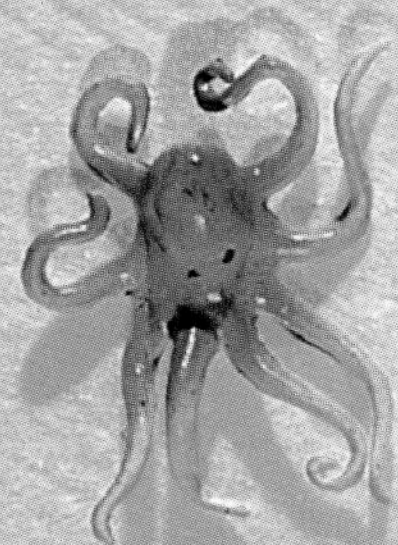

- **Divergent thinking.** This is where lines of thought come from various different directions and might produce lots of different answers, all of which would be equally valid (see pp. 54-55).

Find one right answer

Convergent thinking is best suited to the type of questions where there can be only one right answer, for instance mathematical sums or crossword puzzles. Although this approach may include trying to recognize patterns within a problem, grouping information in some way in order to speed up the problem-solving process, it is concerned only with exploring the path that will lead to the correct solution.

Getting stuck in a rut

Convergent thinking—useful as it is in specific situations—can occasionally be a stiflingly rigid problem-solving technique. For instance, the problem solver approaches a familiar quandry in exactly the same satisfactory way as he or she has done in the past—a tried and tested approach to the problem. In doing this, he or she may be ignoring all kinds of new, more imaginative ways of looking at a situation; ways that might yield more effective and innovative results. Relying on patterns of thought that have worked only adequately well in the past will continue to present you with similar mediocre results. It is only through stretching your perspective that you will be able to realize creative solutions.

Even if you are using convergent thinking in the kinds of logical situations in which it performs best, such as solving crossword puzzles, take care not to let it blind you to other avenues of thought. So if you get stuck on one line of thought that seems to be leading you nowhere, try restructuring the way you view the problem by changing tack and looking at it from a completely different angle.

Fishing for answers
Using convergent thinking for problem-solving, such as throwing a single line when you want to catch one fish at a time, can hook satisfactory solutions.

SHOWDOWN IN DODGE CITY

The following story, based on a scenario by psychologist Michael Posner, is a good example of the way you can use convergent thinking creatively. The towns of Tombstone and Gopher's Gulch are 30 miles apart on a straight stretch of road. At 1:00 p.m. on Saturday, Butch Cassidy robs the bank in Tombstone and the Sundance Kid robs the bank in Gopher's Gulch. The gunslingers planned to meet in Dodge City, which is half way between the two towns.

Just as Butch is heading out of Tombstone, a nearsighted deputy sheriff named Seymour thunders out of a side street on a somewhat out-of-control horse, right under Butch's nose. Seymour is very earnest, but unhappily not very competent. He is really a wealthy kid from back East who wanted to prove his manhood to his father. Too frightened to tangle with Butch, who has now drawn his pistol, the young deputy rides off down the road toward Gopher's Gulch.

When he reaches the Sundance Kid, whose gun is also drawn, Seymour turns around and rides hell for leather back in the direction of Tombstone. The deputy continues to ride back and forth between the outlaws without ever getting up the courage to confront either one of them, until Butch and Sundance meet up in Dodge City.

And now the problem...

If both desperadoes travel at 15 miles per hour, and the deputy thunders along at 40 miles per hour, then how many miles will Deputy Sheriff Seymour have ridden before he finally has to square up to the outlaws in Dodge City?

Problem-solving strategies

The question "How far has the deputy ridden?" structures the problem in terms of distance. It can be solved by concentrating on distance, but that is not the most efficient approach. You will get the answer faster if you focus on time instead.

Rephrase the question as "How much time will it take for the outlaws to meet?" Since the towns they start in are 30 miles apart, and they are riding at 15 miles per hour, they should meet in one hour, each having traveled 15 miles to get to Dodge City, which is right between the two. You know that Seymour is tearing through the desert at 40 miles per hour. In one hour, the time you know it will take for the two outlaws to travel to Dodge City from their respective starting points, he will travel 40 miles.

A flexible approach

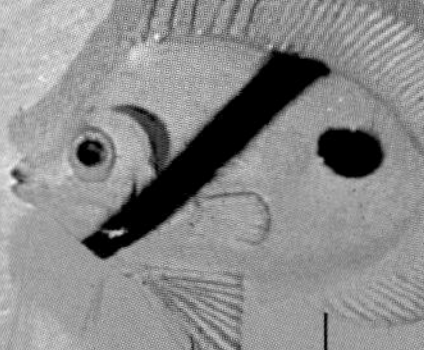

By consciously changing your problem-solving approach, you were able to avoid having to solve the mathematical equation needed to answer the question from the distance angle. So, always keep an open mind—the most obvious path isn't necessarily the most straightforward.

MATRICES

When searching for the answers to certain types of problems, you may find it hard to juggle all the relevant information in your mind while you figure out a solution. One highly effective way of organizing large amounts of information is to externalize it in some way. There are many ways to do this—you might try taking notes or drawing pictures that lay out the problem visually. One very useful visual method—especially where mathematical puzzles such as those shown here are concerned—is to draw a simple grid known as a matrix. By putting the basic data down on paper in a clear, concise way, you can free up space in your short-term memory for solving the obtuse parts of the problem. The following two problems are good examples of the matrix in action. When you have looked at them, turn to "Solutions," on pages 133-134, for the answers.

1. A tale of two cities

In the North Atlantic sits a small island famous for its natural beauty as well as for the two very distinctive but odd towns that contain its total population. Barter Port, a quaint seaside hamlet, and Trading Town, a farming and mercantile village with olde worlde charm, have very different identities and have endured a strange and silent feud for centuries. Cooperation between the two communities is rare; in fact, each has its own currency. However, because of the close proximity of the towns, there have been occasions when the currency of Barter Port, which is comprised of fish, shells, dolphins, and ships' wheels, has been accepted in Trading Town, where the local currency is carrots. But to discourage exchange of currencies neither village has published an exact exchange rate. At the entrance to its marketplace,

Trading Town—perhaps the slightly more pragmatic of the two—has erected a sign (see below) that cryptically sets out the conversion. People who live in the two villages understand it, but tourists to the island find the sign extremely confusing.

One enterprising visitor, who was told that a dolphin was worth 3 carrots, managed to work out the rest of the conversions by drawing a matrix with numbers based on the sign. Using a similar technique, can you figure out the Trading Town carrot values for the remaining Barter Port currency?

2. Does love conquer all?

A new scriptwriter, Jennifer, has just come onto the team of the soap opera *Love Conquers All*. She joined at very short notice, after the previous writer stormed off the set when the producers changed the hairstyle of one of the lead characters. Jennifer has got to make changes to the next day's episode, but she can't remember who is married to whom. Still in a fit of pique, the last writer left her the following cryptic synopsis of the relationships in the series.

An introduction to Everydayville

In the town of Everydayville, Ralph, Gerald, Blake, and Sam are married to June, Vicki, Erica, and Saskia. Vicki is Gerald's sister; a wonderful mother with five beautiful children who mean everything to her and a husband who sells life insurance. Ralph and his wife, who always sports a gingham pinafore and bakes cookies, want to wait a few more years before starting a family. Ralph has never introduced his wife to Erica, the town's leading lawyer and a notorious seductress, because she wears slinky clothes and drives a fast car. Erica is having an affair with Gerald. Everyone seems to know about this apart from Gerald's wife, but her best friend, June, is considering breaking it to her. Gerald and Blake are twin brothers, although Gerald is a handsome rake, and Blake is shy and wears thick glasses.

With the aid of the above matrix, can you help Jennifer discover who is married to whom? You could try using an X in the relevant box to denote a couple who cannot be married, and a 0 to denote a married couple.

Conversions
By looking at the information in this matrix, you can figure out the rates of exchange between Trading Town and Barter Port.

DIVERGENT THINKING

IN SITUATIONS THAT DEMAND more creative mental processes, where convergent thought would be too narrow and limiting, you can adopt the approach often known as divergent thinking. Divergent thinking can be seen as casting your net wide over the water, picking up all kinds of relevant ideas, as opposed to convergent thinking (see pages 50–51), where you might throw out just one line in search of one solution.

Creative solutions

Divergent thinking differs from convergent styles by allowing several different paths to be considered simultaneously, rather than rigidly pursuing one path toward one solution.

If you are not used to divergent thinking, it can sometimes be very difficult to liberate your mind to start looking at a problem in different ways. Once you get used to thinking divergently, however, all sorts of new insights will come to mind, often providing you with more interesting, appropriate, or satisfactory solutions to your dilemma.

This kind of thinking can be applied to all kinds of tasks, from writing a novel or an advertising jingle, to designing a building. On a smaller scale, you could use it to solve storage problems in your home or office by moving beyond the idea that storage facilities need to be attached to the floor, and hanging shelves from the ceiling. Or, you could build your bed on a platform, and use the space underneath it for storage. Everyone is capable of divergent thought, and most people already use it more often than they might suppose.

Netting a large profit

If you allow yourself to spread a huge net over a large area, taking in all kinds of different ideas and possibilities, then your solutions can be much more creative.

Breaking the rules

Humor is a common part of divergent thinking, putting a surprise twist on an accepted set of rules. In the Marx Brothers' movie *A Night at the Opera,* Groucho is hiding his brothers in a hotel suite, and they keep moving pieces of furniture in order to hide themselves from the police. Finally, a police officer walks into one of the rooms and points to a bed that wasn't there before. "What's that bed doing there?" he demands. Groucho, ignoring the obvious interpretation and adopting a different one, replies, "I don't see it doing anything."

Since creative problem-solving can be thought of as breaking set patterns, it may seem a difficult skill to develop. However, there are things you can do to help open up your mind—such as the exercise that appears on the opposite page.

One of the most important things about divergent thinking is that it does not look for a single answer, discarding all other options as soon as it has found a likely path to that answer. Instead, it will search for and look at many possible solutions, giving each one equal weight, even those that, on the face of it, would seem to be unlikely.

FISHING FOR ANSWERS

To exercise your divergent-thinking muscles, try to come up with as many possibilities for each problem as you can. Don't throw any out, just concentrate on making a list. The following puzzle will give you a taster of how to approach the task.

At first glance...

Three women in swim suits are standing together. At first glance, two appear to be sad and one happy. The two seemingly sad women are trying to smile and the happy one has tears streaming down her face. Why? Some possible answers might be:

Solution 1. All three are mothers watching their children having a swimming lesson. One of the women is so proud of her child's progress that tears of happiness have come to her eyes. The other two are sad because their children are struggling; nevertheless they force themselves to smile.

Solution 2. The three women are at college together and are close friends. Unknown to each other, they are all in love with the same boy. An important party is coming up, and none of them has a date as yet. They are hanging out beside the pool when he comes by. He asks one of them if he can talk to her for a minute, and then asks her to the party. When he leaves, she is so happy and excited she starts to cry. Her friends make a big effort to smile because they do not want to spoil her happiness.

Solution 3. The women are contestants in the Miss Universe pageant. The one who is crying has won, and is doing what is expected of the winner. The other two smile because they are on camera, and are supposed to be gracious and charming about losing.

This problem is based on one that appears in Paul Sloane's *Lateral Thinking Puzzlers*, and any of the solutions could be "correct," depending on why you needed an answer to the question. For example, if you were given a photograph of the women and asked for your interpretation, your conclusion might depend on whether you thought the women looked most like mothers, students, or beauty-pageant contestants.

Tossing ideas around in this way is called "brainstorming." It involves organizing facts in different ways and staying open to alternative views. Brainstorming is most effective when used by several people tossing out ideas. Opening yourself up to different points of view can stimulate creative thinking, and produce various satisfactory solutions.

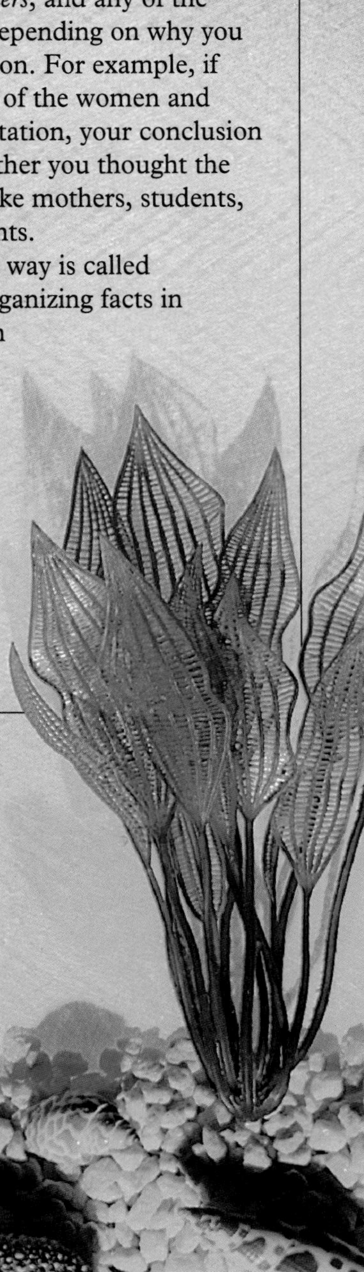

BRANCHING OUT

Do you find that you have to devote considerable effort to acquiring knowledge or solving problems, only to find that, far too often, the information seems to leave your head as fast as you try to acquire it? In *The Mind Map Book*, British researcher and writer Tony Buzan theorizes that this is because you tend to study all the relevant facts in relative isolation and try to commit them to memory. He believes that we can learn and retain information much more efficiently, and use what we have learned more productively, if we begin to study and think in a different way, using a technique that he calls "radiant thinking."

Expand your mind

In order to facilitate this process, Buzan suggests the use of what he calls Mind Maps—freely drawn diagrams in which information is set out in the form of key words and, especially, key images, all branching out from, and connecting with, a central idea. Each idea or image then inspires its own associations and connections, branching off in yet another direction, and so on.

The point of radiant thinking and its practical expression—the Mind Map—is that it encourages the ability to develop an overview, to see things in a broad context, and to analyze ideas and facts in relation to one another and to wider issues. In addition, knowledge absorbed like this is retained much more fully, more accurately, and for much longer, than isolated facts learned by rote. Studying in this way is enormously satisfying in that it enables and encourages you to engage with your chosen subject in an active way, using your right-brain capacity to make unexpected discoveries and unearth fascinating links between one seemingly separate area of knowledge and another.

Mind Maps have a wide variety of potential applications in everyday life—as a problem-solving tool, for example, or to clarify and strengthen your memory. However, one of their most useful functions is as a form of note-taking and organization during a course of study.

How to Mind Map

To develop your understanding of the whole Mind Map concept, and discover how it could be of use to you, try making a Mind Map yourself. In the center of a large sheet of paper, place a key word and image. This could be a political or historical situation such as the war in Bosnia, a scientific process like photosynthesis, or the subject of a speech or essay you are working on. The straightforward example on the right is designed as part of a high-school art project about the artist Leonardo da Vinci. The Mind Map covers not only his art works, but also other parts of his life and creative work to give a more all-round picture of him as a Renaissance Man.

Now connect the images and ideas most closely associated with your central image, using key words to clarify the link. You can see how this works by looking at the Leonardo Mind Map. Then, branching out from these secondary concepts with further ideas, link any other relevant ideas and images, making sure that you note when there is an interconnection between any of them. Afterward, carry on filling the page with interrelated words and images, punctuated, whenever possible, with color-coding, linking arrows, and lines of varying thickness. Include any other clear, graphic means you can think of to incorporate all the elements, bring them to life, and construct a complete picture of your subject or project.

Keep at it

The more you practice this technique, the more natural and effortless it will feel, and the more new associations you will become aware of. You will also be able to apply it to an ever-wider range of uses, as Mind Maps can be a fruitful way of looking at a wide variety of problems and decisions. And while you might not be happy with your original Mind Maps, you can keep improving on them. Mastering the technique of radiant thinking using Mind Maps in this way will help you to develop your brain to its full potential, and to enhance the creativity in every area of your life.

Find the connections

After you have decided on the subject for your Mind Map, you will find that your brain makes connections to it automatically—whether it is a study aid, like the one opposite, or a problem-solving device.

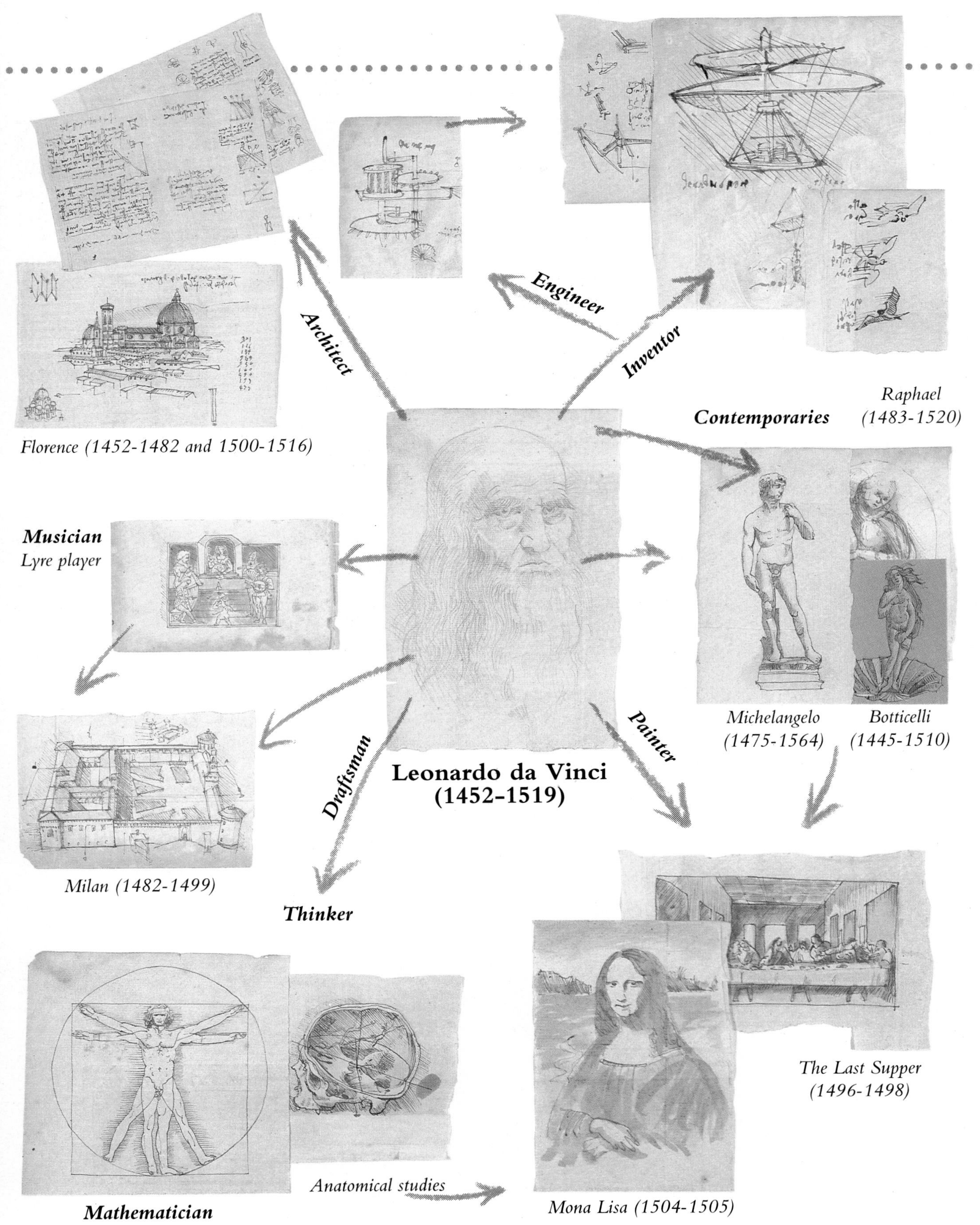

Architect
Engineer
Inventor
Florence (1452-1482 and 1500-1516)
Contemporaries
Raphael
(1483-1520)
Musician
Lyre player
Michelangelo
(1475-1564)
Botticelli
(1445-1510)
Draftsman
Painter
Leonardo da Vinci
(1452-1519)
Milan (1482-1499)
Thinker
The Last Supper
(1496-1498)
Anatomical studies
Mathematician
Mona Lisa (1504-1505)

THE EUREKA MYTH

IN THE LAST FEW PAGES we have discussed ways of thinking that depart from a strictly logical construct as if they were mutually exclusive. In reality, our mental resources are most efficient at problem-solving when they are used in combination. The human brain can apply logical, divergent, and radiant thinking techniques to all kinds of problems, switching in and out of different modes of thought at the point where it gets bogged down in one particular method.

Accumulating knowledge

Flashes of insight, however dramatic, do not happen in a vacuum. Often they are the final leap in a chain of attempts to solve a problem, a chain in which each link has been examined to see how it holds up in different circumstances. This type of logical thought process, in which results are constantly modified by testing and discarding premises that do not account for the observed phenomena, is typical of much of scientific discovery.

When we chronicle the history of science, we rarely linger along the obstacle-strewn path a scientist trod before arriving at a stunning conclusion. We carry the image of the ancient Greek mathematician and inventor Archimedes leaping out of the tub and shouting "Eureka!" when he finally understood the concept of water displacement—that a body immersed in water displaces an equal mass of water. We don't picture him wrestling with the problem of mass for long days, months, or years before it finally clicked. The truth is, each step along the road to discovery is indispensable to the final illumination of a concept or theory.

Scientists often make simultaneous use of a range of problem-solving techniques such as brainstorming (see pages 27 and 55) and radiant thinking (see pp. 56-57). For example, James Watson and Francis Crick, who discovered the structure of DNA in the early 1950s, were working at Cambridge with others also studying DNA. The Cambridge group was in friendly competition with a further group working at King's College on the same subject. The scientists went to hear each other's lectures and used each other's techniques in their respective research. While this exchange of ideas may not have constituted formal brainstorming, the effect was the same—Watson and Crick discovered the vital double-helix structure as a result of the interplay of their own work with that of several other scientists.

Inspired errors

It was a lecture by Rosalind Franklin of the King's College group about the water content of DNA molecules that inspired Watson to create his first (incorrect) three-stranded model. As it turned out, Franklin came close to discovering the correct structure herself, but in her research she failed to use the variation of radiant thinking employed by Watson and Crick that helped them to perfect their DNA model. Watson and Crick did not actually invent the model-building idea, but adapted it from another scientist named Linus Pauling, whose work they also followed.

As these scientists worked on their own and communicated with each other, they kept testing and discarding different solutions. In each experiment, they simply pushed a set of premises to its logical conclusion to see if it held up. This process, although usually associated with scientific method, is also used in some more traditionally "creative" arenas.

In the nineteenth century, the Impressionist painters worked as a group much like Watson and Crick and their King's College colleagues. Manet, for example, influenced younger painters such as Monet, Renoir, Pissarro, and Seurat. Although the Impressionists did not necessarily socialize with each other, they borrowed elements from one another's work to further their own innovations.

Much of what they were doing was in reaction to the stuffy Académie Française, whose critics were unable to break from an older tradition to embrace this new style. As a result, the Impressionists exhibited their own works in the Salon des Réfusés; building on a collective body of knowledge, they changed the course of Western art.

These painters arrived at their revelations, not overnight, but in incremental steps, just as scientists do; when Seurat, for instance, painted over the same canvas countless times, and filled hundreds of sketchbooks, he was trying out hypotheses and discarding those that did not work. In short, finding the answer to a creative problem is reliant not so much on inspiration as on the processes of gathering information, running trials, applying different problem-solving techniques, and perseverance.

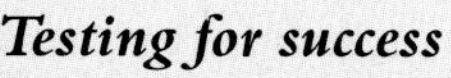

Testing for success

The great scientific discoveries happened not as a result of spontaneous revelations, but from long, frustrating, periods of experimenting, gathering data, and analyzing results.

Powers of Deduction

The chances are that you have often had to make decisions without being sure whether or not you were in possession of all the relevant information. From deciding whether or not to take a new job, to considering where to go on vacation, you can learn to assess when vital facts are missing. However, it is not always easy to recognize such a situation when you are in it—your own biases tend to get in the way. The following scenarios illustrate the pitfalls of making ill-informed decisions.

Party politics

Sonia let her friend Terry talk her into going to a party where she knew no one. She was apprehensive: Terry had dragged her to some dire events in the past. True to form, this party was full of ultra-conservative-looking men in suits, but, making the best of the situation, she headed for the bar.

As she got near, she spotted, among a group of "suits," a tall, handsome man wearing a faded denim jacket, a white T-shirt, scruffy blue jeans, and a pair of trendy mountain-climbing boots. His deep, throaty chuckle encouraged Sonia to take a closer look. As she approached the group she noticed that the man wasn't wearing a wedding ring. She was attracted to him on the basis of the following assumptions:

- he had a relaxed, friendly manner
- his dress was casual and stylish
- he was unattached

When she got nearer, she found that he and his friends were talking about tax loopholes and venture capital—financial matters in which she had no interest. After listening to the stranger for several minutes, Sonia discovered that he had only called in to change out of his suit and have a quick drink before heading off to a costume party. Even though he found the idea embarrassing and ridiculous, he was being forced by his wife to attend. That evening, Sonia learned a useful lesson about jumping to conclusions based on superficial impressions.

House-hunting blues

Gerry, who was living in a furnished room, had been trying without success to find an apartment. One day, he saw an ad for what sounded like an ideal property, on a residential street in a neighborhood that was in the process of gentrification.

Gerry wanted to view it one evening, but as the owners could not see him then, he took a morning off work. The inconvenience was forgotten when he saw the stunning rooms full of rich colors, exquisite paintings, and huge, glittering mirrors. Captivated, he offered the asking price, although it was higher than he had in mind. He assumed:

- The owners were genuinely unable to show the apartment in the evening.
- It was the way the apartment was constructed that provided its warmth and style.
- The rooms were a reasonable size.

The paperwork was processed quickly, and on the evening the previous owners moved out, Gerry hurried around to inspect his new home. As he approached, he was horrified to hear loud drum music coming from the apartment above his. This, he discovered, was a nightly event, and the reason he was only allowed to view during the day. Inside, he found a series of dark, tiny rooms; their charm had been the result of clever decorating tricks such as the use of mirrors. Making such an important decision without uncovering all the facts had been a very expensive mistake indeed.

Not what he seems

Making judgments on the basis of partial information is inevitable from time to time. But take care that important decisions are made with as much knowledge as possible.

INDUCTIVE REASONING

The kind of logical reasoning we have discussed in this chapter moves from the general to the particular. It does this by starting with a set of general premises and trying to apply them to a specific set of data. This mode of reasoning is also known as deductive reasoning. Often, however, we look at things the other way round. Rather than deducing something about a set of data given certain premises, we invent a general rule or premise from a group of observed data. This is a perfectly natural —yet often misleading—thought process called inductive reasoning.

Test the theory

There are some good reasons to use inductive reasoning. For instance, scientists use inductive reasoning to explain the results of a group of experiments. But good scientists are careful to put both the positive and negative sides of their hypotheses to the test. The difficulty with proving anything through inductive reasoning is that all data that adheres to a rule does not necessarily make it true, while one piece of evidence that does not fit the rule proves it false.

You can see how this works by trying to solve the following problem, first demonstrated by the British psychologist Peter Wason. You are presented with four cards from a set and told that each has a capital letter on one side, and a number on the other. The cards you are shown are: E, T, 4, and 7. You are going to test if the following rule holds true with respect to the four cards: if there is a vowel on one side of the card, on the flip side there is an even number. So which cards would you need to turn over to see if the rule applies?

Most people would immediately reach for the E. In addition, many would also reach for the 4. In fact, you need to flip over the E and the 7. If the E does not have an even number on the other side, or if the 7 has a vowel on the other side, the rule is untrue. Whether or not the 4 has a vowel on the other side is irrelevant, because there is no reason to think that consonants, as well as vowels, cannot be backed by even numbers.

Here be dragons

Faulty inductive reasoning led societies to believe for centuries that the world was flat, because they could not see what lay over the horizon. They thought perhaps dragons and other fantastical creatures lurked beyond the horizon—or maybe even the end of the world.

The experiment shows something about human nature. Unlike scientists who are conducting experiments, in daily life people tend to look for confirmation of a hypothesis. They do not look for potential pitfalls. In the case of the cards, of course, this tendency is not very dangerous. However, there are other situations in which it can be considerably more harmful.

Prejudice

One extremely prevalent form of this type of blinkered thinking is prejudice—that is, a preconceived opinion based on limited, and selective, evidence. A male bigot, believing women to be of limited intelligence, and universally incapable of logical thought, might say, "Women don't understand money," or "Women don't have what it takes to be leaders," or "Don't bother women with science—they don't want to know about it."

These sorts of remarks may sound obviously prejudiced, but if you ask the bigot who makes them, he will be able to cite many instances that serve to support and confirm his belief. There was the time he was short-changed at the checkout counter by a 17-year-old girl. He will tell you how he makes all the financial decisions for his family, and his wife likes it that way because she doesn't want any pressure. Then, there is the fact that when he gave his children a chemistry set, his son played with it endlessly, but his daughter ignored it altogether.

In rattling off this evidence, he will have overlooked the many examples that show his beliefs to be nonsense. If women don't understand money, how have tycoons like Anita Roddick created flourishing businesses that spread all over the world? If women don't have the ambition and aggression to be political leaders, what about Golda Meir, Indira Gandhi, or Margaret Thatcher? If women don't want to know about science, how can you account for Marie Curie?

Accurate reasoning

Most people would like to avoid letting themselves down in this thoughtless fashion. So how can you train yourself to avoid jumping to conclusions? Try to follow these rules and you will go a long way toward avoiding faulty reasoning:

1. Don't make a hard and fast judgment from a tiny pool of evidence.

2. Once you have become convinced of a given point of view, force yourself to argue the opposite conclusion. (Notice, too, the evidence on which you are drawing.)

3. Don't lump problems together without examining their differences.

4. When you are considering a problem, list the factors that are pushing you toward a certain conclusion. Try to consider whether these are based on reliable evidence, gut feeling, or inexplicable bias.

5. Beware of statistics that support the vested interest of the group offering them as evidence. This also applies when you are a member of the group concerned. Remember, statistics can be manipulated to support a certain view.

6. Try to be flexible when it comes to trying a different approach.

7. Shed assumptions that limit your thinking.

8. Don't be afraid to question your own judgment, and listen when other people challenge you.

WHO DONE IT?

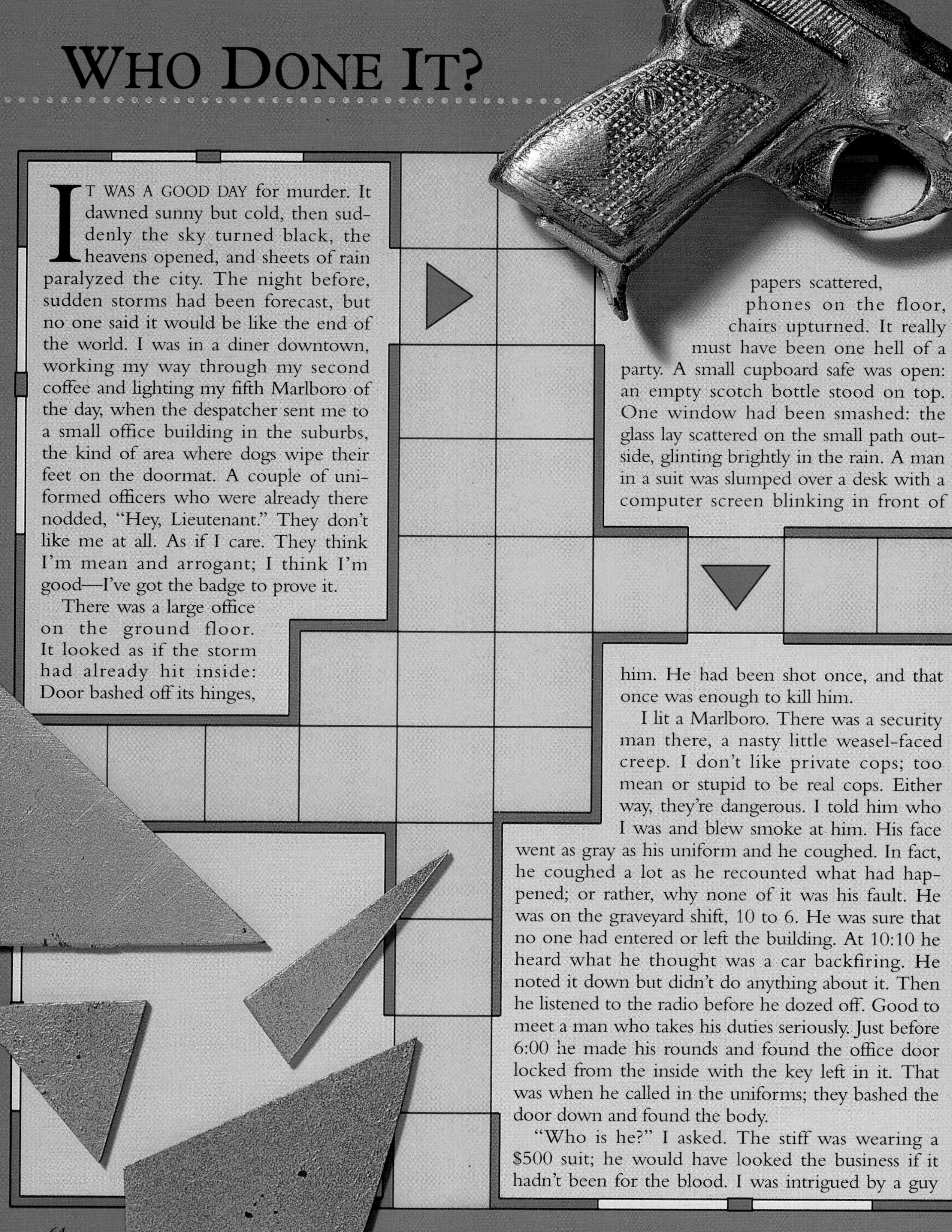

IT WAS A GOOD DAY for murder. It dawned sunny but cold, then suddenly the sky turned black, the heavens opened, and sheets of rain paralyzed the city. The night before, sudden storms had been forecast, but no one said it would be like the end of the world. I was in a diner downtown, working my way through my second coffee and lighting my fifth Marlboro of the day, when the despatcher sent me to a small office building in the suburbs, the kind of area where dogs wipe their feet on the doormat. A couple of uniformed officers who were already there nodded, "Hey, Lieutenant." They don't like me at all. As if I care. They think I'm mean and arrogant; I think I'm good—I've got the badge to prove it.

There was a large office on the ground floor. It looked as if the storm had already hit inside: Door bashed off its hinges, papers scattered, phones on the floor, chairs upturned. It really must have been one hell of a party. A small cupboard safe was open: an empty scotch bottle stood on top. One window had been smashed: the glass lay scattered on the small path outside, glinting brightly in the rain. A man in a suit was slumped over a desk with a computer screen blinking in front of him. He had been shot once, and that once was enough to kill him.

I lit a Marlboro. There was a security man there, a nasty little weasel-faced creep. I don't like private cops; too mean or stupid to be real cops. Either way, they're dangerous. I told him who I was and blew smoke at him. His face went as gray as his uniform and he coughed. In fact, he coughed a lot as he recounted what had happened; or rather, why none of it was his fault. He was on the graveyard shift, 10 to 6. He was sure that no one had entered or left the building. At 10:10 he heard what he thought was a car backfiring. He noted it down but didn't do anything about it. Then he listened to the radio before he dozed off. Good to meet a man who takes his duties seriously. Just before 6:00 he made his rounds and found the office door locked from the inside with the key left in it. That was when he called in the uniforms; they bashed the door down and found the body.

"Who is he?" I asked. The stiff was wearing a $500 suit; he would have looked the business if it hadn't been for the blood. I was intrigued by a guy

who would spend my month's pay on a suit. His name was Andrew Moody, and he was the manager of a small computer department that was under contract to a branch of the government.

Moody often worked late, but Weasel-face never checked up on the office. Moody had been a bit too buddy-buddy with one of his staff, an Alison Thurston, and Weasel-face once caught them doing something that wasn't computer programming. Another time he heard them yelling at each other. Nice to know that everyone affiliated with the government is as professional as I am.

"When will she be in?" I asked. But she had called that morning to say she was sick, and would be late. "Was she here last night?" Weasel-face didn't know. He said Moody must have been alone, and the burglars came in through the window, since no one went in or out. If Weasel-face looked like a man who slept with his eyes open, I'd have taken more notice of him.

Three other people worked in the office. There was Moody's second-in-command, Alan Preston; a programmer, Jennifer Arthur, who Weasel-face said was fond of the bottle; and a junior, Lee Mullard, a young biker with a leather jacket and a reputation for being tough.

The three of them had arrived while we were talking, and the uniforms had taken them straight into another room, where they were drinking tea and coffee. As soon as I went in, Preston started moaning. It always happens—the only guy who never moans is the stiff. Everyone else finds that murder is a big inconvenience. That's why my first wife left, and my third; the second left because she didn't like Marlboros.

Preston's suit was soaked through and he wanted to change. "I came without a coat" he said, "It didn't look like rain." I told him I had a few questions, then he could go home or maybe to his tailor. God, I was good at handling these sensitive situations. "I don't know anything about the robbery," he said. I told him it was just procedure. I learned that line from the movies. What would a thief be after? Jennifer Arthur

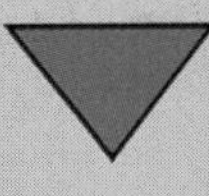

shook her head and said "Nothing much. We're developing a new memory chip, but we haven't gotten very far. There's nothing worth anything." "I don't know," said Preston. "My project was pretty advanced. The plans in the safe would be very useful to someone else." No one seemed upset about Moody. I wondered what it would be like to be so unpopular at work, then decided no one at the precinct would care if it were me.

I talked to each of them separately. Jennifer Arthur was a pleasant-looking, matronly type, carrying a few pounds more than she should've, with the kind of mousy tight perm she probably had 25 years ago. Weasel-face was right: She had a drink problem. Her eyes were red and lined—they reminded me of looking in the mirror every morning—and she had the ruddy, broken-veined cheeks that come from years of staring down an empty bottle. I asked her

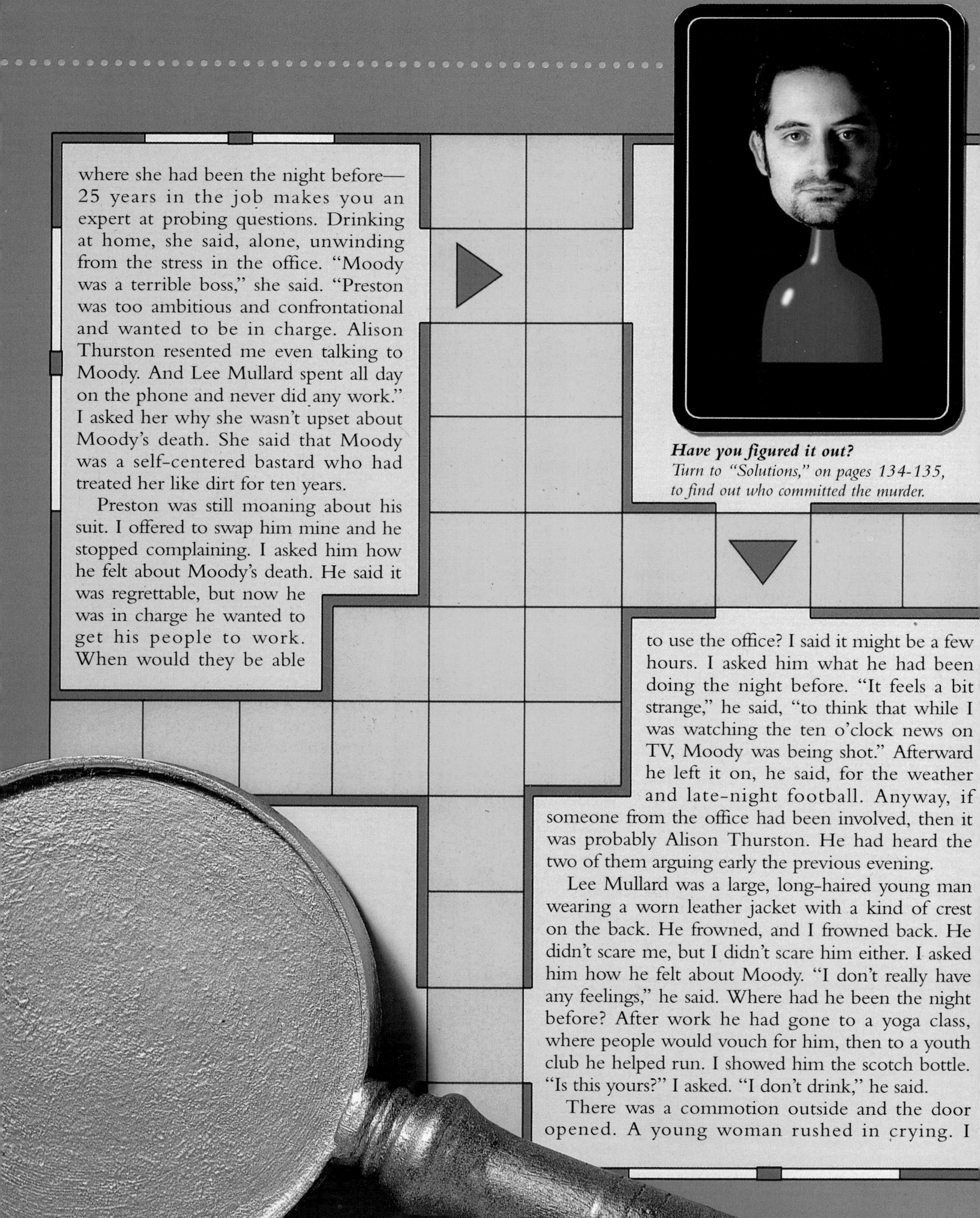

where she had been the night before—25 years in the job makes you an expert at probing questions. Drinking at home, she said, alone, unwinding from the stress in the office. "Moody was a terrible boss," she said. "Preston was too ambitious and confrontational and wanted to be in charge. Alison Thurston resented me even talking to Moody. And Lee Mullard spent all day on the phone and never did any work." I asked her why she wasn't upset about Moody's death. She said that Moody was a self-centered bastard who had treated her like dirt for ten years.

Preston was still moaning about his suit. I offered to swap him mine and he stopped complaining. I asked him how he felt about Moody's death. He said it was regrettable, but now he was in charge he wanted to get his people to work. When would they be able to use the office? I said it might be a few hours. I asked him what he had been doing the night before. "It feels a bit strange," he said, "to think that while I was watching the ten o'clock news on TV, Moody was being shot." Afterward he left it on, he said, for the weather and late-night football. Anyway, if someone from the office had been involved, then it was probably Alison Thurston. He had heard the two of them arguing early the previous evening.

Lee Mullard was a large, long-haired young man wearing a worn leather jacket with a kind of crest on the back. He frowned, and I frowned back. He didn't scare me, but I didn't scare him either. I asked him how he felt about Moody. "I don't really have any feelings," he said. Where had he been the night before? After work he had gone to a yoga class, where people would vouch for him, then to a youth club he helped run. I showed him the scotch bottle. "Is this yours?" I asked. "I don't drink," he said.

There was a commotion outside and the door opened. A young woman rushed in crying. I

Have you figured it out?
Turn to "Solutions," on pages 134-135, to find out who committed the murder.

guessed it must be Alison Thurston—detective's intuition. She was a petite blonde with a tight red sweater and a tighter pencil skirt, and she was hysterical. In other circumstances I would have liked to comfort her. I got no chance. "It's that Arthur woman," she cried. "She killed Andrew. She's always hanging around the office when he's working late, drinking and trying to steal him. If she can't have him, she doesn't want anyone to." She broke down; I gave up the idea of offering my shoulder and had one of the female uniforms take her to another room. Lee Mullard looked at me. "What do you think?" I asked. "Not sure," he said. "Alison's more likely to be jealous than Jennifer. But Jennifer is usually drunk—often she can't stand up or know where she is. I don't approve of alcohol; it poisons the body." I pitied him; such ignorance in one so young. I lit a Marlboro: he glared at me. I wasn't impressed: I glare better in my sleep.

Just then, the chief arrived, excited as a dog with two tails. I deduced that the words government and promotion were linked in his mind, and he wanted things wrapped up. I reviewed the evidence: the wrecked office, the witness statements. "If they took any sensitive papers, that has to be our first priority," he said. "We should set up roadblocks. Has the room been dusted for fingerprints? We may be dealing with professionals, even terrorists." Such insight: no wonder he sits in a big office while I walk the streets smoking myself to death.

"That's not necessary," I said. "This was obviously no robbery. The murderer has given the game away. Come on—let's go make an arrest."

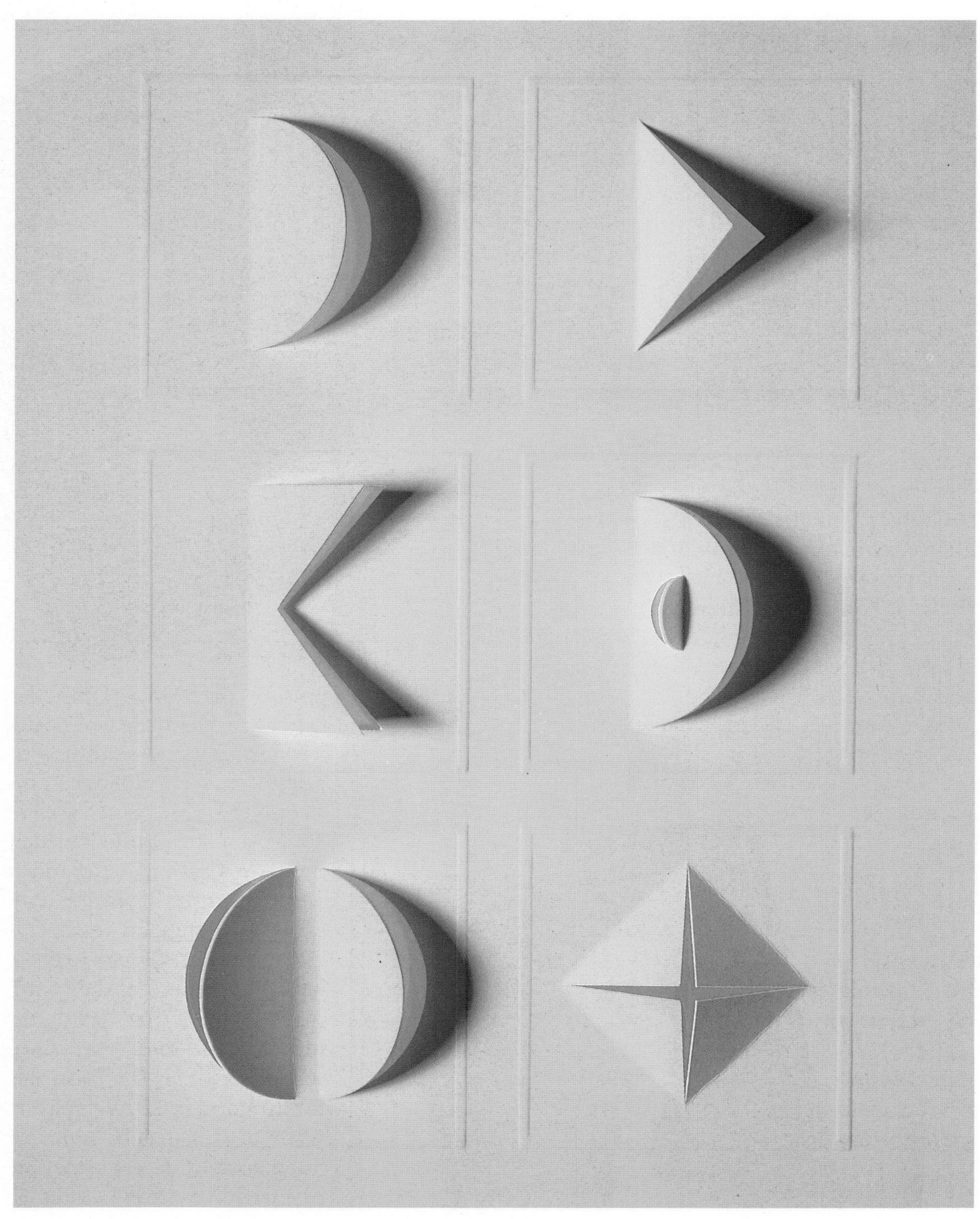

CHAPTER THREE

WORD POWER

WORDS—WHETHER THEY'RE used for expressing emotion, explaining ideas, or simply asking for directions—are the most powerful means of communication we have. Mastering the basics of language, as well as its infinite subtleties, will help you in daily life, both in expressing your own thoughts and ideas, and in understanding other people's.

One invaluable skill is that of processing information: knowing where to find it, extracting it from a mass of extraneous material, and organizing it clearly. This skill is particularly useful when, for instance, you are called on to present a report, but it also helps in activities ranging from reading the newspaper to constructing an argument. "Getting the Point," on pages 70-71, will provide a wealth of useful guidelines.

For those who have trouble finding the right words, all spoken and written communication is difficult. If this applies to you, there are many ways you can improve your language skills. Through games and handy tips, this chapter will help by revealing where your verbal strengths and weaknesses lie, and enable you to enhance your ability to speak, read, listen, and comprehend (see "Do You Understand?" on pages 72-73).

The knack of understanding what people are telling you—rather than picking up only part of what you hear, or, worse, misunderstanding it—will ease communication and help you to learn. Equally important is being able to present facts so that others will understand them. "Putting Your Case," on pages 74-75, explains how to lay out information clearly and precisely.

Following this is a guide to improving your verbal skills. Listening to how words sound, discovering their meaning, playing word games, reading more quickly—all these can increase your mastery of language. Begin by turning to "Choose Your Words" (pp. 76-77).

Concentration is another vital part of learning and retaining information: "Apply Yourself" (pp. 78-79) will show you how to master it. Finally, we introduce you to cryptograms and codes, flexing your mental faculties with a collection of puzzles, tricks, and riddles, such as "Wordplay," on pages 80-81.

Working through the exercises in this chapter will dramatically increase your facility with words. As a result, you are likely to enjoy greatly enhanced powers of communication—and increased success in your dealings with other people.

WORDS ARE ONE OF THE KEY ELEMENTS OF LEARNING AND COMMUNICATION. EASE AND SKILL IN USING LANGUAGE WILL BRING A WIDE RANGE OF PERSONAL AND PROFESSIONAL REWARDS.

GETTING THE POINT

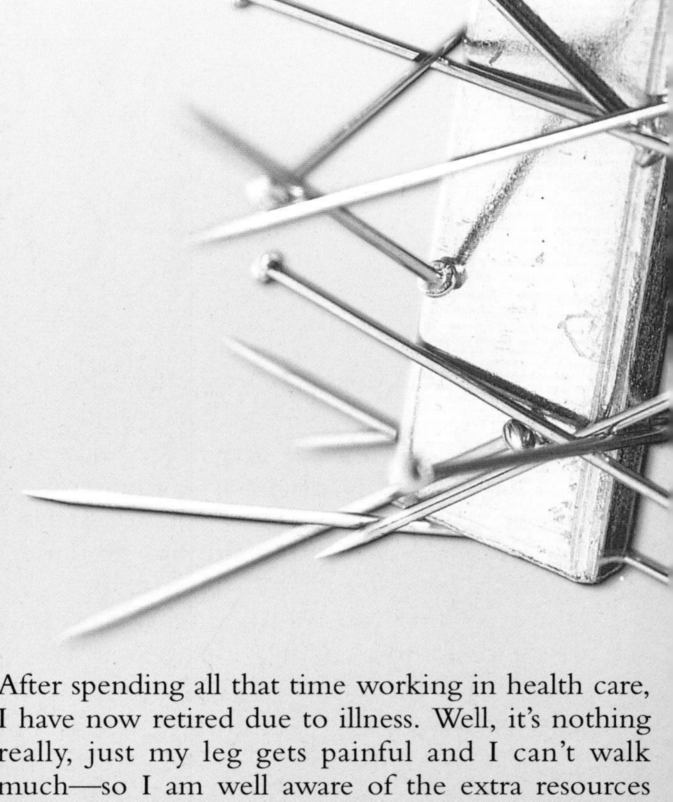

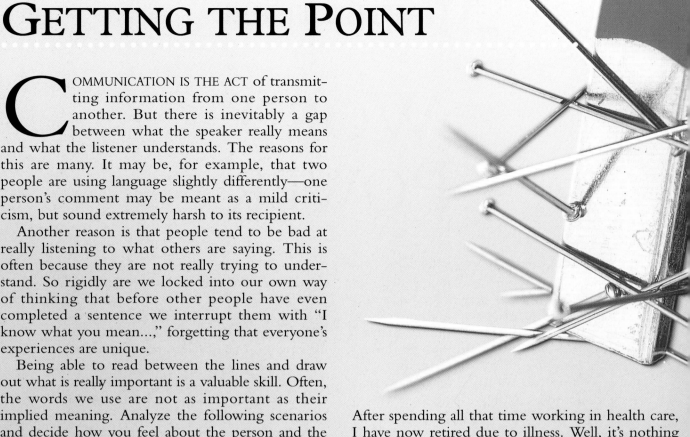

COMMUNICATION IS THE ACT of transmitting information from one person to another. But there is inevitably a gap between what the speaker really means and what the listener understands. The reasons for this are many. It may be, for example, that two people are using language slightly differently—one person's comment may be meant as a mild criticism, but sound extremely harsh to its recipient.

Another reason is that people tend to be bad at really listening to what others are saying. This is often because they are not really trying to understand. So rigidly are we locked into our own way of thinking that before other people have even completed a sentence we interrupt them with "I know what you mean...," forgetting that everyone's experiences are unique.

Being able to read between the lines and draw out what is really important is a valuable skill. Often, the words we use are not as important as their implied meaning. Analyze the following scenarios and decide how you feel about the person and the case he or she is making. Then, work through the questions that follow; they might change the way you feel about what you've just read.

Election candidate

"My name is Brenda McTavish and I am applying to be the local Action Party candidate in the forthcoming elections. I have lived in this area for 35 years and worked in the local hospital for most of that time. So I know the concerns of local people and think that I am well suited to this post. Let me say that I am as concerned about the recent crime wave as anybody and, if I become the candidate for this area, I will make sure that I allocate more resources to policing—and particularly to setting up neighborhood-watch initiatives to keep our streets safe. After spending all that time working in health care, I have now retired due to illness. Well, it's nothing really, just my leg gets painful and I can't walk much—so I am well aware of the extra resources that the hospital needs. And believe me, I shall be getting more money for our kidney dialysis project from central party funds."

- What are Brenda McTavish's credentials for the job of local party candidate?
- What information does she offer about the Action Party's policies for local government, and its stand on major national and international issues?
- What effect did her age and sex have on you?
- Does she have realistic plans for the area?
- How important is her ill-health to the campaign?
- Do you feel sorry for her?
- Would your commitment to another candidate be influenced by what she was saying?

Lending a hand

"I'm sorry, but I won't be able to make your party on Saturday night after all—my life is in complete chaos at the moment. My brother phoned me last night just as I was sorting out something sexy to wear. He has a huge problem because he's moving on Saturday; he can't afford to hire a van so he was planning to shift everything himself. But that fell through because now his car has broken down.

I told him that I was really looking forward to your party, and I offered to get a cab so that he could borrow my car. But apparently that won't work either because of the insurance or something. Anyway, I didn't feel I could refuse to help him. I didn't think you'd mind that much. I'm sure nobody will miss me. Actually, I won't know anyone else who'll be there, will I?"

- Do you believe this story? If not, why not? What do you feel is the real reason for canceling?
- If you think the story is an excuse, what are the implications for your relationship with this person that such a lie was felt to be necessary?
- How would you feel if the story were true?
- If the story is an excuse, were you wise to invite this person to your party in the first place?
- How would you feel if you learned that there was another, more serious, motive for canceling—one that this person felt unable to let you know?

Because language is such a dynamic and often times ambiguous tool of communication, deciphering what someone is really trying to tell you —or to conceal from you—can be extraordinarily difficult. By patiently training yourself to be alert to subtle nuances of meaning, however, or to the underlying message behind what someone else is saying—or writing—you will find that interaction with other people becomes more interesting, more effective, easier, and richer as a result.

Choose your facts

It is very important to be able to pick out the vital or relevant information from among the many facts with which you are presented.

Do You Understand?

How many times have you read something and not really understood what it was telling you? Have you been tempted to learn facts by rote rather than really trying to get to grips with them? Do you write yourself notes that later appear to make little sense? This happens to everybody when words—and their meaning—escape them.

Comprehension, which is understanding what you are reading or listening to, is not simply about being familiar with individual words. It is also about being able to use the words themselves as a vehicle to make sense of the essential meaning that the writer or speaker wants to convey.

Two-way traffic

Failure to understand a passage of text can come about for a variety of reasons—it may be because the message isn't being conveyed clearly enough, or because you are not making enough effort to interpret the words.

Comprehension is a two-way process between writer and reader. Good writing encourages the reader to "see" the story or the character being described. Good reading involves the reader using his or her imagination to "see" what the writer is saying. The key to comprehension is to engage with the words, giving them a chance to paint a clear picture in your mind.

To demonstrate just how hard it can be to understand a passage of text when you are unable to form any image of what is going on, read the following two paragraphs and try to work out what is being described:

1. The object involved mustn't be either too heavy or too light. A big one is easier to handle, but a small one will do the job. Also, small ones tend to be very hard. If you put a hole in some you have to stop. Sometimes you can mend it yourself. Looking for it is no fun. Using one hand is much more awkward than using two. Open spaces are more suitable. It's important to beware of

Conjure up a picture
When you understand a story, you will draw an image of what it says in your head.

breakables. If you aren't careful, you can be hurt. Some people earn lots of money this way. It can be great fun for old and young alike.

2. Some people are gifted at it and find it a pleasure; others do it because they have to. It can take a lot of time if you do it properly. It's better to do it in your own home. Sometimes you need a book to help you. You need to be well prepared or it can easily end in failure. Safety is crucial. Disaster can strike if you run out of time. Young children usually enjoy it. If there are too many people involved, confusion is likely to occur.

In the case of these two passages, you have not been provided with enough information to understand the material. It has not been possible to paint a picture of the scene because key words and explanations are missing. In fact, the first passage is about playing ball and the second one about cooking. Go back and reread them. This time you will be able to "see" everything clearly in your mind. The passages suddenly make sense.

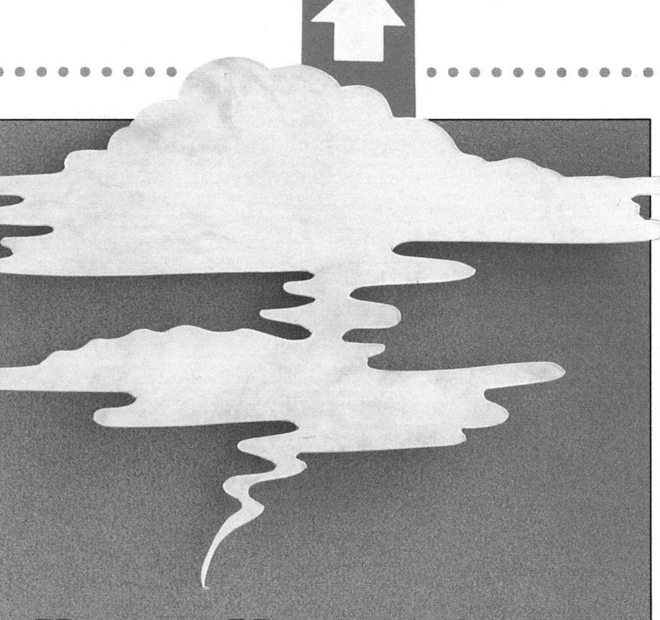

KEYS TO UNDERSTANDING

There are many ways in which you can improve your comprehension skills. The simple techniques that follow, if practiced frequently, will help you to understand both the written and spoken word more easily and clearly:

- Be sensitive to your own confusion, and don't ignore things you don't understand. Allow a bell to ring if something occurs that puzzles you.
- If you are reading text, look up any words you don't understand, and write them down.
- Reread any complex sentences, underlining the important phrases, until the meaning is clear.
- Go out of your way to get to the bottom of what you are reading. Look up information you don't really understand, and ask friends what they think.
- If you are listening, don't be afraid to ask for clarification of anything that doesn't make sense to you. Speakers are often pleased by this—as it shows you are really listening to them.
- Use pen and paper, if necessary, to clarify any concepts you find confusing. For example, draw a map showing the positions of several buildings in relation to one another.
- Whether you are reading or listening, try to let the words paint a picture in your mind.
- If you are dealing with facts, aim to understand them rather than learning them by rote. Try to relate them to facts you already know. Asking other people to test you often helps.

PUTTING YOUR CASE

No collection of facts, no matter how pertinent, can be fully absorbed if they are presented in a muddled and disjointed way. The ability to present information clearly and logically is invaluable in many areas of life, whether you are called on to produce a professional report, relate an incident, or pass on instructions of some kind.

Organizing your material

There are many ways to organize data for presentation. In some cases, such as describing an accident, details are best communicated chronologically. For other purposes, like asking for a salary increase, it is more useful to list the pertinent facts in order of priority. Or, if you are preparing a report on the needs of your department, arranging points thematically—space, equipment, staff, etc.—is likely to be most effective. Before you begin to communicate, therefore, it's important that you are clear about the overall purpose of the exercise.

Collecting your thoughts

To help you assess your ability to present information effectively, try the following exercises. Firstly, imagine that you were a passenger in a car involved in a serious road accident. You have been asked by the police to write down everything you remember about the incident. Still feeling shocked and confused, your thoughts flowing in a haphazard way, you note the following points:

1. I smelled fuel.
2. My husband John and I were driving along a busy street.
3. Suddenly, everything went deathly quiet.
4. John swerved and braked.
5. It was a sunny day.
6. The terrifying crash seemed to last forever.
7. I was lifted into an ambulance.
8. John's arm was covered in blood.
9. I heard the screeching of brakes.
10. I could hear a Madonna tape playing.

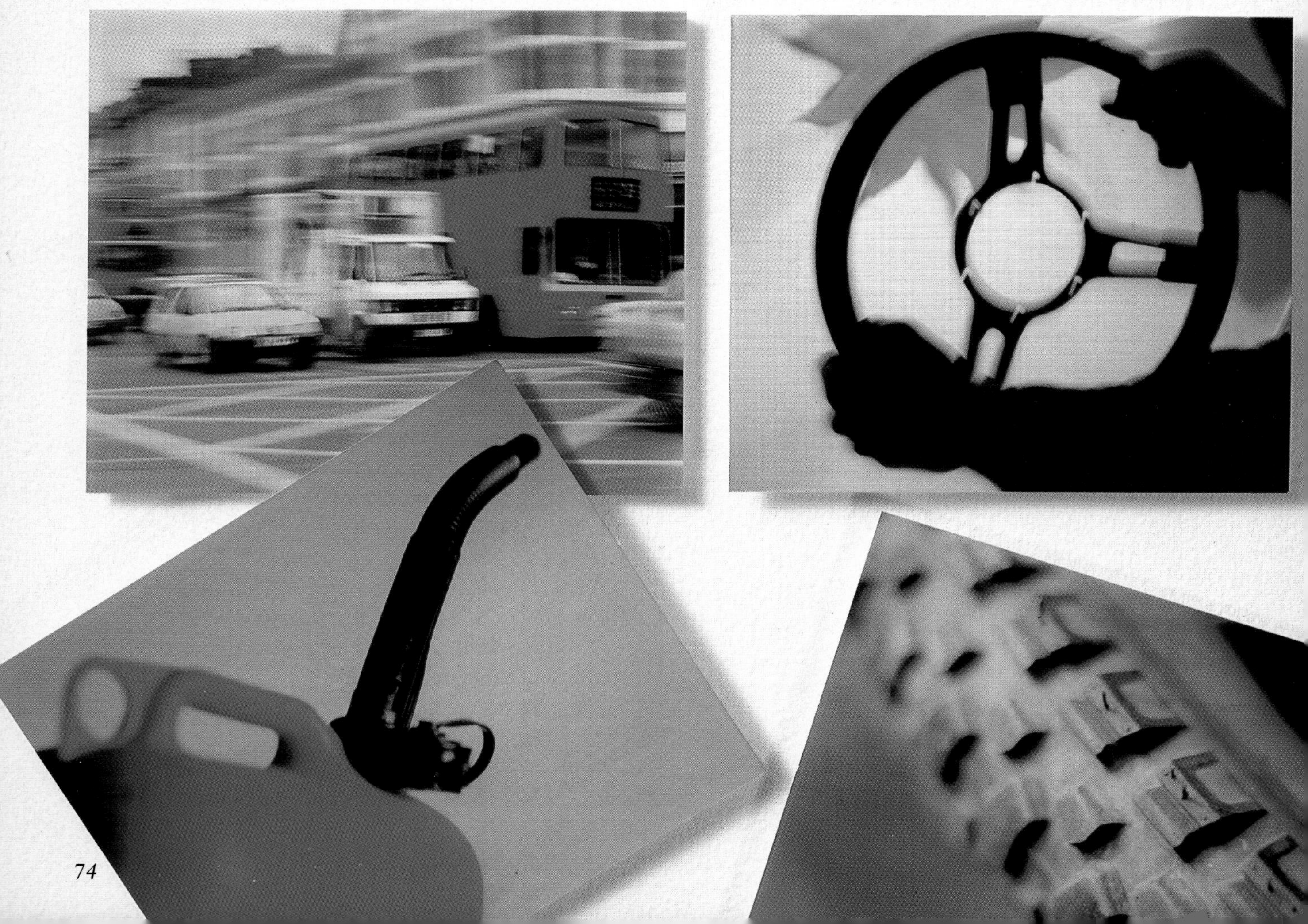

11. Someone shouted, "Call an ambulance!"
12. We pulled out to overtake a parked bus.
13. Firemen cut the roof off the car.
14. Someone asked "Are you OK?"
15. I saw a car speeding toward us.
16. The sidewalk was crowded with pedestrians.
17. I saw John's airbag inflate.
18. Someone was groaning.
19. I felt hands touching me.
20. I was hungry.

Go back through these notes, deleting any irrelevant points, and reorganize the rest in chronological order. When you have finished, turn to "Solutions," on page 135, for the answer.

Making your point

In the same way, imagine you want to ask for a salary increase. In preparation, jot down some reasons you think you deserve it. Now, arrange them in order of importance. Again, turn to page 135 for the answer.

1. I have been doing the job for three years.
2. My son needs more pocket money.
3. I have taken on much more responsibility.
4. Some colleagues earn more than I do.
5. It was agreed that my salary would be reviewed at this time.
6. You said you like my work.
7. I've been offered another job at a higher salary.
8. I'm getting bored.
9. Co-workers often ask me for help and advice.

The right order

After a serious incident like a car accident, it is vital that you get your facts straight, even if they are jumbled at first.

DRAFTING YOUR IDEAS

When you set out to produce any kind of document—an essay or a speech, for example—it's seldom an effective strategy to take a blank piece of paper and plunge straight in. Firstly, you should be absolutely clear about your subject, your audience, and the length of the item required. Is a short, incisive piece, or a long, detailed one called for?

Note down the main points, ensuring you organize them in a logical and cohesive way. Illustrate the facts with colorful details and examples. The most effective tactic is to tell people what you are going to say, say it, then recap on what you have said. In other words, sandwich your information between a strong introduction and conclusion, emphasizing the most important facts.

CHOOSE YOUR WORDS

WORDS ARE THE MEANS by which you express what you are thinking. The more limited your range of words, the less clearly and coherently you will be able to convey the complexity of your thoughts and feelings. Perhaps you notice yourself saying "you know" repeatedly, feel you don't communicate what you really mean, or find that you are often at a loss for words. If you want to express yourself more fluently and to use a wider array of words with more flexibility, ease, and dexterity, you'll find you can improve your verbal skills quite simply: the key is to have a systematic plan.

Get prepared

To begin with, equip yourself properly. Buy a good dictionary and thesaurus and keep them handy so that you can refer to them each day. Find yourself a small notebook and pen that you can keep in your pocket or handbag to use for jotting down words and expressions. Join your local library and become familiar with its sections; borrow a varied range of books on a regular basis, perhaps trying ones that seem harder to read than books you normally look for. Take out a subscription to a periodical that interests you in addition to purchasing—and reading—a quality daily newspaper.

These measures alone will not increase your verbal skills. They will, however, provide you with the essential tools; the rest is then up to you. You need to develop a curiosity about your own language and a willingness to learn. How accustomed are you to thinking about the words you use? Consider, for example, whether you can define the following words: ankle, continuous, eyelet, indulgent, parasite, series, trunk, yell. Even if you think you know their meaning, look them up. Become familiar with using a dictionary and understanding its definitions.

Build your vocabulary

Listen to yourself over a period of a few days and jot down in your notebook words and phrases that you repeat many times. When you have a quiet moment, review those words and phrases and, using your dictionary and thesaurus, try to find a range of replacement words and phrases you could use. Jot them down in your notebook and learn them, perhaps using them in a sentence. Whenever you catch yourself about to use one of your cliché or slang expressions, recall the alternatives you have noted and try to use one or other of those instead.

Look up one word in common usage every day. You can use your notebook to jot down words you hear or read and whose meaning you are not clear about. Next to it write its meaning. In everyday life

WORD BLINDNESS

Dyslexia, or word blindness, is a mild brain dysfunction that affects a person's ability to read and spell. It is not associated with intelligence. It is a life-time condition that tends to run in families and may show itself in problems with, among other things, reading.

Usually, sufferers don't understand the logic behind the way words are put together, confusing words like "form" and "from," or "on" and "no." Letters are reversed—"b" and "d," "p" and "q," for example. Spellings can be bizarre—either phonetic, as "ptrad" for "betrayed," or idiosyncratic, as "yr ti" for "your tie."

Dyslexia is not usually diagnosed until a child is at least seven, because all children learning to read and write produce dyslexia-like mistakes up to that age. Once this form of learning difficulty has been diagnosed, however, a wide range of teaching techniques can be employed to deal with it.

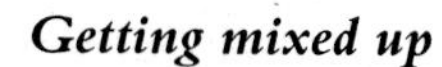

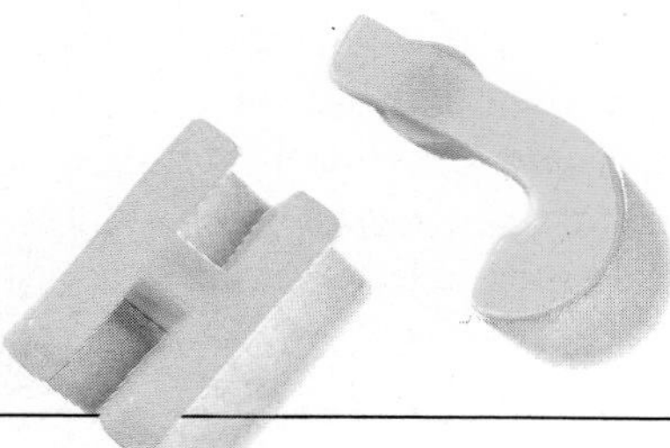

Getting mixed up
In addition to letters, dyslexics often confuse directions and spatial relationships such as push and pull, north and south, and left and right.

Eat your words
Consulting a dictionary and taking part in word games will increase your vocabulary.

people are accustomed to understanding the meaning of a sentence even if it contains one word they do not know. Take the opportunity not to let any strange word escape you. Then try to incorporate this new word into your vocabulary. This will increase your active vocabulary—the words you understand and use—quite quickly. Many people never take the opportunity to extend the variety of words they learned at school. Make sure that you are not among their number.

Trace your roots

Use a comprehensive dictionary to learn about the roots, or origins, of words. Developing a grasp of word origins opens up whole families of new words. For example, the Latin word gradus—"step"—lies behind a huge range of words in English, including aggression, congress, degrade, degree, digress, egress, grade, gradation, gradient, gradual, graduate, ingredient, ingress, progress, regress, retrograde, and transgress. Understanding that the original concept "step" is behind each one will help you to define them more accurately but also to learn new words in the same family.

Have fun finding synonyms and antonyms for common words, making feminine forms of masculine nouns—for example "actor" and "actress." One very good way of building your vocabulary is by doing crossword puzzles and other word games. For instance, what seven-letter word means "container for liquid" and "position in baseball?" It is "pitcher." Allow crosswords to make interesting word connections for you, increasing your understanding of language and improving your vocabulary.

Use your ears

Get into the habit of listening to the words and phrases that other people use. Jot down any interesting ones that you wouldn't have thought to use, and try to incorporate them into your speech. Listen to their pronunciation: figuring out the root of a word that is otherwise unfamiliar to you can help you to understand it.

Get into the habit of listening to documentary programs and news bulletins on the radio rather than watching them on television. In this way you will have to rely on your auditory skills to understand and interpret the information and events portrayed, creating images in your head rather than seeing the story unfold with your eyes. This should also help you think about the meanings of different words, and the power one word has to conjure up an entirely different image from another one that, superficially, has the same meaning.

APPLY YOURSELF

Do you find that you just can't settle to a task? Do you put off the evil moment of getting down to it, find your attention wandering, or keep having to break off to do "more important" tasks? If so, you need to develop your concentration.

Concentration

All of us have the ability to apply ourselves 100 percent to the task in hand, whatever it is. Everybody's concentration span, however, is different. Some people find they can concentrate on a task for an hour or more, that the time whizzes by while they are engrossed in work. Others find that after only a few minutes their mind starts to drift.

Most people have an optimum attention span: it may be longer when they are feeling rested, and interested in their work; similarly, it may be shorter if conditions are not ideal. However, no matter how long or short your concentration span, no matter how easy you find it to get down to a task and focus your attention on it, you can improve your skill with a few simple techniques.

Concentration combines speed with accuracy. It is a common misapprehension that in order to concentrate on a task, you must work slowly. On the contrary, researchers have found that the faster you read the more you are engaged, the more you concentrate, and the more you understand.

Prepare yourself

It's a good idea to make a list of all the things you need to do and prioritize them. Before you start, make sure you have all you need.

Clear your work space of clutter so that you have room to spread out and to avoid having other jobs compete for your attention. In order to do this, complete any nagging chores right away. Be careful, however, that you don't use these as an opportunity to put off the larger task.

It's wise to work on only one activity at a time: trying to keep three or four balls in the air wastes time and effort since you may jump from one task to another, repeating work unnecessarily.

Get going

Once you have completed your preparation, you are ready to apply yourself by doing the following:

1. Get clear in your mind your motivation for doing the job, and decide how much time you are going to devote to it. If you are bored, you may have trouble staying focused.

2. Briefly go over what you already know about the subject so your brain starts off in the right mode. This makes it easier for you to tackle complications and take in new information.

3. Jot down the questions to which you need to find answers and keep this list in front of you. Read actively for the answers. Keep referring to this list if you find that your mind starts to wander.

4. If you are reading a nonfiction book, don't dive in at page one; instead read the summary, conclusion, or contents page and decide what interests you most. Then read the beginnings and ends of chapters, sections, and paragraphs where much information is condensed. Mark in pencil any areas to come back to for a closer read.

5. Know your concentration span. If your attention span runs out after only ten minutes, don't force yourself to concentrate for an hour: 50 minutes of that will be wasted. Allow yourself to work hard for just ten minutes. Then, slowly, you can build up your ability to concentrate.

6. If you find your concentration slipping, review what you are working on, and the purpose behind what it is that you are doing.

7. Have frequent breaks, but don't get involved in any other activity for so long you lose your train of thought.

8. Work on the job until you have got all you can out of it. Don't simply give it up as soon as you lose interest.

Good preparation

When you are getting ready to work, make sure that you have everything you need around you.

Speed Reading

Most people read at a rate of about 240 words per minute. However, we all have the ability to read at up to 1,000 words per minute—and still comprehend what we are reading.

Speed reading is not about reading quickly for its own sake; it involves reading more efficiently, so that you can absorb more information in a shorter space of time. The key to speed reading is to skim for meaning rather than analyze every word.

Other ways you can increase your reading speed are to improve your vocabulary and grasp of grammar so you don't have to stop and consult a dictionary or ponder over the meaning of a sentence. Get into the habit of reading, for pleasure as well as business; this is something that will improve your reading skills in general as well as increasing your speed.

Tips for speed reading

Here are a few techniques to speed up your reading. Some of them will take time to perfect, but by practicing speed reading at every opportunity, you'll find you soon get quicker and will be able to absorb information more rapidly.

- Don't allow your eyes to stop on every word; instead try to read groups of words—anything up to six words at a time.
- Don't skip back to previous words and phrases, just keep moving on to the next thing.
- Move your eyes smoothly across the page.
- Use your finger or a pen as a guide, moving it quickly underneath the lines of text: this alone can increase your speed by up to 100 percent.
- Take in more than one line of text at a time, particularly if doing light reading.
- Use a metronome to provide a regular rhythm for your reading. This stops your eyes from slowing down and lets you increase your speed by quickening the pace.

WORDPLAY

TO MAKE THE PROCESS of improving your vocabulary and your facility with words more enjoyable, you can supplement conventional study techniques with a range of absorbing games and puzzles. Whether you use them to pass the time during long car journeys, or to enliven a family get-together, word games can provide educational fun for no more than the cost of some pencils and a few sheets of paper.

On the following pages is a series of games—to play on your own or with others. The next time you have a spare few minutes, find a pencil and get cracking!

Fun for one

Word games are ideal for when you're on your own.

• **Letter scrambles.** Pick a word—the longer, the better. Then, by rearranging all or some of its letters, see how many different or smaller words you can make. To increase the challenge, ban one, and two-letter words, or set yourself a time limit. Try going back to the same word every day for a week, attempting to reach or improve on your total more quickly every day.

Two or more can play

The first two games in this section are ideal for adults and children alike; the last one is more complicated.

• **A is for...** Pick a letter of the alphabet, then take it in turns to think of a word beginning with the chosen letter. To make the task more difficult, allow only words with a minimum number of syllables—two or three, for example, are good targets to aim for. The first person who fails to produce a word within a limited space of time—say five seconds—loses. This game is more difficult than it sounds, especially after several minutes' play.

• **Free association.** One person says a word—any word—then the next player says whatever related word first springs to mind. This might be one that rhymes with the previous word, or is directly opposite in meaning, or that describes some aspect of it. For example, the flow of words might run as follows: dog, cat, black, brown, gown, dress, shoes, boots, roots, tree, me, you, glue, stick, beat, and so on. The essence of this game is speed: Try not to think too hard and you'll find the words will come more easily. If you wait too long or if your word is not in sequence, you're out!

• **Letter by letter.** The first player chooses a letter—say "c." The next player has to think of a word that contains that letter—octopus, for example—and add an appropriate letter before or after the original one; in this case that could be "oc." The next player then has to think of a word containing those two letters—elocution, for instance—and add an appropriate letter, either in front of or after the existing two; for this example, the new sequence of letters would be either "loc" or "ocu." The object of this game is to carry on playing as long as possible without actually completing a word, however short. Once you do—or you can't think of a word that incorporates the particular sequence of letters you've been given, and so are unable to add a letter—you're out. If you suspect another player of adding a letter without having a word in mind, you may issue a challenge. If the other player cannot produce a suitable word, he or she is out. You can also play this game by writing down your sequences on paper and passing it from player to player.

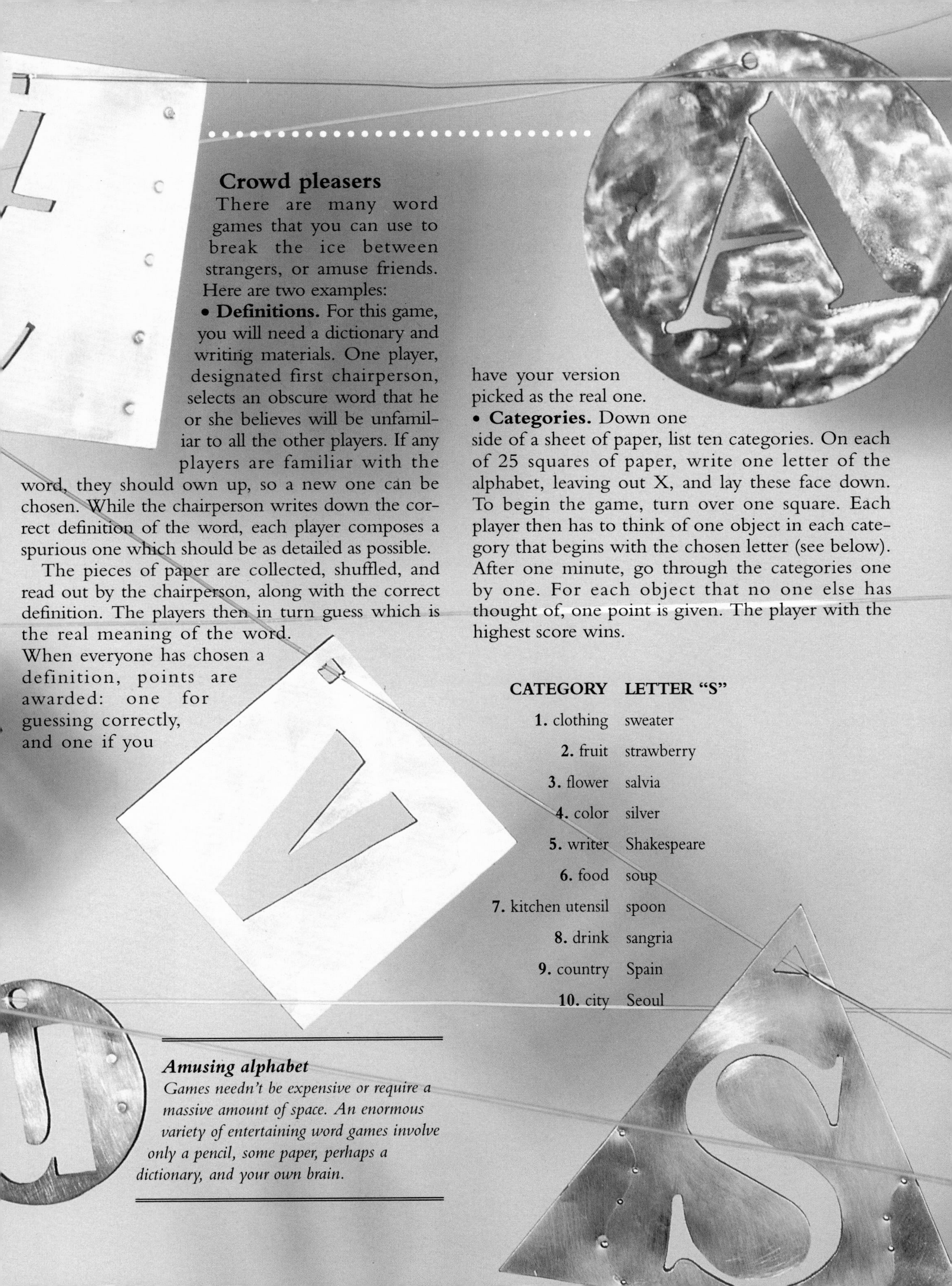

Crowd pleasers

There are many word games that you can use to break the ice between strangers, or amuse friends. Here are two examples:

• **Definitions.** For this game, you will need a dictionary and writing materials. One player, designated first chairperson, selects an obscure word that he or she believes will be unfamiliar to all the other players. If any players are familiar with the word, they should own up, so a new one can be chosen. While the chairperson writes down the correct definition of the word, each player composes a spurious one which should be as detailed as possible.

The pieces of paper are collected, shuffled, and read out by the chairperson, along with the correct definition. The players then in turn guess which is the real meaning of the word. When everyone has chosen a definition, points are awarded: one for guessing correctly, and one if you have your version picked as the real one.

• **Categories.** Down one side of a sheet of paper, list ten categories. On each of 25 squares of paper, write one letter of the alphabet, leaving out X, and lay these face down. To begin the game, turn over one square. Each player then has to think of one object in each category that begins with the chosen letter (see below). After one minute, go through the categories one by one. For each object that no one else has thought of, one point is given. The player with the highest score wins.

CATEGORY	LETTER "S"
1. clothing	sweater
2. fruit	strawberry
3. flower	salvia
4. color	silver
5. writer	Shakespeare
6. food	soup
7. kitchen utensil	spoon
8. drink	sangria
9. country	Spain
10. city	Seoul

Amusing alphabet

Games needn't be expensive or require a massive amount of space. An enormous variety of entertaining word games involve only a pencil, some paper, perhaps a dictionary, and your own brain.

More Wordplay

There are many other word games that can be played by groups of people, including "Your time's up," "I went to market and bought a...," and "Who is it?" The instructions for playing are listed below. Now get some of your friends together and have fun with them!

• **Your time's up.** This game is simple in theory, but surprisingly difficult in practice! Every player has to speak for one minute (or start with 30 seconds if you prefer) on a given subject without repetition, hesitation, or digression; if another player detects any of these faults, he or she can issue a challenge.

As soon as this happens, the clock is stopped; if the challenge is ruled unfounded, the speaker continues. If the challenge is allowed, the challenger takes over and must go on speaking, on the same topic, for the length of time left. The person who is speaking when time runs out wins a point. When each player has opened a round, the one with the greatest number of points is the winner.

There are several variations to this game. In one, the players, as before, are required to speak on a particular subject. In this version, however, they are forbidden to use, say, four key words relating to that subject. For instance, if the chosen topic is "hospitals," the banned words might be "doctor," "nurse," "operation," and "drugs."

In yet another version, the players are divided into two teams, each of which is asked to come up with a list of ten topics with corresponding forbidden words, and write them down on ten separate slips of paper. The first player is then given one of these papers by the opposing team and has to describe the topic specified to his or her own team without using any of the words that were banned. This can be much harder than it sounds! If the team guesses correctly, then they will score a point; if, however, the player utters any of the banned words, he or she will automatically be called out and the play will then pass to the other team straightaway.

Use your imagination
For word games that involve memory, visualization tricks can be extremely helpful. To remember a list of "purchases" for the market game, for example, imagine them passing in front of you on a supermarket conveyor belt.

To save time, you might like to prepare for these games in advance by devising a list of suitable topics with appropriate forbidden words.

• **I went to market and bought a...** The players take it in turn to say what they bought at the market, in each case adding their own purchase to the list of items bought by the previous players. For example, "I went to market and bought a dog," "I went to market and bought a dog and an armadillo," "I went to market and bought a dog, an armadillo, and a fresh pineapple," and so on. If any player forgets an item on the list, or gets the order wrong, he or she is out, and play continues until only one player—the winner—is left.

This simple game, suitable for playing with young children, is a good test of memory skills. One way to make it easier is to try visualizing the growing pile of "purchases;" alternatively, create a mental tableau that is striking enough to stick in your mind—an armadillo standing on a dog's back eating a slice of pineapple, for example.

• **Who is it?** Divide the players into two teams and have each person write the names of ten famous people—real or fictional—on a piece of paper. Tear the papers into strips, each one bearing a single name, and fold these strips tightly. Put them into a hat, and pass it to the other team.

From each team in turn, one player pulls a name from the hat and describes that person to his or her own team without mentioning the name. A time limit of one minute is set. If the team guesses this name correctly, the player selects another one; if that is also guessed, another is taken, and so on until the minute is up. One point is awarded for each name that a team guesses correctly, and play continues until the hat is empty.

Whose hat are you wearing?
Word games are not only great fun but can also help you to enhance your thinking skills. Communicating someone's identity without using a name, for example, can strengthen your powers of description as well as your general knowledge.

CRYPTOGRAMS

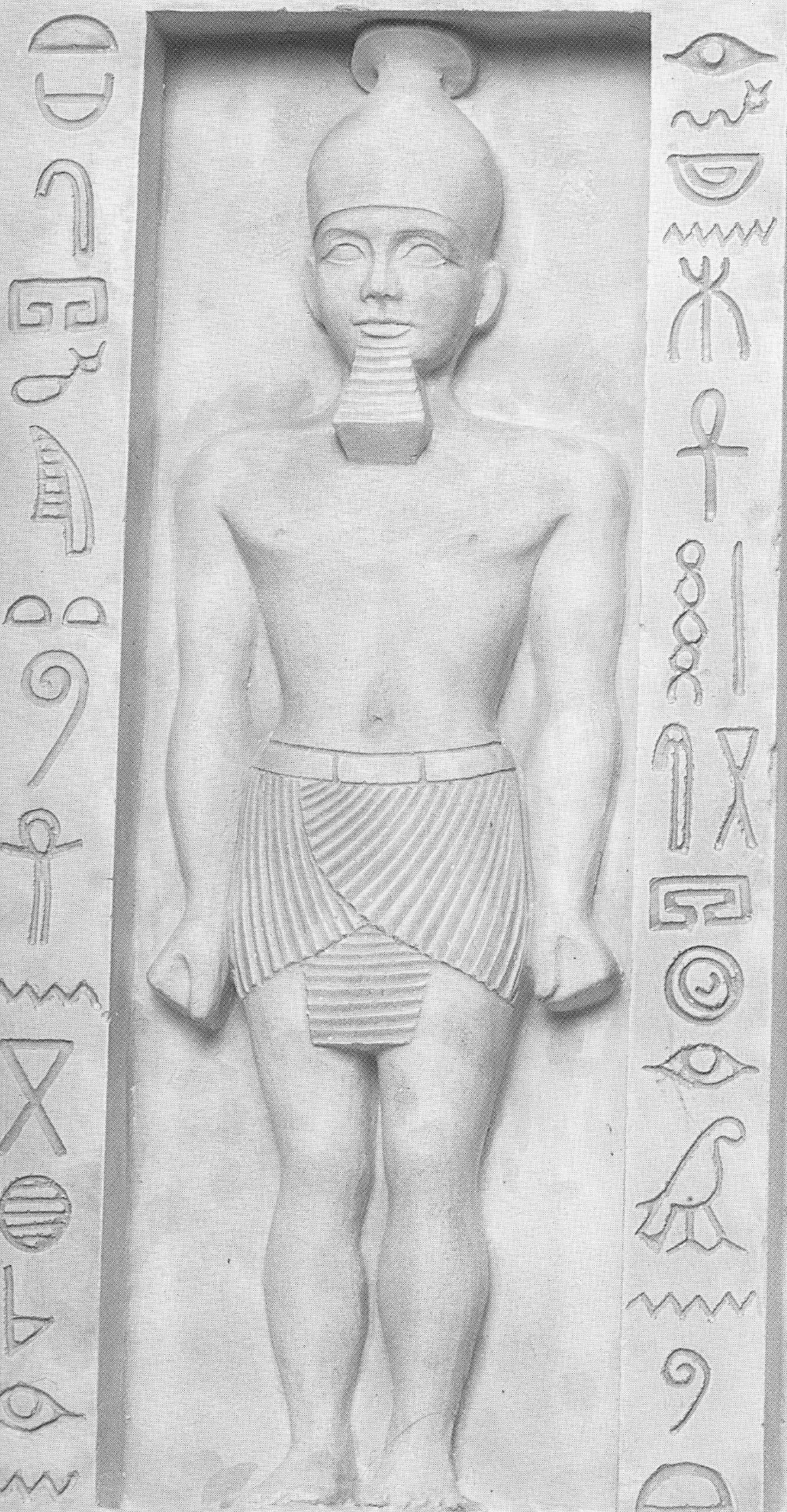

CRYPTOGRAMS ARE communications in cipher or code. One of their best-known uses is in time of war, when coding makes it possible for messages to be sent without their contents being revealed to the enemy.

Cryptograms can be very simple or extremely complex. They can be constructed by substituting one letter for another, a number for a letter, a shape for a letter, or a combination of all three.

A catalogue of codes

The simplest cryptograms are those like REWOPDNIM, in which the letters have just been set out back to front. Once the device has been identified, the original word, MINDPOWER, and any others that come after it, are easy to decode.

A similar trick involves altering the position of the spaces so a message appears to make no sense. Using this code, the phrase ENHANCE YOUR THINKING SKILLS might be written as EN HANCEY OURTH INK INGSK ILLS.

Another common cipher consists of numbers that replace the letters of the alphabet. At its most basic, this means that A = 1, B = 2, and so on. So, the code 3 1 20 represents the word "cat," and 4 15 7 is "dog."

More complex versions shift the numbering system along, so instead of A = 1, B = 2 etc., 10 might stand for A, and 11 represent B, through all 26 letters to 9, which replaces Z. By this system, "cat" would be 12 10 3 and "dog" 13 24 16.

To create a more sophisticated cryptogram using a similar structure, write the letters of the alphabet down the side of a

Easy to interpret?
The ancient Egyptians used hieroglyphics, a form of cryptogram that remained undeciphered for centuries.

sheet of paper. Beside them, write out another set of letters, but this time put, say, R at the top, to stand for A. By this system, Z will be represented by Q. The phrase, "the cat sat on the mat," therefore, would be encoded as "Kyv trk jrk fe kyv drk."

To decode cryptograms like this, begin by looking for a pattern. Here, the letters "rk" occur three times, and the word "kyv" comes up twice. The first word "Kyv" is likely to be the start of the sentence because it has a capital letter, so you might guess that it—and the identical fifth word—is "The." "K" would therefore stand for "t," "y" for "h," and "v" for "e." Now the code has effectively been broken, since once you jot down the letters from A to Z, then write beside them the decoded ones, you can quickly fill in the others.

Brain teasers

More complicated again are codes that replace letters with other letters, numbers, or symbols—not according to any system, but randomly. With cryptograms like this, the only constant factor is that all the letters, numbers, or symbols stand for the same letter each time they appear.

Breaking random codes is a tedious process that often begins with making use of known characteristics of the language involved—in English, for example, "e" is the most common letter, and there are only two single-letter words—a and I. Some knowledge of the context of the message also helps. When you're trying to break a military code by trial and error, for instance, if you see a four-letter word that begins and ends with "b," then it is far more likely to be "bomb" than "blob."

Using these guidelines, see if you can decipher the following letters to reveal a familiar aphorism: J rdees xjgdn vx j rdees djtedn. For the answer turn to "Solutions," on page 135.

The Rosetta Stone

Perhaps the most famous code-breaking tool in history was discovered in 1799, by Napoleon's forces in Egypt. Now on display in the British Museum, this slab of carved black basalt was found near the ancient town of Rosetta, west of the River Nile, after which it was named. The unique value of the Rosetta Stone is that it holds a single inscription reproduced in three different ancient scripts: Greek, which was familiar to the scholars of the time, plus the then-impenetrable Egyptian script called hieroglyphic, and a form of it called demotic. This was considered less mysterious because, like our own alphabet, it operated on the principle of phonetics—shapes representing particular sounds. Hieroglyphs, in contrast, were thought to be purely symbolic, using stylized pictures to represent ideas.

Breaking the code

A number of contemporary scholars contributed toward deciphering the hieroglyphs, but the final step was taken in 1808 by brilliant young French Egyptologist, Jean-François Champollion.

Previous research had revealed that the rings or cartouches common in Egyptian texts, encircled royal names. By comparing the two Egyptian scripts with the Greek version, and using as a key the royal name Ptolemy, which he had deciphered in both Greek and demotic, Champollion unearthed the secret of hieroglyphics—they are neither purely phonetic nor wholly symbolic. Instead they *combine* signs representing sounds with others that represent ideas. In 1822 the Frenchman published his results. They provided the key to unraveling the language of the ancient Egyptian world, and as a result, information about a whole civilization.

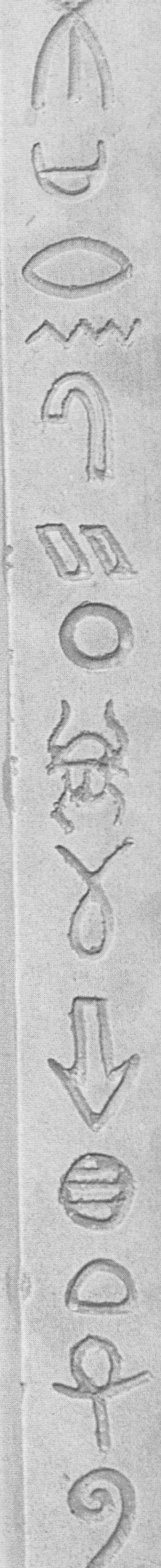

Working It Out

Once you have understood the basics of how cryptograms work, try your hand at decoding those featured here. As you have already seen, it is often possible to figure out words and phrases when you have only some of the information. This is partly guesswork, and partly logical deduction.

On these two pages you will be able to practice your deductive skills, and improve your ingenuity with words. You can play some of the games on your own—or try them out on a friend. Other puzzles will need two people to play them. For answers turn to "Solutions," on page 135.

New word games

To sharpen your skill with words, try playing these games with a friend:

1. Think of a six-letter word—for example "window." Do not tell your friend this word. Ask her to suggest letters that she thinks may be included in the word: for example, does it contain a W? Answer honestly, without revealing the position in which the letter occurs. Your friend will need paper and pen to work out the answer.

2. When you get the hang of puzzle one, make it slightly more complicated. Ask your friend this time to suggest other six-letter words. Whenever the same letter comes up in the same position, say yes; for example, if your chosen word is "window" and your friend says "watery," say yes because the position of "w" is identical in both. Do not tell your friend which is the matching letter. Take it in turns to complete the words.

Smoke signals
Native Americans used to communicate by a complex code of smoke signals.

Decipher these!

Listed below are a variety of cryptograms that you can try to decipher. Rearrange or interpret the symbols, letters, or numbers as appropriate, in order to make words or phrases.

1. ?M A R G O T P Y R C S I H T D N A T S R E D N U U O Y N A C

2. 13 9 14 4 16 15 23 5 18

3. 23 5 12 12 4 15 14 5 25 15 21 8 1 22 5 23 15 18 11 5 4 20 8 9 19 15 21 20

4. J vrbb rb jb pxxm jb j vrun

5. If:

✂ ☎ ✈ ✉ ☞ ✏ ✔ ✚ ★ means "beautiful," and

❄ ☞ ✈ ✂ ✏ ★ ✏ ☞ ◆ means "stability,"

what does the following mean?

✂ ☎ ✈ ✉ ☞ ◆ ✈ ✣ ▲ ☞ ➽ ☎ ✂ ☎ ✈ ❄ ☞

Now work out how would you write the following words: hand, fatty, table, dainty, sane

6. KNI HTVUOYY ANE HTEV OR PMI

Find the missing letter

The game "hangman" involves completing a word in a limited time, knowing only how many letters there are. Here, we have adapted it to give you a start. See how quickly you can fill in the gaps—you may discover more than one word that fits:

e - e - - - - e -
- - - g - - g e -
i n - - - - - - - - - i - n
- - - l i o - - - - - y
- - - - - - g - - -

What Does It Mean?

It is sometimes possible to work out the meaning of words in other languages by noting their similarity to words you already know, and the context in which they are used. For instance, the English word "amorous," meaning "in love" or "motivated by love," has its roots in the Latin "amor," to love. Other European languages use "amor" as a root for words with similar meanings—for example, the French word "amour," the Italian "amore," and the Spanish "amor," all mean "love."

The title "dame," awarded in Britain to notable women, is echoed in German (damen), and French (dames), both meaning "ladies." Similarly, "equal" (English), "égal," (French) and "iguál" (Spanish) all mean "the same."

RIDDLES GALORE

Riddles are puzzling or mystifying questions or statements posed as problems to be solved or guessed. They can often seem misleading and impenetrable until you know the answer—when they appear obvious. What makes riddles fun—as well as difficult—is that although the question seems straightforward you cannot find the answer by taking a simple approach; solving them requires a certain amount of ingenuity.

Ancient intelligence tests

For thousands of years, riddles have been considered a test of intelligence. In ancient times, creating and solving riddles was a popular pastime in many parts of the world. For instance, the Jewish King Solomon, famed for his wisdom throughout civilization, was visited by the Queen of Sheba, who wanted to catch him out with hard questions, or riddles. When he was able to answer them all, his reputation as a wise and virtuous king grew even more. The ancient Greeks also enjoyed the intellectual pleasure of solving riddles. Their riddles were usually short verses, full of obscure imagery, ambiguities, and plays on words.

One of history's most famous riddlers was the Sphinx, a mythological creature who was represented in Greek and Egyptian art as a female lion with a human head. She would ask travelers riddles, killing them if they failed to answer, as they invariably did. However, according to legend, when the Greek King Oedipus managed to answer the riddle correctly (see riddle eight, below right), the Sphinx killed herself.

A popular game

Riddles have an aura of mystery, and have passed into the realm of legend and religious faith. In ancient times, people consulting the oracle for advice and guidance on a problem they confronted in their life were often given an answer in the form of a riddle. Their task would be to unravel the mystery to find the solution to their problem. Although riddles were taken seriously, they also became the stuff of humor. Later, they became popular with a wide range of people, from the common folk up to learned monks, kings, and courtiers. The first published collection dates from 1538 and was compiled by an Italian blacksmith.

In the modern Western world, many of our most enduring jokes are based on riddles. In some circles they have taken on a poetic quality, and their air of mystery and surrealism has been used to great effect. They also form part of popular culture: One of Batman's most notable foes is called the Riddler. In order to fight him, Batman has first to solve the riddles he poses.

The meaning behind the words

The better a riddle is, the harder it is to solve. Nothing is as simple as it appears in a riddle: You cannot take its words at face value, and you need to look beneath simple words to find their real meaning. If you take them too literally, you will not solve the riddle.

This is demonstrated in a typical riddle from Italy, which was originally written in rhyming local dialect. It runs as follows: "Two fathers and two sons went hunting and each killed one hare. How many hares does that make?" You probably think that the answer is obvious—four hares. However, riddles are seldom so swiftly solved, and the correct answer is not four, but three. That's because there were three men in the hunting party—grandfather, father and son—the father being both son of the grandfather and father of the son.

Einstein, in writing about creative thinking, said "The same thinking that created the problem will not solve it. Think differently!" This advice can be applied to solving riddles. If you think in a straightforward way a riddle appears ridiculous. In order to solve it, you need to make a mental adjustment, shift your perspective, and look at the problem from a different vantage point.

To solve the riddles in the box below, try considering them from a different angle. They need to be solved with reasoning—and patience. Remember that although riddles are logical, their central idea has to be teased out.

SOLVING RIDDLES

Try your hand at solving these riddles. You will find the answers in "Solutions," on page 136.

1. What grows bigger the more you take away?

2. What kind of ear cannot hear?

3. Who makes me, sells me; who buys me, does not use me; who uses me, does not know me. What am I?

4. I have a comb but am not a barber; mark the hours but am not a bell; have spurs but do not ride. What am I?

5. What can you spend but never buy?

6. What gets wetter as it dries?

7. What has three hands, the second hand really being the third?

8. What walks on four legs in the morning, two at noon, and three in the evening?

9. What has 21 spots but is never ill?

10. What walks on its head all day?

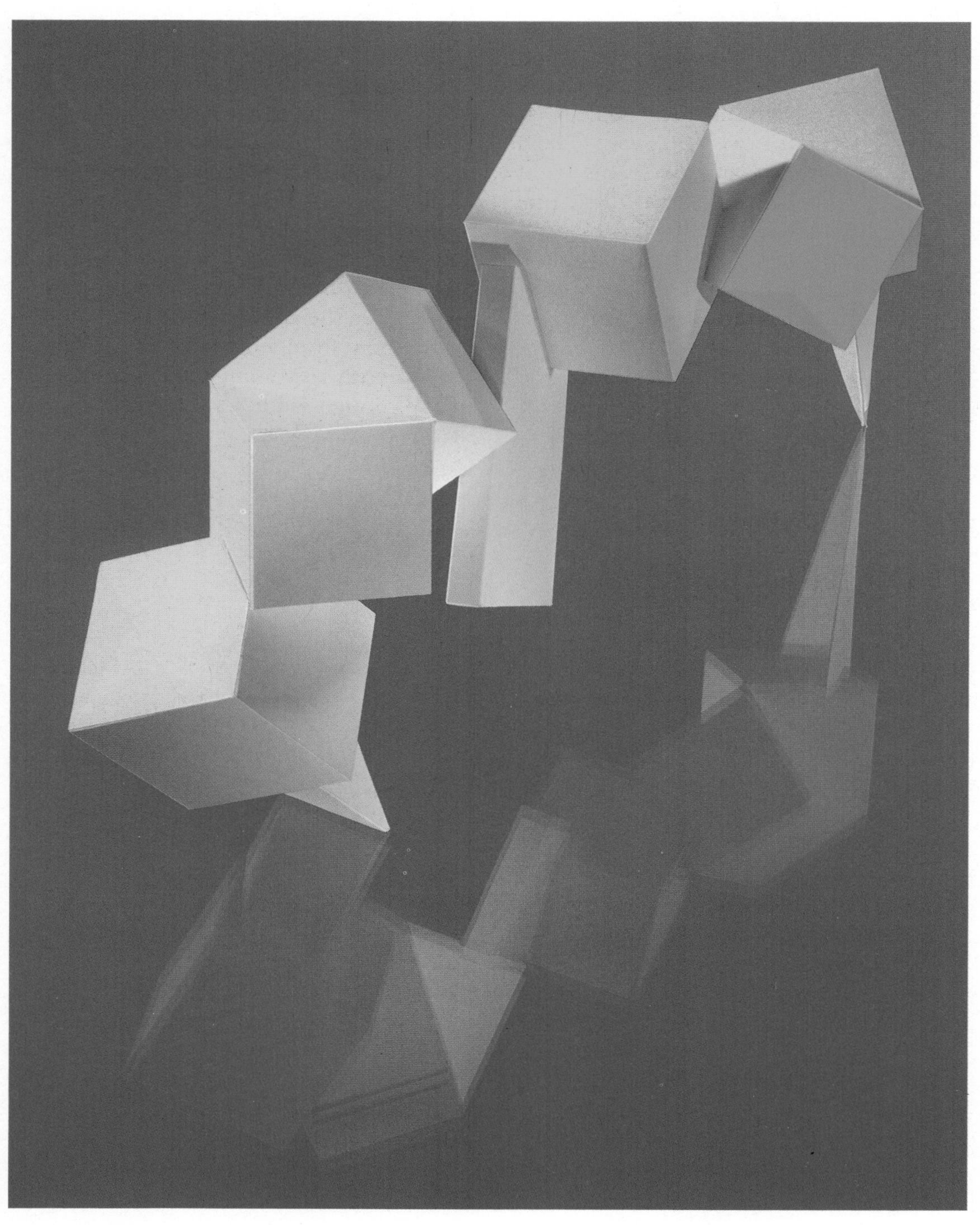

CHAPTER FOUR

FIGURE IT OUT

NUMBERS ARE PART OF our lives. We need them when we go shopping, when sorting out our personal finances, when calculating a service charge, and in many other everyday contexts. Yet while some of us are happy using numbers, many more are intimidated by them. However, everyone has basic mathematical ability, and it is easy to improve the skills you already have. If you do not feel excited by this idea, the chances are that you do not enjoy numbers; nevertheless, as this chapter illustrates, numbers can be fun.

Playing number games, such as those in "Fun with Numbers," on pages 94-95, will encourage you to make connections between numbers, and also to think logically. Number play is also a good form of mental workout, one that will dramatically improve both your mathematical ability and your confidence.

Understanding how numerical systems work is another important step in increasing your facility with numbers. On pages 96-97, we take a brief look at some familiar and less-familiar systems, from the decimal to the binary, the latter commonly used in computer programming. We also explore other systems, from counting and calculating on your fingers to Roman numerals, that are still used today.

But what is it that makes some people exceptionally good at math? Is it the way they use their brain, or do they have a mental ability that others lack? As we discuss on pages 102-103, math geniuses may be driven by a passion for numbers, a heightened appreciation of the sense of order in the world of numbers, or the ability to "see" numbers in a different way from most of us. "Spectacular Math," on pages 104-105, offers a fascinating insight into numerical mind tricks.

It is interesting that some math geniuses talk of "seeing" numbers, because scientists believe thinking is made up of two elements—perceiving visual or non-verbal events, and interpreting verbal systems or language. Our perceptual skills enable us to interpret our physical environment and to get our bearings; one weakness in this area that many people suffer from is a poor sense of direction. Is this true of you? Test your map-reading skills with "Lost in Space," on pages 108-109.

By working through the basic numerical puzzles in this chapter, you'll sharpen up your basic skills, and gain the confidence to tackle the more complex calculations. Once you refuse to be intimidated by numbers, you'll discover you're capable of much more than you realized.

THE WORLD OF NUMBERS IS FASCINATING AND FUN, YET SOME PEOPLE FIND IT FRIGHTENING. THERE IS NOTHING TO FEAR: YOU MAY LACK CONFIDENCE, BUT EVERYONE HAS MATHEMATICAL ABILITY.

MATHEMATICS FOR ALL

EVERY DAY OF YOUR LIFE, whether you like it or not, you come into contact with the world of mathematics. For instance, at the supermarket, you calculate the approximate cost of your purchases to make sure you can pay for them; in a restaurant, you have to work out your share of the bill and the size of the tip. Surveys continue to show, however, that most adults, irrespective of their educational background, have some fear of mathematics.

It would be logical to assume that, since so many people have these worries, there might be some reason for them—that their brains are inadequate for the task. This is not the case, however—everybody can learn how to deal with numbers. The balance between left and right brain (see pp. 20-21), as well as varying between individuals, alters if one side is used more than the other. The principal cause of numerical illiteracy is simply a failure to exercise the left brain—whether intentional or not.

In the end, attaining basic mathematical skills is much the same as developing any other skill, from playing the piano to driving a car. It is essentially a case of understanding the techniques involved and putting them into practice. To help you do this, work through the exercises shown here, which cover many of the basic mathematical functions that you are likely to come into contact with in everyday life.

The correct change
Mathematics is a necessary part of our everyday lives. Learning to use even the most basic calculations can save you time—and money.

NUMBER TRICKS

The multiplication table that gives people the most problems is probably the 9-times table. However, there are ways in which you can remind yourself how it works. Firstly, look at the list below:

1 x 9 = 9	2 x 9 = 18
3 x 9 = 27	4 x 9 = 36
5 x 9 = 45	6 x 9 = 54
7 x 9 = 63	8 x 9 = 72
9 x 9 = 81	10 x 9 = 90
11 x 9 = 99	12 x 9 = 108

Now, look at the answers. You will see that their digits all add up to 9, with the exception of 11 x 9, which leaves two nines. When you are looking at multiples of more than 12, you will see that the figures in the answer still add up to 9. For instance, 13 x 9 = 117 (1 + 1 + 7), and 25 x 9 = 225 (2 + 2 + 5).

Percentages

Many people find percentages tricky, yet they are actually very straightforward. The word percent means literally "for every hundred." Therefore 15 percent of a dollar is 15 cents. If you're in a restaurant and you want to leave a 15 percent tip on a $20 meal, you can think of the tip as simply being 20 lots of 15 cents—$3.00. Everyday percentages, such as a tip, are easy because they tend to be in multiples of 5 or 10: For example, 10 percent off a $500 suit is $50. To calculate 40 percent off an $800 table, work out 10 percent, then multiply by 4 to arrive at a discount of $320.

Similarly, to calculate percentages that are a multiple of 5, add half of 10 percent at the end of the sum. So, to calculate 35 percent of $120, work out that 10 percent of $120 is $12, so 30 percent would be $36. Half of 10 percent is $6, so the total is $36 + $6 = $42.

Rounding

Many everyday situations that on the surface require a complex calculation will only require an answer that is roughly accurate. For example, if you are about to buy items that cost $38.99, $10.21, $33.57, and $10.49, and you have $100 to spend, you don't really need to know that the answer is $93.26, simply that it's less than $100. In a case like this, the most effective way is to forget adding up the cents, but just concentrate on the dollars. In each case look at the number of cents—if it is 50 or above, then increase the number of dollars by one. Now, the mental calculation is much more manageable: 39 + 10 + 34 + 10 = 93.

Rounding can also be very effective with percentages. For instance, imagine you have been told your salary of $41,000 a year is about to rise by 9.8 percent. By rounding the figures you can treat the calculation as being 10 percent of $40,000. Then you will be able to work out immediately that your pay rise will come to around $4,000 (or $4,018 exactly).

FUN WITH NUMBERS

Whether you find the idea of solving number puzzles daunting or intriguing, here are some simple and enjoyable examples. Their solutions can be found by spotting repeating patterns, or turning parts of the sequence into smaller calculations. Be warned: Some of these puzzles may require you to approach the problem from a less obvious perspective. For example, the sequence 60, 60, 24, 7, 52 is a series of mathematically unrelated numbers; a little lateral thinking reveals that it alludes to the number of seconds in a minute, minutes in an hour, hours in a day, days in a week, and weeks in a year.

Also included are some mathematical stories. Even people who are quick with figures may find these difficult: Try reading through the problem to change it into a calculation. When you have finished, turn to "Solutions," on page 136, for the answers.

Missing numbers

Find the missing numbers in the following group of sequences:

a)

b)

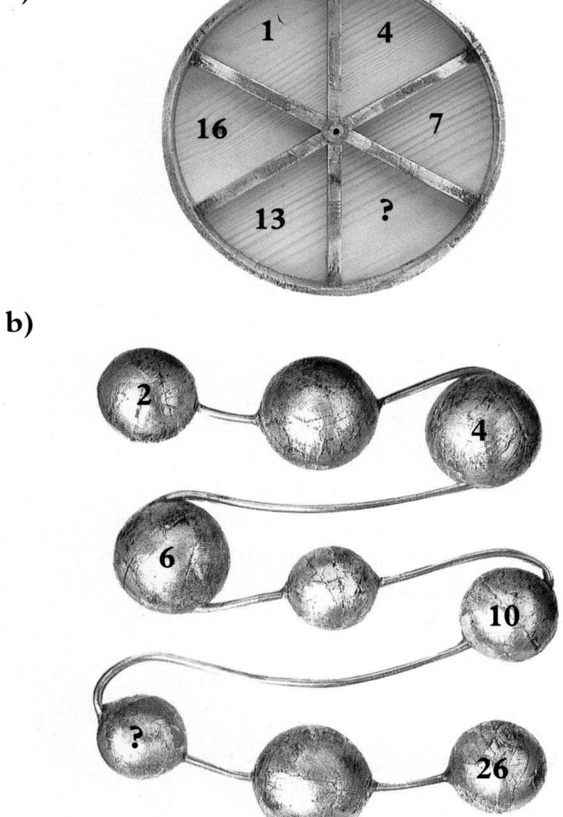

c)

d) The grid below contains five empty boxes. See if you can fill them. A clue is to look for patterns that run both horizontally and vertically.

1	1	2	3	_
2	4	4	_	8
3	9	_	9	12
4	_	8	12	16
_	25	10	15	20

Making connections

a) This is a puzzle to challenge your ability to find number patterns. Look at these four rows of figures. Which figure is the odd one out, and why?

12	6	4	8	10
8	4	3	4	6
20	10	8	16	18
34	17	15	30	32

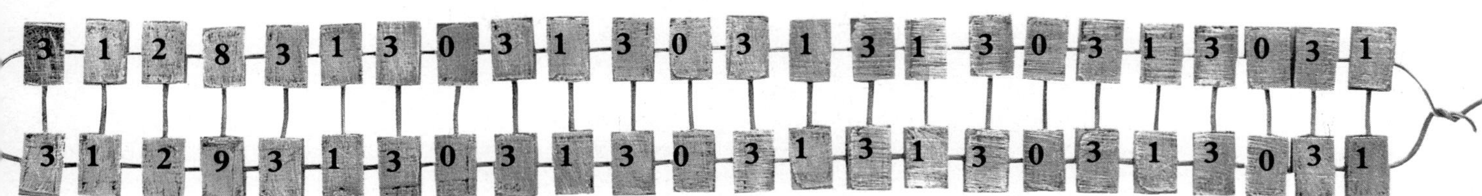

b) At the top of this page are two lists of numbers. Can you see how they are connected? A clue is to try to break each list down into smaller groups.

Complements

Look at the two lists of numbers appearing on the right. Each number in the left-hand column has a "complement" in the right-hand column, which, added to it, makes 100: for example, the number 17 has a complement of 83. Try to match all the pairs in less than a minute.

16	79
29	59
37	58
18	95
61	86
4	27
73	39
65	67
21	63
36	82
42	84
14	71
19	96
33	81
41	64
5	35

Logic

The next two questions require you to work out what information is relevant. The best way to approach them is to turn them into simple sums. Beware: not all the information is necessary.

a) Redfield Town and Orgone City are 200 miles apart, linked by a single road. Jim lives exactly halfway along that road. He has to meet his bank manager in Redfield at 12:45 p.m. tomorrow. If Jim leaves his home at 10:00 a.m. and drives at a steady 50 mph, will he arrive in time?

b) Janet is picking berries with her son Mark and her daughter Wendy. Janet works twice as quickly as Mark, who works twice as quickly as Wendy. Janet can fill eight boxes of berries an hour. If they work from 11:00 a.m. to 4:00 p.m., how many boxes will they fill altogether?

PROBABILITY

Every day of our lives, we try to predict the likelihood of a certain event or series of events taking place—for instance, the chance of the numbers we have chosen winning the lottery. Mathematics provides logical ways to predict the likelihood of an event occurring. This can only be calculated with total accuracy when all outcomes are known. The simplest example is tossing a coin. We know that whatever the outcome it will be one of two possibilities—heads or tails. This can be referred to as a 1 in 2 probability, or 50 percent. Probabilities are also shown as a decimal fraction of 1 where 1 represents complete certainty. The likelihood of calling either heads or tails is 1 divided by 2 = 0.5. The probability of calling heads is 0.5 and the probability of calling tails is also 0.5. These are the only two possibilities—if you add up these numbers they equal 1, which is the probability that either heads or tails will appear.

Here are some probability problems for you to solve, involving shaking a die. Remember that there are six possible outcomes. What is the likelihood of:

a) Rolling a 6.
b) Rolling a 4.
c) Rolling a 6 or a 4.
d) Rolling anything except a 1, 3, or 5.

Counting Systems

Have you ever wondered why our counting system is based on ten digits: 0, 1, 2, 3, 4, 5, 6, 7, 8, and 9? Centuries ago Aristotle theorized that we find it convenient to count in tens because we have ten fingers. When the need arose to count higher than 9, rather than creating symbols for each new number, a higher order was introduced: 9 is therefore followed by the number 10, indicating 1 unit of ten and 0 single units. The sequence continues up until the number 99, when you move up to the next higher order, 100—i.e., 1 unit of a hundred, 0 units of tens, and 0 single units. This ten-digit system is known as base-10 or "decimal," from *decima*, the Latin word for ten.

Quinary counting

In a number of ancient cultures, such as that of the Tamancos people of South America, the number system had a base of 5. Such systems, known as "quinary," almost certainly developed in the same way as the decimal system, except that they were based on the use of one single hand, rather than both hands together, for counting. This theory is reinforced by the knowledge that, in some of the early languages, the words used for hand and five were interchangeable.

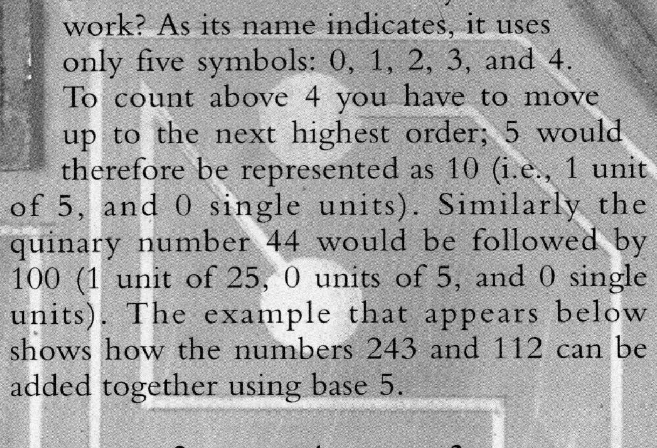

So how would a base-5 system work? As its name indicates, it uses only five symbols: 0, 1, 2, 3, and 4. To count above 4 you have to move up to the next highest order; 5 would therefore be represented as 10 (i.e., 1 unit of 5, and 0 single units). Similarly the quinary number 44 would be followed by 100 (1 unit of 25, 0 units of 5, and 0 single units). The example that appears below shows how the numbers 243 and 112 can be added together using base 5.

2	**4**	**3**
+1	**1**	**2**

Step 1. Begin with the digits that appear on the right. In quinary, 3 + 2 = 10. So, in the usual way, enter 0 beneath that column, and then carry the 1 over into the next column.

2	**4**	**3**
+1	**1**	**2**
		0

Step 2. In quinary, 4 + 1 = 10. But here you need to add the 1 to 1 that you carried across. In quinary, this adds up to 11. So put 1 in the middle column, and carry 1 over into the next column.

2	**4**	**3**
+1	**1**	**2**
	1	**0**

Step 3. Finally, 2 + 1 + 1 = 4 (the 1 is carried from the previous column). The answer will come to 410.

2	**4**	**3**
+1	**1**	**2**
4	**1**	**0**

Use the same principle for calculations involving any base, remembering that when you reach the last digit of that base, you must move up to the next order. So, in base 8, the number after 7 is 10.

Converting bases

Try this example, which is to convert the decimal number 59 into base 5.

Step 1. Begin by calculating the quinary equivalents of the decimal orders by multiplying the previous order by five: This gives you the quinary orders 1, 5, 25, 125, etc. When you have worked out the first quinary order that is greater than the decimal number you want to convert (i.e., 59) stop and space them out in a row reading right to left: **25** **5** **1**

Step 2. Divide 25 into the decimal number 59. Don't worry about decimal places, just work with the integer (the whole number) and the remainder. 59 ÷ 25 = 2 with a remainder of 9. Write down 2 under that column.

25	**5**	**1**
2		

Now divide 9, the remainder, by 5, which is the heading of the next column to the right. 9 ÷ 5 = 1 with a remainder of 4. Write down 1 under the column headed 5. As the next column to the right deals with single units, no further calculations are necessary, so write down the remainder under the column headed 1.

25	**5**	**1**
2	**1**	**4**

59 in base 10 = 214 in base 5. You can check that figure back by adding together in base 10 the product of each column:

2 x 25 = 50
1 x 5 = 5
4 x 1 = 4
59

This principle adapts readily to other bases. For example, if you want to use base 8 (octal), the column headings you need are 1, 8, 64 (8 x 8), and 512 (64 x 8); if you want to use base 2 (binary) the headings will be 1, 2, 4, 8, 16, and 32.

Systems in technology

At the heart of all computer technology is the binary number system, the second most common base after the decimal system. Binary has a base of 2 and uses only the numbers 0 and 1. In computers these equate to the two states in a circuit, either on or off where 0 equals off (i.e., no current passing through the circuit) and 1 equals on. All types of information can be coded for a computer in this way.

Another system used in computers is hexadecimal, which uses base 16. Here, the letters from A to F represent the numbers between 10 and 15. In hexadecimal, therefore, number 13 is shown as D.

Test yourself

Now see if you can use what you've learned to calculate the following. Turn to "Solutions," on page 137, to find the answers:

1. Using base 5, add 2432 to 1442.
2. Convert 87 in decimal to base 8.
3. If you are using base 7, what would be the sum of 6453 + 214?
4. Convert the decimal number 71 into its equivalent in binary.
5. In binary, what is the sum of 101000 + 1011?
6. In base 8, what is 777 + 1?
7. What is the greater number, 724 in decimal or 1324 in octal?
8. Using base 5, add the sum of 1432241 to 3224314.

Other routes

Using a base of 10 is only one way to count; try using other bases too.

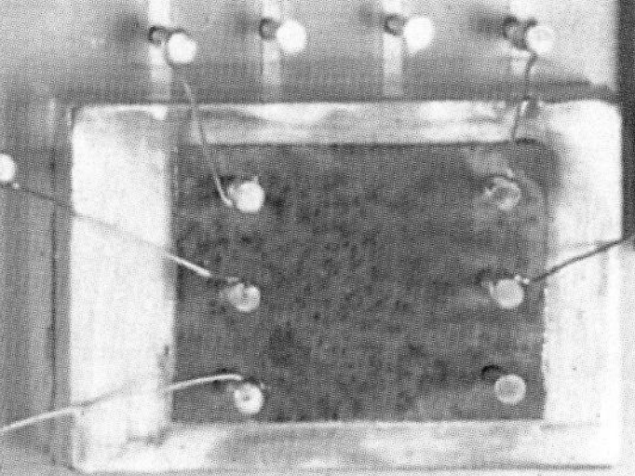

INDIGITATION

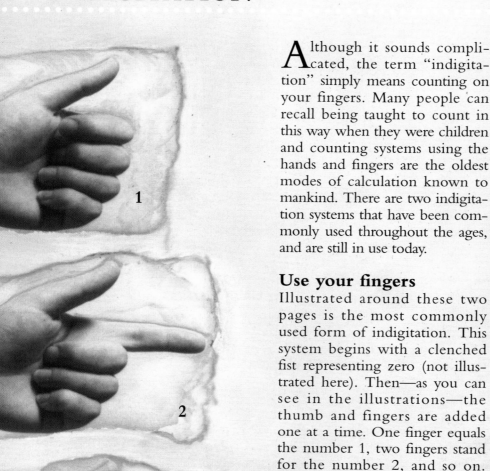

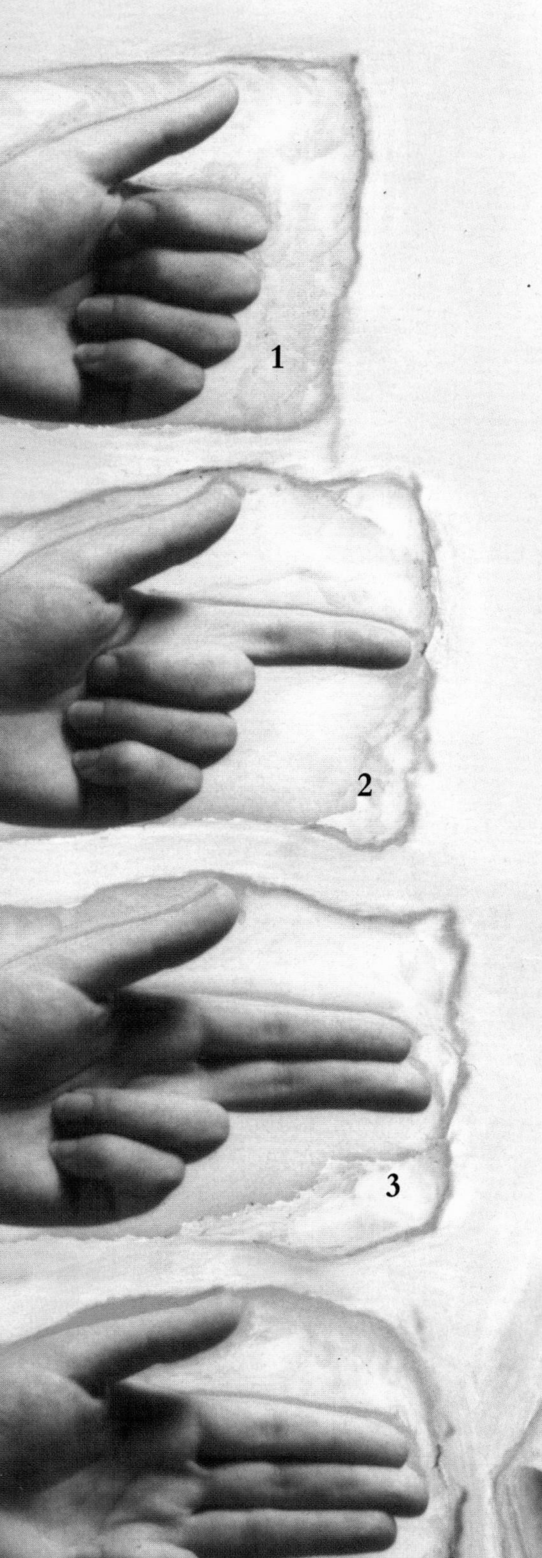

Although it sounds complicated, the term "indigitation" simply means counting on your fingers. Many people can recall being taught to count in this way when they were children and counting systems using the hands and fingers are the oldest modes of calculation known to mankind. There are two indigitation systems that have been commonly used throughout the ages, and are still in use today.

Use your fingers

Illustrated around these two pages is the most commonly used form of indigitation. This system begins with a clenched fist representing zero (not illustrated here). Then—as you can see in the illustrations—the thumb and fingers are added one at a time. One finger equals the number 1, two fingers stand for the number 2, and so on. The other hand is used for figures above 5. This is probably the way you learned to count when you were a child.

Another form of indigitation works in the opposite manner to the one that is illustrated here. This method begins with an open hand and subtracts from the little finger downward. Therefore the little finger folded in equals 1, the next finger folded in equals 2, and all fingers down to form a fist equals 5. On the same basis as the other system, two clenched fists stand for 10.

Advanced indigitation

Of course, in an era where electronic pocket calculators and computers are commonplace, the methods shown above may seem a childish or cumbersome way of performing simple calculations. In fact, during the Renaissance period, long before the creation of logarithm tables or slide rules, mathematicians developed extremely sophisticated ways of performing long multiplication using the hands.

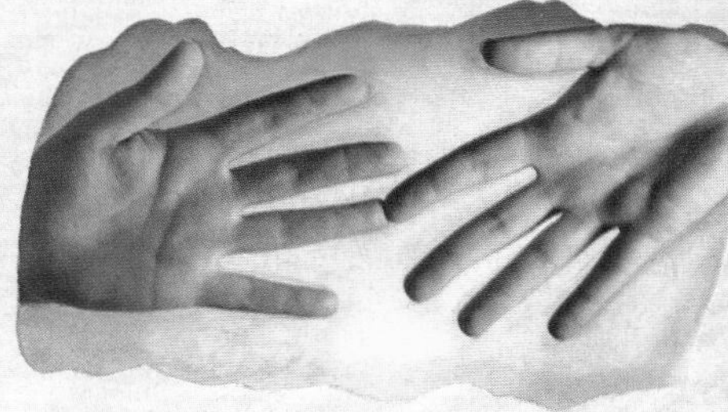

One way of doing this is as follows. Look at the two hands pictured directly above. The method shown here uses the concept of a "complement," (see "Fun with Numbers," pp. 94-95) this time for the number 10.

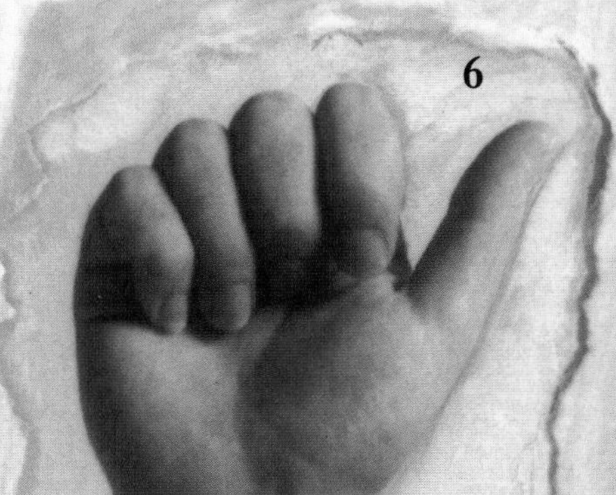

ROMAN NUMERALS

In the Western world, before the fourteenth century, the Roman numeral system was in common use. The symbols that we are familiar with now derive from the Middle-Eastern Indo-Arabic system, which is why they are known as "Arabic" numbers.

Roman numerals comprise seven main symbols: I (1), V (5), X (10), L (50), C (100), D (500) and M (1,000). In order to work out a number given in Roman numerals, you add and/or subtract the given symbols, thus:

Whenever you see a lower-value symbol to the left of the next-highest symbol you subtract the lower value from the higher one: e.g., IV is 4, and XL is 40. When a lower-value symbol appears to the right of a higher symbol you add the two together: e.g., VI is 6, and LX is 60. If you have a series of high, low, and high symbols then subtract the low symbol from the high symbol following it instead of adding it to the high symbol that precedes it. As an example you can see that XXIX is 29.

The following is a list of the Roman numerals 1-10 and their Arabic counterparts:

I	—	1	VI	—	6
II	—	2	VII	—	7
III	—	3	VIII	—	8
IV	—	4	IX	—	9
V	—	5	X	—	10

Now, using this information, see if you can figure out the Roman numeral equivalents for each of the following numbers: 33, 45, 101, and 1998. Then turn to "Solutions," on page 137, to see whether or not you have the correct answers.

In this example, we will multiply 9 x 7. To do this, hold your hands out with the palms facing you. Each hand represents (from the thumb downward) the numbers from 10 to 6. Move your hands so that the tip of the third finger, 7, is touching the tip of the opposing index finger—which represents 9.

Now, take the first number, 7, and work out its complement to 10 by counting up to the thumb—the complement is 3. Repeat this for the second number, 9—the complement is 1.

The next step in this indigitation problem is to take the difference between either number and its opposing complement—in this case either 7 - 1, or 9 - 3. This tells us that the "tens" number of the answer is 6.

To get the final number you simply multiply both the complements (3 x 1 = 3) and place the product after the tens number answer. Therefore the final answer to the indigitation problem is 63. (This multiplication technique works best for equations above 5 x 5.)

Point to the answer
People have always used their fingers to solve mathematical problems.

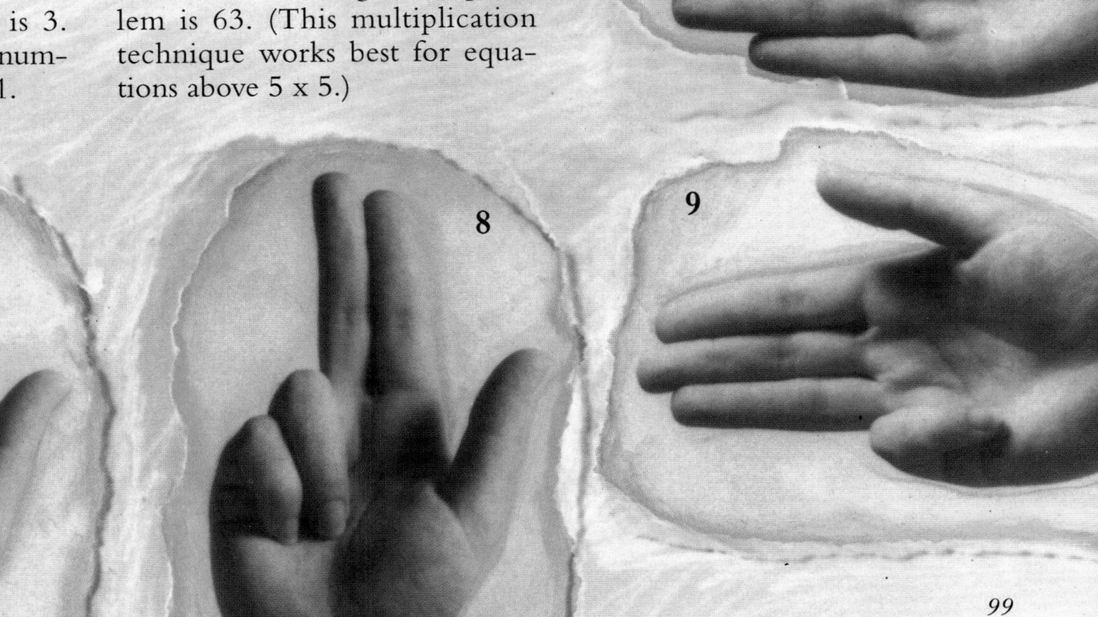

PROCESSING DATA

Some number puzzles are more involved than others, and even though you may consider yourself good at some of them, there are others that you may find difficult. One tip is that when you encounter complicated problems like the ones on these pages, it's a good idea to jot down the details as you read through them so you can build up a picture of the information you have. Beware, though—in some cases you may not have enough information to formulate an answer. Turn to pages 137-138 for the solutions.

Sweet sales

The following is a table of figures for sales of candy, to accompany the graph below.

	Last year	*This year*
Humbugs	19,680	21,899
Smarties	21,087	22,645
Treacle	3,098	4,090
Jelly Beans	1,367	4,867
Hard Candy	27,867	21,867
Liquorice Allsorts	9,786	14,234
Wine Gums	9,754	9,786
Rock	12,876	11,345

Using the data presented, see if you can tell which of the following statements are true.

1. More Hard Candy was sold this year than last.

2. Wine Gums sold better this year than Liquorice Allsorts did last year.

3. Sales of Hard Candy fell by more than 20 percent this year.

4. The total sales of Humbugs increased by less than 10 percent.

5. If next year's sales change at exactly the same rate as this year's, then Smarties will no longer perform better than Humbugs.

Bill and Ted's money adventure

Bill: Let's go out tonight. How much money do you have in your pocket?

Ted: Well, remember that when we counted our money this morning I had twice as much as you did. Have you spent any of it?

Bill: Yes, I spent $10 on a new CD.

Ted: OK, well I haven't spent anything today, and I noticed that I had enough to pay my telephone bill, with $20 left over.

Bill: Oh, wait a minute, of course, I paid my telephone bill today. That was $60.

Ted: Cheap! Mine was only half what it cost last year.
Bill: So how much was that, then?
Ted: Well, that's ten times my own age and I'm four years younger than you.
Bill: And I'm 32, so... oh, I just remembered, Jeff paid me back the $50 he owed. You know that he still owes me my age and your age put together, though.
Ted: Now I can work out how much money you have...or can I?

Is this true?

1. Ted is 28 years old.
2. Ted's phone bill last year was $290.
3. Bill has exactly $60 left in his pocket.
4. Ted doesn't have enough information to work out how much money Bill has.
5. His friend Jeff now owes Bill a further $60.

The match makers

This year, SureFire, based in Chicago, produced 120 million boxes of matches. This accounted for 60 percent of all the matches produced in the States. A quarter of all matches made in the U.S. are exported. The other U.S. companies producing matches are SuperStrike of Detroit and SuperFire, from Seattle. Their shares in the U.S. match market are identical. However, SuperStrike and SuperFire both export twice as many matches as SureFire. SuperStrike get 10 cents a box for their matches in the U.S. Half of all matches produced by SuperFire are exported to Canada. The income from each box of SureFire is twice that for SuperStrike. Income from exported matches is 50 percent higher.

Which of these statements are true?

1. SuperFire only exports matches to Canada.
2. SuperStrike has a total income of $400,000.
3. SureFire's match sales in the U.S. were worth $22 million.
4. SuperFire exported $300,000 worth of matches.
5. 200 million boxes of matches were produced in the U.S. last year.

Rise and fall

Look at last year's figures (left) and this year's (right) to see the change in candy sales.

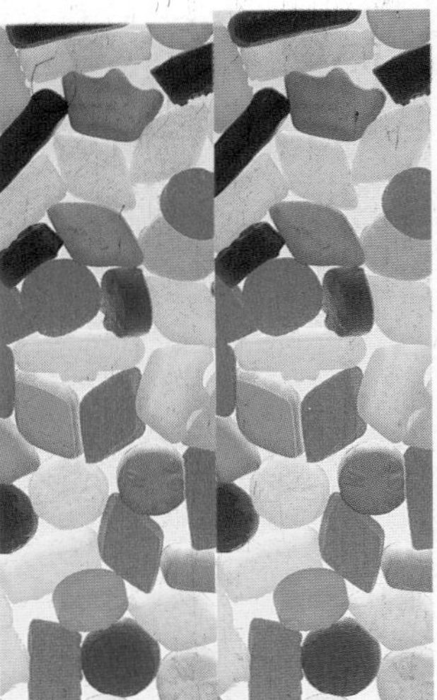

Hard Candy | *Liquorice Allsorts* | *Wine Gums* | *Rock*

Math Genius

From time to time reports appear in the media about remarkable individuals with a mathematical facility so astounding that it seems almost magical. Are these people somehow different from everyone else, or have they simply developed to a very high degree skills that any one of us could learn?

Human computers?

Scientists have started to take steps toward examining why and how some people are mathematically brilliant. Do such people have some extra faculty, which is missing in the rest of us, or do they simply use their brains in a different way? While there is no conclusive answer to these questions, some clues can be gained by looking at the following three people who seem to be math geniuses. The first is Shakuntala Devi, famed throughout the world for her incredible demonstrations of mental arithmetic. In 1981, Devi—known as "the human computer"—was registered in *The Guinness Book of Records* for multiplying two 13-digit numbers in her head, and giving the answer in 28 seconds. Devi had grown up in near-poverty in Bangalore, India, with no formal education. Her explanation for this amazing capacity was quite modest. She claimed that she simply fell in love with numbers and calculations. This was not a self-conscious act—Devi viewed "her" numbers as toys with which she could play endlessly. They also provided her with emotional security since any of her calculations would always give a predictable outcome. As she herself said, "Two plus two always made, and would always make, four—no matter how the world changed."

Successful and unsuccessful

It seems likely that some people have unconsciously developed their mathematical skills at the expense of everything else. This would seem to be the case for Oscar Verhaeghe, who at age 20 could neither read nor write, and had the vocabulary of a small child. However, when he was tested by a committee of mathematicians, they found that when they asked him to calculate 689 cubed, he was able to give the answer—327,082,769—in six seconds.

Brilliantly normal

Sir Isaac Newton was a math genius—with striking abilities evident in other parts of his life too.

However, other math geniuses are generally intelligent, sometimes extremely intelligent, and their interests cover a vast range. They seem to be highly successful through most areas of their lives, and achieve a great deal. According to Tony Buzan and Raymond Keene, who have written extensively on the subject of genius, many people who fall into this category are able to live very full and interesting lives, both as regards their careers and personal relationships. For instance, the mathematician Sir Isaac Newton achieved three substantial scientific breakthroughs in his early 20s: mathematical calculus, the discovery that white light is composed of all the colors of the spectrum, and a universal law of motion, connected to his best-known discovery—gravity. He was also a member of parliament, president of the Royal Society, and master of the Royal Mint, and was the first scientist to be knighted. Newton was a mathematical genius, but his capabilities were unusual rather than abnormal. This is in stark contrast to people who appear to function more or less as human calculators.

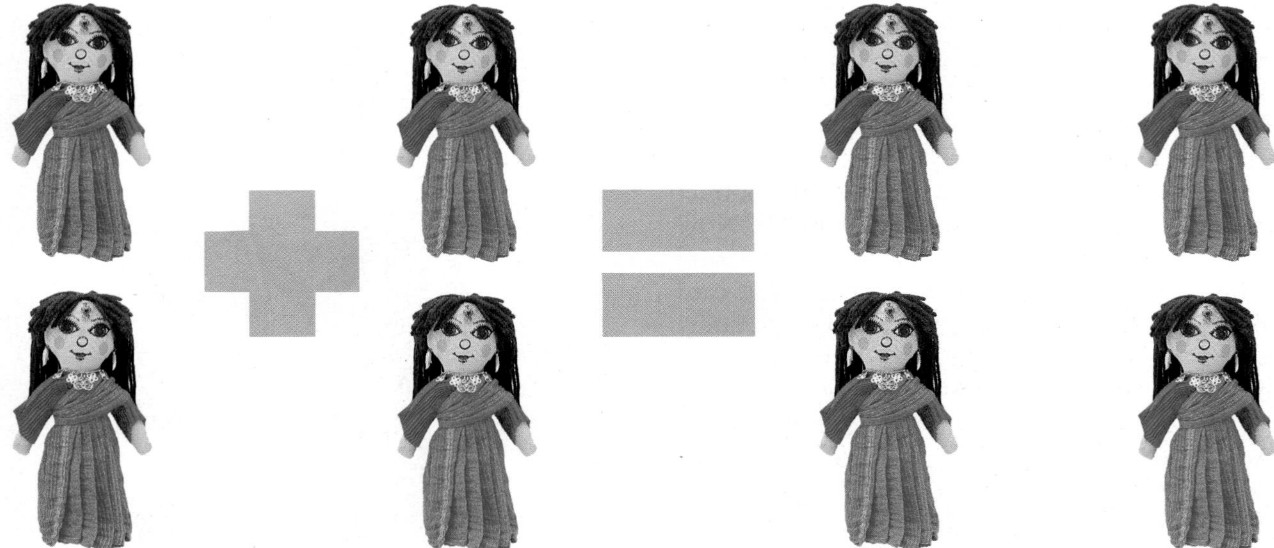

BRAIN MAN

In the film *Rain Man*, Dustin Hoffman portrayed Raymond Babbitt, an autistic man who possessed extraordinary mathematical skills. Autistic individuals are often totally cut off emotionally and they tend to be unable to communicate with other people, even close relatives. In effect, they are completely detached, neither happy nor sad, and unconnected to absolutely everything that goes on around them. Although it was once considered to be a psychiatric problem, autism is now thought to be a disorder of the central nervous system. As yet, however, its causes are not understood, and there is no cure.

While most people with autism have a very low IQ, about 10 percent exhibit outstanding artistic, musical, or mathematical abilities, and approximately one percent are profoundly gifted in one very narrow field. For this reason, they are sometimes called "autistic savants," or "idiot savants"—learned idiots. Autistic identical twins Charles and George were two such extraordinary individuals. They could hardly speak, or cope with even basic sums, although, within seconds and with total accuracy, they were able to work out the right day of the week for any date, even for thousands of years in the past or future.

SPECTACULAR MATH

Clearly some people do have an astounding facility—even genius—for dealing with numbers. However, not all math tricks are great feats of mental arithmetic. You may be surprised that some extremely impressive tricks can be performed with very little numerical agility. Here are two examples that anyone could perform.

Math or magic

The following trick was performed by Marvo the Magician. Marvo first chose two assistants from the audience, Janet and Derek, handing a pack of cards to Janet and asking Derek to blindfold him.
Marvo: "Janet, please shuffle the cards. Now I'm going to ask you to do some simple arithmetic. Think of number between 1 and 10, add 5, add on 3. Now think of another number between 1 and 5. Add that number. Subtract 4. Now, think of one other number between 1 and 5 and subtract it from the total. Don't tell me the number. Now take that many cards from the top of the deck and hide them in your pocket. Lastly, look at the card on the top of the remaining deck, show the audience, and then put it back on the deck and pass the cards to Derek." She showed the Jack of Clubs, placed it on the deck and passed the pack to Derek.
Marvo: "Derek, choose a celebrity, anyone you like."
Derek: "Clint Eastwood."
Marvo: "Excellent. Now, deal some cards from the top of the deck and spell Clint Eastwood aloud as you deal—one card for every letter." Derek spelled the name and dealt 13 cards.
Marvo: "Put those cards back on top of the deck, but first, Janet take the cards you chose from your pocket, and place them on the deck. Then hand me the cards." She took out the cards, and then Derek did the same.
Marvo: "Now, I'm blindfolded. I don't know where the cards are, as I don't know the numbers Janet thought of, but..." He turned over the top 13 cards—revealing the Jack of Clubs. How did Marvo do this?

Easier than it looks

Even the most impressive-seeming tricks can often be reduced to simple math.

Naming the day

This next trick will teach you how to select any date from the year 1900 onward and name the day of the week on which it fell, IN YOUR HEAD. To perform the calculation, all that is required is that you memorize the four tables shown below. Tables 1 and 3 will probably require little or no effort. However tables 2 and 4 may pose more of a challenge to you, especially if you are not used to memorizing numbers. Take a brief look at pages 16-19, which will help in this exercise.

Table 1
7, 14, 21, 28

Table 2

January = 0	April = 6	July = 6	October = 0
February = 3	May = 1	August = 2	November = 3
March = 3	June = 4	September = 5	December = 5

Table 3

Sunday = 0	Tuesday = 2	Thursday = 4	Saturday = 6
Monday = 1	Wednesday = 3	Friday = 5	

Table 4
This is a list of leap years from 1900 onward.

1900 = 0	1920 = 4	1940 = 1	1960 = 5	1980 = 2
1904 = 5	1924 = 2	1944 = 6	1964 = 3	1984 = 0
1908 = 3	1928 = 0	1948 = 4	1968 = 1	1988 = 5
1912 = 1	1932 = 5	1952 = 2	1972 = 6	1992 = 3
1916 = 6	1936 = 3	1956 = 0	1976 = 4	1996 = 1

The calculations consist of 4 simple steps. Don't worry if you haven't memorized the tables, start off on paper. First, select a date—say April 18, 1996.

1. Turn the day of the month (18) into a single figure that is less than 7. To do this you must use table 1 and subtract the highest possible entry in the table. In this case it is 14. Therefore 18 - 14 = 4.

2. To the resulting number you add the number that corresponds to the month from table 2. The number for April is 6. The resulting addition gives an answer of 10. As in step 1, this figure must be expressed as being less than 7 using table 1. 10 - 7 = 3.

3. As the year is a leap year—one of the years listed in table 4—add the previously calculated figure (3) to the value that corresponds to the selected year in table 4, reducing it again if necessary to a number under 7. In this instance, as the year is 1996, the resulting number is 4 (3+1). (If the month to be used is January or February in a leap year, you would subtract 1 from this addition, which in the instance above would naturally add up to 3). Now look for the day in table 3 which corresponds to 4. The table shows us that April 18, 1996 was a Thursday.

4. If the year concerned is not a leap year, use the value of the previous leap year shown in table 4 and add the difference between that leap year and the chosen year, reducing the number if you need to until it is less than seven. So had the year been 1995, the figures would have been 3 (for 1992) + 3 (1995-1992).

Test yourself
Here are four examples to try for yourself. You can either work them out on paper or try to do the calculations in your head! The answers appear on page 138.

1. July 11, 1920
2. February 19, 1948
3. September 29, 1930
4. May 4, 1969

VISUAL THINKING

HOW DO YOU SEE THE WORLD? Early theories about the way our minds work tended toward the view that all thought processing involved some form of visual imagery. Being able to think without creating mental pictures was considered impossible. Current research, however, suggests that there are two systems at work while we think: the perceptual system, which deals with visual or non-verbal events, and a second system which makes use of verbal symbols or language. This process is called "dual coding." What seems to happen is that these two separate processes interact continually while we are thinking.

Size and distance

You can begin to understand how visual awareness affects the way people think if you consider the following questions:

- Is an eagle bigger than a sparrow?
- Is a sparrow bigger than a thrush?

In order for you to answer these questions you will have first conjured up mental pictures of the three different birds, and then you probably made visual comparisons allowing you to reach a conclusion. You will also have answered the first question a good deal more quickly than the second. This is because the difference in size between an eagle and a sparrow is vast, but the second pair of birds are much more similar in size.

This is what psychologists R. S. Moyer and R. H. Bayer call the "symbolic distance effect." Mental comparisons between two items take place on a dimension that is relevant to both items—in this case, the dimension happens to be size, but it could equally be color, weight, or unmeasurable qualities like attractiveness or sense of humor. The speed at which we make the comparison is dependent on their distance apart on that scale. Therefore you can see that, in terms of size, the eagle and sparrow are almost at opposite ends, whereas the sparrow and thrush are quite near to one another. This research has also provided a good deal of information about the way such imagery is used when we think.

Which way to go?

Imagine that you are in your local town, and a stranger asks you for instructions to get from, say, the hospital to the railway station. You are likely to respond with a set of instructions, such as, "...walk to the corner, turn right, and carry on until you reach the traffic lights, then cross over the bridge and the station is straight ahead." Without this type of visual thinking you would be unable

Birds of a feather

At first glance you might assume these birds are the same size—but that's because the perspective is distorted. Likewise, comparing similar things in your mind's eye can make it difficult to determine differences accurately.

to give such a set of instructions. These thought processes do not use verbal symbols—the mental process involves the creation of a series of mental maps for each section of the route as you give out each instruction. Research has shown that when mental images like this are generated, we "scan" this panorama in much the same way as we do when we encounter the real images in the real world. These mental images can be powerful and long-lasting. For example, it's likely that you would be able, even now, to give directions from your childhood home to your school.

Think and draw

To test out how well you can think visually, here is an exercise for you to try. In principle, the process is identical to the mental map-drawing process described above. To begin with, read through each step, trying to build up in your mind a gradual picture of the overall shape. Now take a pencil and paper and try to draw this shape. You can refer back to the steps if you want to.

1. Draw a large square.
2. Draw a line up from the center of the top edge of the square, perpendicular to it. The line should be the same length as each side of the square.
3. Around the line, draw a circle whose diameter equals the length of the line, and whose center point is also the center point of the line.
4. Inside the square, in each one of the two bottom corners, draw a small circle that touches the two sides of the square.
5. Starting from the center point of the large circle, draw a horizontal line that extends to the right well beyond the perimeter of the circle.
6. Using the outside end of this line as a center point, draw a very small square.
7. Draw a line from the bottom right corner of the small square to the top right corner of the large one.
8. Draw a triangle whose base is the shortest line that can be drawn between the two small circles, and whose third point is where the large circle intersects with the large square.

Now turn to "Solutions," on page 138, and take a look at the image. How closely matched are the two pictures? Don't worry if you think your drawing is not very good—that isn't the point of this exercise. If you have all of the components drawn correctly and in roughly the right position, then your abilities to think visually are well developed. If they differ considerably, go back over each step to find out where you might have gone wrong. To develop your ability to think visually, you could try getting someone to read out similar instructions.

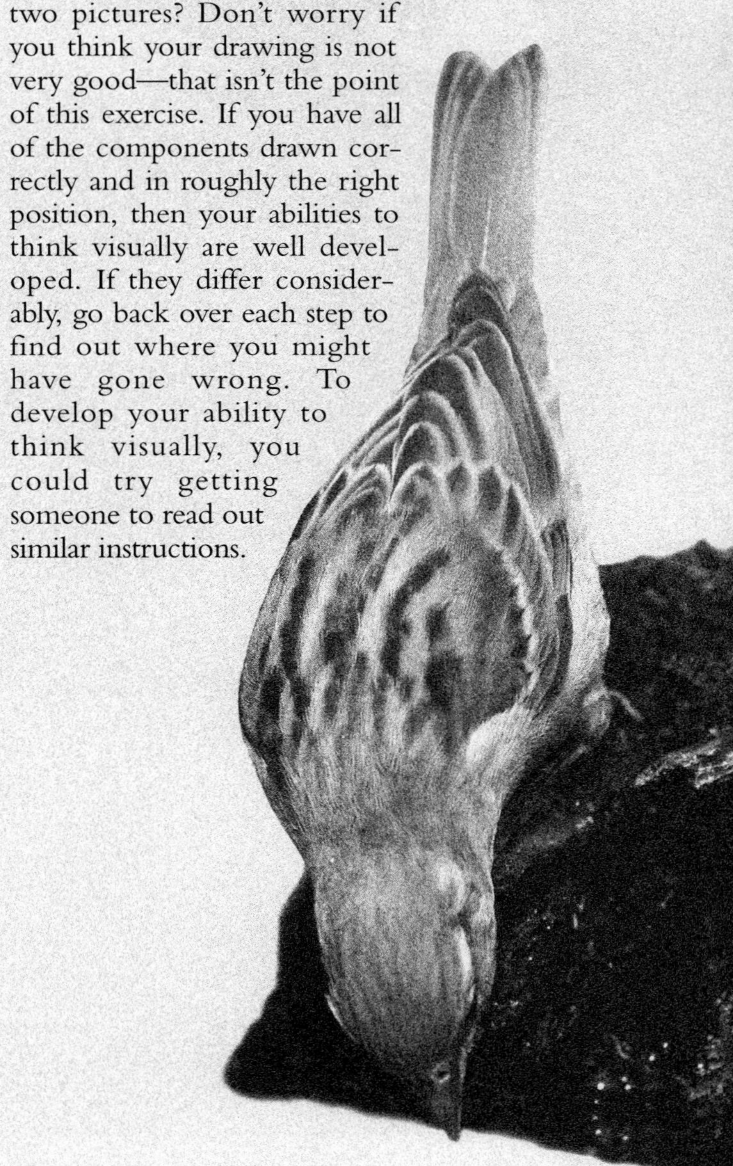

Lost in Space

Do you sometimes find it hard to give or take directions, getting your right hand confused with your left, your north with your south? Many people consider that they need to develop these faculties further. Test your sense of direction with the following map-reading exercise. Starting at entry point A, follow the directions carefully and make a note of where you end up. Keep the page upright; don't switch it around in order to make more sense of the instructions! Then, turn to "Solutions," on page 139, to see if you arrived at the intended destination.

Where are you going?

You are at the edge of a little village—but no one has given you any directions, so you can't find your way around. Starting off at point A, walk due south until you reach a tree between two houses. Turn onto the road opposite, and then when you reach a footpath, continue going due south. After you see a house, you wonder whether you are walking in the right direction, so you turn back. But soon you realize that you were right after all, and continue along the footpath again until you reach the road.

At this point, you turn left, then first right, until you reach a river. You turn north again until you get back to the T-junction, then you walk east. After a while, you see a footpath running off to the left; you walk along this path until you see another one joining it. Turn right along that path until you reach the road. Now, go south along this road, until you see another road that leads eastward. Think about going along this road, but don't—instead keep going due south until you see a footpath turning off to the left. Turn to the west, then take the

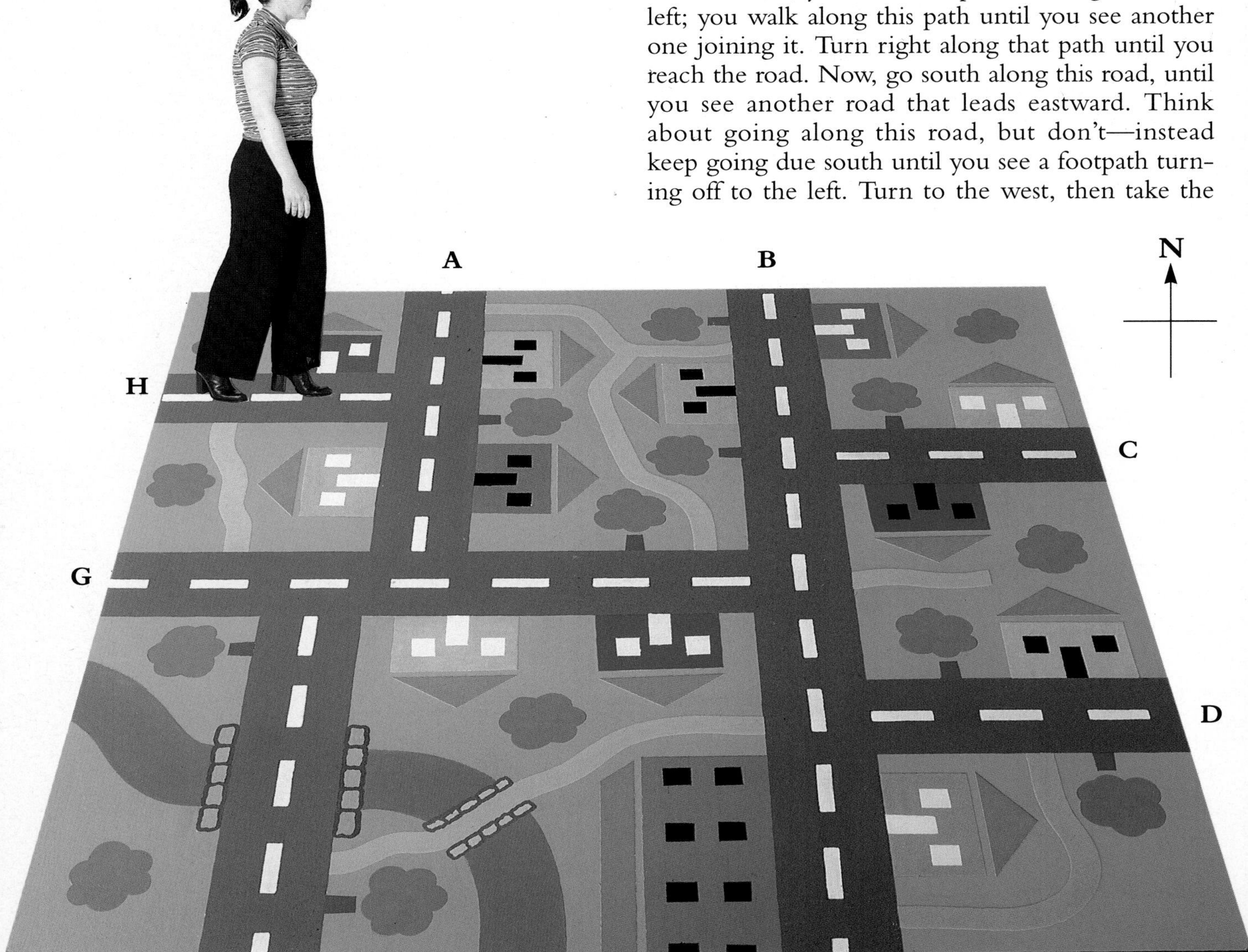

Straight ahead
Look at the picture at the top of this page. What are the potential hazards awaiting the driver of this car? Take note of everything you think might cause an accident—or otherwise make driving difficult. How many hazards can you spot in one minute? A list is in "Solutions," on page 139.

first road on the left, walking down past a river, until you reach a footpath. Taking the footpath, you walk slowly up it, pausing for quite a while at the bridge, where you throw sticks into the river.

Carry on along this path until you arrive at the road, turning right and walking south until you see a footpath on the other side of the road which seems to be opposite a factory. Go along this footpath until you reach a road, then turn west, then first right, until you see a road that seems to be turning to the east. You are starting to feel tired, so instead of taking this turn, you decide to sit down to have a rest.

After a while, you continue to walk along the road you're on; when you come to a footpath, you follow it for a while, until you see it join up with another path. At this point, you realize that you have been there before, so you turn back the way you came. At the main road, therefore, you turn back northward and eventually you reach an entrance to the village. So do you know where you have got to now?

WHAT'S ALONG THE EDGE?

When you are driving, you need to make good use of your peripheral vision, so that you can anticipate hazards like those in the picture above. Peripheral vision is the part of your field of vision that enables you to see what is happening on either side of you, while at the same time being able to pay attention to what is going on in front. It stops you bumping into objects around you, and makes you aware of things you had not anticipated.

The area of the retina used for peripheral vision has a much higher proportion of light receivers than are found in the area used for sharp-focus vision. Researchers have discovered that peripheral vision is actually stronger at night because this group of light receivers is sensitive to lower levels of light than those that are meant for sharp focus. So, if you want to see more clearly in the dark, try not to look directly at an object. You will probably see it more clearly if you view it from an angle.

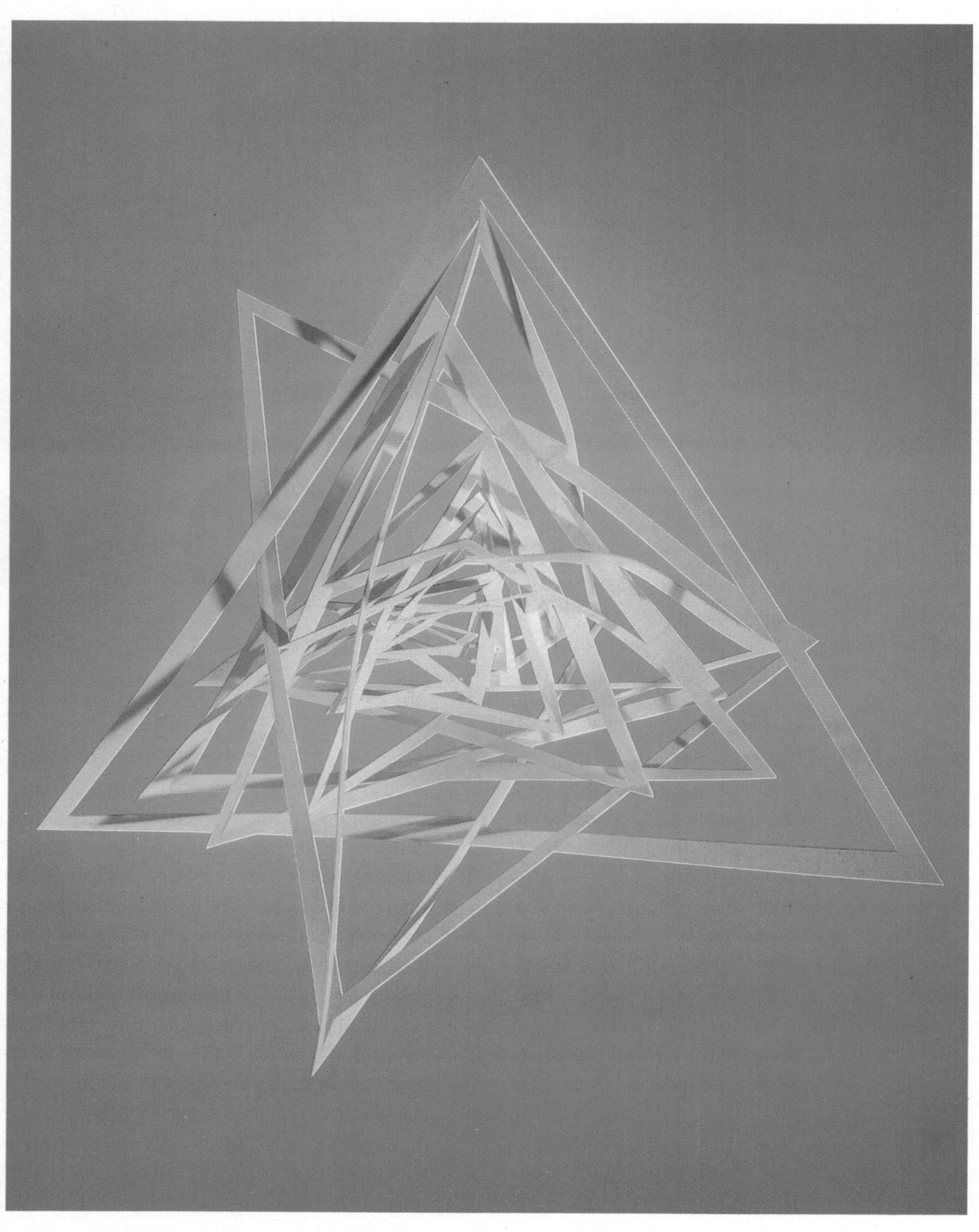

CHAPTER FIVE

FURTHER DIVERSIONS

MANY PEOPLE ENJOY PLAYING intelligence games of one kind or another. They are fun because they are a way of expressing your personality, intelligence, and creativity, and because you get a sense of pleasure when you prove equal to a challenge. But games are also important because they improve your mental agility and your sense of awareness—skills important in every area of life. This chapter has a range of games to amaze and amuse you—visual games, word games, number games, even juggling!

Some games are very simple, others are very complex; some use dice to introduce an element of chance, others, such as chess, are purely a question of skill. We offer you many different types to try—the subtle, mathematical game of hex on pages 114–115, games to test your discipline, concentration, and observation on pages 116–117, and puzzles using matches on page 122–123.

The chapter also has a range of visual games. These are particularly fascinating because we find it hard not to "believe our eyes," so it is striking to discover how easily you can be tricked. This is often because the mind begins to understand what it is seeing in conventional ways that can lead to false assumptions. Although such tricks can be unsettling, it is also exciting to battle with your mind to make sense of the image before you. Turn to "Watch This Space" on pages 118–119 for a selection of visual tricks, and to pages 124–125 for two Magic Eye visual illusions.

Another way to broaden your perspective is to approach a problem from an unconventional angle. This is done very simply in "What's the Question?" on pages 120–121, where the usual "question and answer" format is turned on its head by giving you answers and then asking you to find the questions. This encourages creative and original thinking, and demonstrates that there may be more than one solution to a problem. It also helps you to be more open-minded—showing you that if people do not respond as you expect, it may be because your question is ambiguous or has several correct answers.

Finally, in "Improve Your Dexterity" on pages 126–127, we teach you how to juggle. Juggling exercises many things—hand-eye coordination, reflexes, concentration, and balance. As you will also discover, juggling is a wonderful example of how improving your mental skills can be exciting, liberating, and fun!

INTELLIGENCE GAMES ARE A GOOD WAY TO IMPROVE YOUR MENTAL SKILLS. SOME TEST YOUR POWERS OF LOGIC, OTHERS HELP YOU APPROACH PROBLEMS FROM NEW AND UNUSUAL DIRECTIONS.

GAMES OLD AND NEW

THROUGHOUT history and across cultures, humankind has devised an astonishing range of games or tricks to amuse, educate, or simply pass the time. Despite the advent of ever more complex computer-based games, many of today's most popular games have been enjoyed for generations and have roots that go back thousands of years.

Back to the beginning

Some of the earliest games were derived from methods of foretelling the future. Ancient writings frequently refer to divination by the throwing of sticks—this tradition has remained, but now we know it as the drawing of lots. It is generally thought that over the years, the divination sticks lost their mystical significance and became more commonly used in games of chance, as dice are used in board games. Later, the element of chance was removed and games of pure skill were developed.

Research has shown that as long ago as the eleventh century, the Chinese practiced divination using pieces of lightly oiled paper known as strip cards. It is from these that present-day playing cards are generally thought to have evolved.

Many games are also remnants of ancient religious or mystic rituals. The children's game of hopscotch, for example, is related to myths of labyrinths, and later came to symbolize the soul's journey from Earth to Heaven. Another ritual involved batting an object into the air as many times as possible without letting it drop. This was said to determine the length of one's life.

Early board games

The evolution of board games also goes back many thousands of years, when they helped primitive people interpret the wishes of the gods. The earliest board games are thought to have used patterns scratched into the sand. Stones were placed on this "board" and moved around in a way that imitated the hunting and combat that were part of people's everyday lives.

Many games have their origins in warfare: The ancient Greeks, for example, made little distinction between sport and war—violence and bloodshed were a feature of the early Olympics. The game of chess, which originated in India or China, is probably the oldest game of pure mental skill—the element of chance does not enter into the game—and one of the clearest examples of a game based on warfare.

Intellectual games

Chess is widely recognized as an intellectual game, and even at the simplest level, it calls upon its players for concentration and the intuitive vision to discover strategic possibilities. For further information on chess, see pages 46-47.

Word games and other puzzles have also been played throughout history. Riddles were often used as an early form of IQ test in the ancient world. One of the oldest and most famous of riddles is in the Old Testament of the Bible, where Samson asks at his wedding feast: "Out of the eater came something to eat; out of the strong came something sweet." His answer was that he had seen bees making honey in the carcass of a lion—and nothing is sweeter than honey or stronger than a lion.

Surprisingly, the crossword puzzle, now thought to be the most widely played word game in the world, only dates back to the early nineteenth century. General knowledge quizzes are a relatively recent phenomenon, but quiz shows now proliferate on television. Their attraction is that they have no complex rules, and allow the viewer to participate from the comfort of the sofa. In the 1980s, this popular trend gave rise to the board game *Trivial Pursuit,* which is now enjoyed by many people in countries around the world.

Playing on screen

The future development of the games industry is likely to be strongly influenced by modern technology. One of the most popular recent pastimes has been the computer game. But however widely they differ in appearance from traditional games, popular examples such as Tetris still combine the classic elements of simplicity and tactical planning, as well as very nimble fingers.

THE GAME OF HEX

Through the ages, scientists and mathematicians have been known to devote enormous amounts of time and energy to solving recreational puzzles. The eighteenth-century German philosopher Gottfried Willhelm Leibniz, for example, was thought to be obsessed with a simple children's peg-hopping puzzle. Similarly, Albert Einstein's bookshelves were said to be well stocked with mathematical games and puzzles. In fact, it is not surprising that such brilliant minds were taken up with these seemingly trivial pastimes—many of mankind's greatest scientific discoveries have begun simply as attempts to solve some of the numerous puzzles that have been put to us by nature.

There is considerable evidence that working through mathematical puzzles can have practical benefits as well as entertainment value. This is because such exercises "train" the mind to take an ordered, analytical approach to the kinds of practical problems which people tend to encounter in their everyday lives.

One of the simplest and most fascinating games played during the last few decades is known as hex. Hex was devised by the Danish physicist, inventor, and poet, Piet Hein. The idea came to him while he was contemplating a famous four-color topology exercise. This game involves allocating one of four possible colors to every country on the globe, in such a way that no two countries of the same color share a border.

The rules of the game

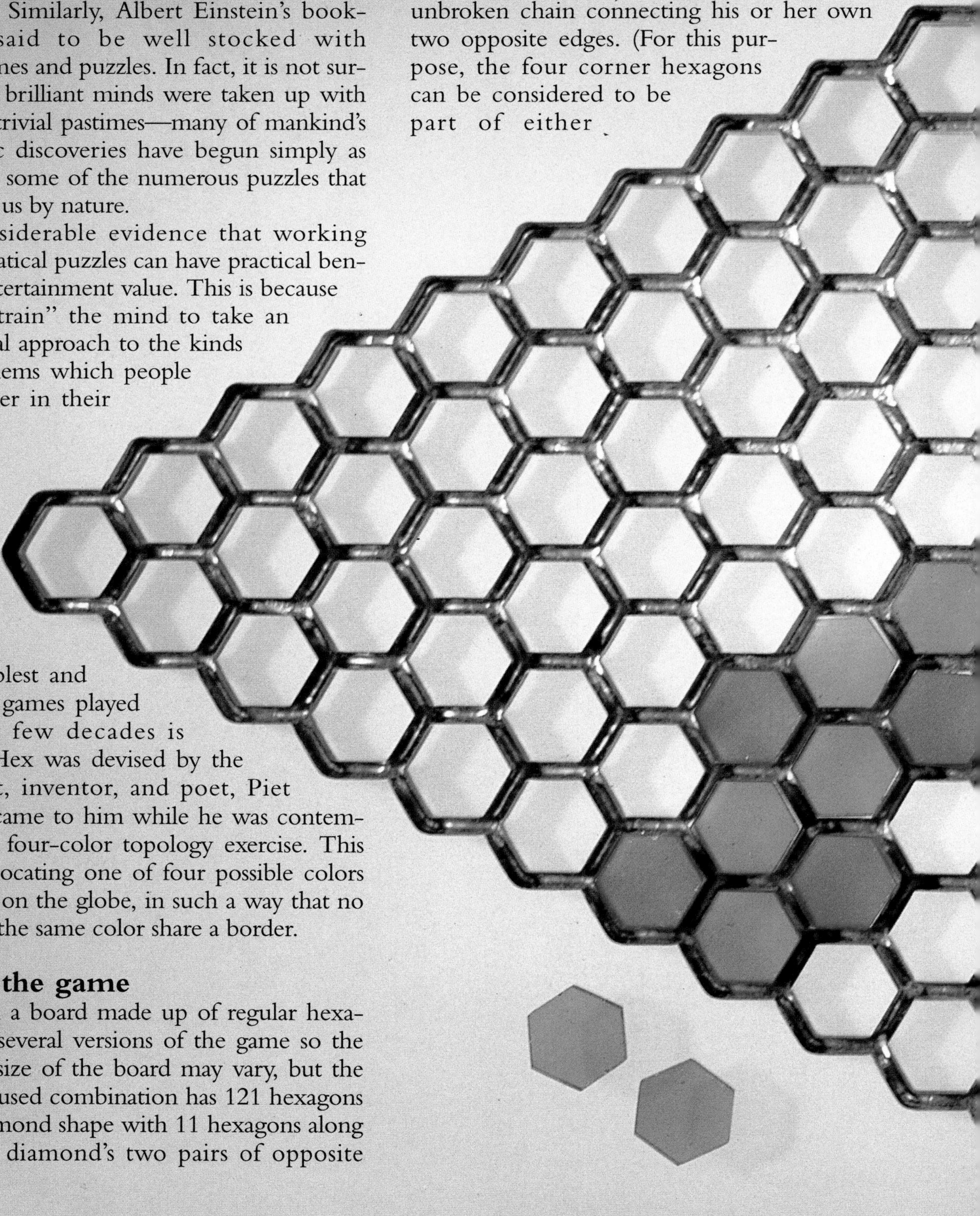

Hex is played on a board made up of regular hexagons. There are several versions of the game so the exact shape and size of the board may vary, but the most commonly used combination has 121 hexagons arranged in a diamond shape with 11 hexagons along each edge. The diamond's two pairs of opposite edges are assigned different colors—say blue and green. The game requires two players, one with a supply of pieces in one of these colors, the other with a supply of pieces in the other. The players take turns placing pieces on the board; the object of the game is for one of them to make an unbroken chain connecting his or her own two opposite edges. (For this purpose, the four corner hexagons can be considered to be part of either adjoining side.) Therefore the challenge of hex lies in balancing the game's two main aspects: although the players have to concentrate on building up their own chain, they must also try to block their opponent's moves at the same time.

A subtle diversion

Like many other games such as backgammon and checkers, hex may seem absurdly simple to begin with. In fact, it is a game of great subtlety that has captivated mathematicians since its invention. As a consequence, game theorists have made repeated attempts to come up with what is known as a decision procedure—a particular set of moves that guarantees victory to the opening player. A number of such procedures have been developed, but to date, they are so complicated that they are meaningless to the non-mathematician.

Even played at a lay person's level, though, hex can pose many interesting challenges. It is also an extremely enjoyable game of which a number of variations have been developed, most of which are aimed at combating the fact that, as in tic-tac-toe (sometimes called noughts and crosses), a simpler "relation" of hex, the player who starts the game has a sizable advantage. For more experienced players, therefore, the challenge is often to see how few moves it takes to win, given the advantage of the first move. Even then, the second player sometimes wins.

Try the game of hex for yourself. As markers, use small bright buttons, borrow the pieces from a game of checkers, or cut out small discs of colored card. If you prefer, simply draw out a board like the one illustrated and run off a number of photocopies; then, instead of playing with loose pieces, issue each of the players with a felt-tip pen with which to color the hexagons in turn.

Challenging shapes
Mastering the game of hex requires considerable planning and skill.

Open Your Mind

Here is a further series of puzzles that will test your discipline and concentration. These puzzles are looking specifically at concentration and the ability to spot tiny differences. In each case you will have to pay careful attention to detail. To begin with there are a series of number puzzles that revolve around simple mental arithmetic—but the time limit will create additional pressure. The word exercises are simple proof-reading, although some of them are made more difficult by the fact that the "words" are random groupings of letters. When you have finished, turn to "Solutions," on page 139, to see if you were right.

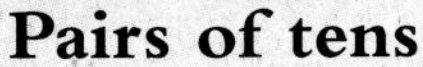

Pairs of tens

Look at the ten rows of numbers below. You have three minutes to work through the list, marking every pair of adjacent numbers in each row that add up to ten. For example, if you see 5 and 5 next to one another, they add up to ten, so you can mark them off.

A. 4 5 1 9 3 6 4 2 2 8 4 5 9 8 2 7 3 8 4 9
B. 9 2 6 9 6 5 4 7 8 3 9 1 7 4 9 8 0 9 8 7
C. 4 7 9 4 6 3 5 1 4 6 8 0 7 9 8 3 1 9 8 1
D. 5 3 4 7 6 5 2 3 9 8 7 6 5 4 8 6 7 4 5 6
E. 9 6 7 4 5 3 7 6 7 4 6 2 8 4 6 3 4 3 5 5
F. 9 7 5 3 4 2 1 9 4 7 2 6 9 1 7 3 5 1 9 7
G. 1 0 6 8 5 4 3 8 6 7 4 9 7 8 5 7 6 4 3 6
H. 7 3 4 6 5 8 7 9 6 8 5 5 3 5 2 4 3 7 5 8
I. 9 9 9 2 9 1 1 9 5 7 6 3 4 2 9 9 8 0 6 7
J. 2 8 6 7 0 8 9 6 7 3 4 2 9 4 6 8 4 3 2 1

Adding triplets

Here is a slightly harder version of the same puzzle. This time you have to mark triplets of adjacent numbers that add up to 10. Once again, you should try to do this in under three minutes. Although this exercise is more difficult than the previous one, because you have to see figures grouped in threes, at least this time there are only five rows to check.

A. 2 7 2 1 6 4 8 1 4 5 5 3 4 2 6 2 3 4 8 7
B. 2 5 4 3 1 4 2 3 5 4 6 3 4 2 4 6 5 3 2 4
C. 8 1 1 7 5 9 8 7 6 4 5 9 7 8 3 2 5 5 3 4
D. 8 7 5 6 3 9 8 6 7 1 9 1 1 7 9 8 7 8 2 4
E. 1 9 6 7 5 4 3 2 4 3 3 1 2 2 2 1 2 1 2 7

Checking nonsense

This exercise should prove more of a challenge—the "words" that you have to proof read are simply random groups of letters that have no meaning whatsoever.

Below you will see three pairs of letter sequences. The adjacent sequences should be identical, but in each case, the second of each pair has three differences. You have three minutes to find them all.

1. aitry hdter nshuf uepgf jnvgc wretr otyug fgdsd khuty bgcfd sdfs

aitry hdter nshuf uergf jnvgc wertr otyug fgdsd khoty bgcfd sdfs

2. qtyre oiuhg nbvfg lmkye pqokj nvyte dtrwe nvygt mkbuy huftr qtire mtire

qtyre oiuhg nbvfg lmkye qpokj nyvte dtrwe nvygt nkbuy huftr qtire mtire

3. fkyre gusbh guygh jghju guyhg gkhjg gjhgf gkhjg gfjhg bkhjk bolorog molog

fkyre gusbh guygh jhgju guyhg gkhjg ghjgf gkhjg gfjhg bknjk bolorog molog

Symbols

The next exercise will test your powers of observation and concentration to the full. Your eyes can often deceive you when it comes to looking at the small differences in words or images.

Below are four paired sequences of letters from the alphabet combined with decorative symbols. In each case the second row has subtle variations. Can you spot them? You have two minutes.

A.
❄ u ✌ f ✌ ✌ r h h f ▼ g u ❄ ✌ i k o e t 6 r
❄ u ✌ y ✌ ❄ r h y f ▼ g V ❄ ❄ i k O e q 6 r

B.
❉ ✖ ✕ ✖ ❉ ❉ ✖ ✕ ✖ ❉ ✖ ✕ ❉ ✖
❉ ✕ ✕ ❉ ❉ ❉ ✖ ✕ ✖ ❉ ✕ ✕ ✕ ❉

C.
d ❉ 1 ✱ ❉ i r y u 8 y ❉ ✱ y t ❉ e p 0 8 y
d ❉ P ✱ ❉ l r y u y 8 ❉ ❉ y t ✱ e p . 8 y

D.
❍ p o p ❑ p p o p p o o ❚ ❐ ❑ ❐ p o p
❍ p ❍ p ❑ p p ❍ p o o p ❚ ❐ ❐ ❑ o p p

Proof-reading

Look at the two blocks of words below. While they may appear in different-shaped boxes, they should contain identical information. However, there are three errors in block B. You have two minutes to find them.

A

apartment
a p a t h y
aperture apex
aphorism aplomb
apogee apologize
apoplexy apostasy apostle
apostrophe apothecary
apotheosis appall apparatus apparel
apparent apparition appeal appear
appease append appertain appetite
applaud apple appliqué appoint appreciate
apprehend apprentice approach approbation
appropriate approve approximate apricot apron apt

B

apartment apathy
aperture apex aphorism
aplomb apogee apologize
apoplexy apostasy apostle apostrophe
apothecary apotheosis appall apparatus
apparel apparent apparrition appear
appeal appease append appertain
appetite applaud apple appliqué
appoint appreciate apprehend
apprentice approach appropriate
approve approximate
apricot apron apt

Don't get distracted!
Developing your concentration so that you can focus completely on the task in hand will mean that you spot mistakes more easily—and make fewer of them yourself.

WATCH THIS SPACE

Whenever we look at anything, our natural instinct is to separate what we see into two separate parts—the principal object and its background. Whenever we focus on an object, the background gets blurred, and when we focus on the background, the object is blurred. Changing your point of focus can play tricks with the rest of the picture. Some of the eight visual illusions on these pages demonstrate this with dramatic results; others are two-dimensional images that give a three-dimensional perspective. All of these visual illusions are known as "unstable images," which means that you may see something different depending on how you look at them.

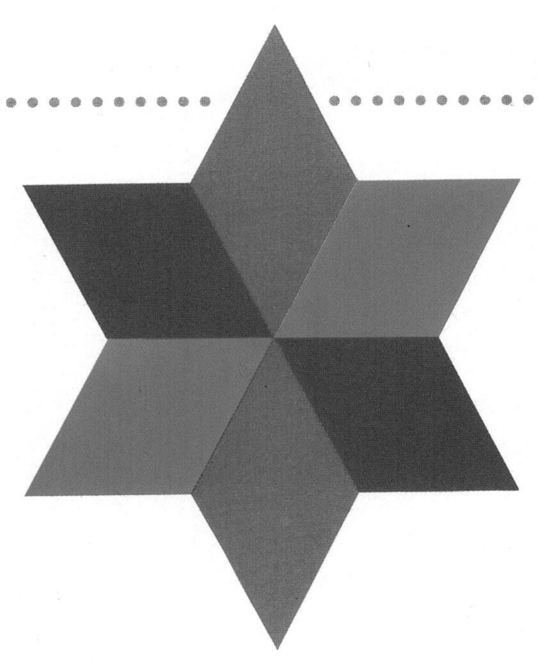

Two dimensions or three?
This design can be seen in three different ways. Firstly, it is a six-pointed star created from six identical diamond-shaped figures. Secondly, it can be seen as a large equilateral triangle with three diamond shapes laid on top. Finally, if you stare at it for a little while longer, a three-dimensional set of cubes emerges.

How many cubes?
Look at the image and see how many cubes you can count. Are you sure about that? Now turn the page upside down and try again. The result may come as a surprise.

Which direction?
If you look at the two small diamond shapes above, they each appear to be at the center of a larger design, perhaps the inside corners of two open boxes that face different directions. If you switch your attention from one diamond to the other, the direction of the box suddenly alters.

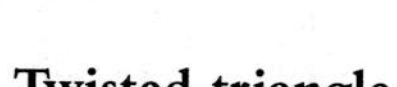

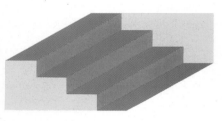

Twisted triangle

The "Penrose Triangle" is one of psychology's most famous visual illusions. If you follow any of the shaded sides, an outside surface becomes an inside surface, and vice-versa.

Which way up?

Turn this image, known as "Schroeder's Staircase," upside down and the image remains the same.

Making sense of shapes

At first, the box above appears to be broken up with a confusion of shapes, but if you study it carefully, a pattern of shapes will begin to emerge. Can you find: one eight-pointed star, two irregular hexagons, four half-hexagons, eight small equilateral triangles, four medium-sized equilateral triangles, four squares, and four large equilateral triangles?

How many stairs?

Starting from the left-hand side, you can count four steps from the bottom to the top. However, if you approach the same construction from the right side, you can get to the top using just one step.

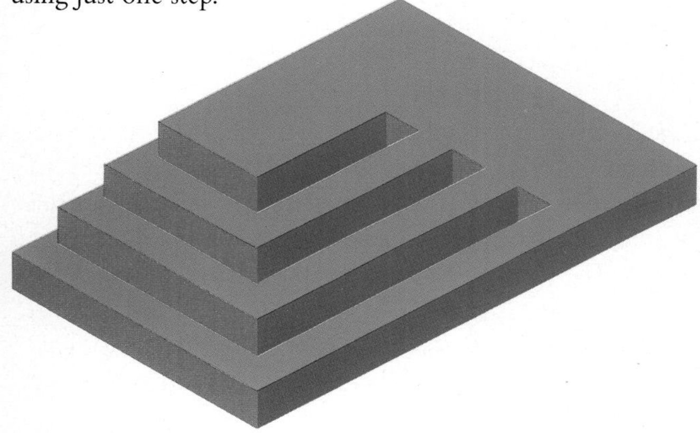

Never-ending stairs

Which is the lowest step? The horizontal lines on the main face show that corner A is clearly lower than corner B. However, you can follow the ascending stairs from corner B counterclockwise until you return to corner A. This principle, a relative of the "Penrose Triangle" shown above, featured in many drawings by the Dutch artist M. C. Escher.

WHAT'S THE QUESTION?

TO IMPROVE BOTH the flexibility and creativity of your thinking skills—and to brush up on your general knowledge at the same time—work through the following quizzes. You'll notice that they have one fundamental difference from those found elsewhere in the volume: here, all the answers have been provided—your task is to work out the questions.

When you have finished the first exercise, turn to "Solutions" on pages 140-141 to check your score.

A fresh perspective
The facility for looking at things in an alternative way, or framing tricky questions differently, can prove useful when your thinking becomes blocked or you find yourself repeatedly going over the same mental territory without success.

Turning the tables

Supply a correct question for each of the following ten answers:

1. 366
2. Caviar
3. Paris
4. George Washington
5. June 28, 1914
6. From 1338 to 1453
7. Yuri Gagarin
8. 3.14159
9. Phil Hill and Mario Andretti
10. Hydrogen, helium, and lithium
11. Judy Garland
12. Austria

Don't worry if, in some cases, your solutions are different from the ones we have given. This does not necessarily mean you are wrong; you may simply have discovered alternative "correct" questions. Paris, for instance, as well as being the capital city of France, is also the name of the suitor rejected by Juliet in favor of Romeo, and of the legendary Greek hero who sparked off the Trojan War by abducting Helen of Troy. In addition, it is the name given to a highly toxic green-colored chemical that is used as both a pigment and an insecticide.

Double jeopardy

Taking this approach a little further, the next quiz sets out a list of answers that are deliberately ambiguous. For each of these, you are required to provide at least two different questions. Again, you may find that more than that number of questions come easily to mind.

Try, if you can, to vary the context or focus of all the questions that relate to a particular answer. With the answer Paris, for example, our suggested questions reflect several different meanings; questions that focus only on the French capital would involve less creativity. Once more, you can check how you did by referring to "Solutions," on pages 140-141.

1. Red and white
2. Turkey
3. 12
4. A mouse
5. 24
6. Florence
7. Diamonds
8. 1600
9. Punch
10. Fiddle
11. Teeth
12. Chestnut
13. 360
14. Match
15. Bridge

(As an additional challenge, see if you can dream up at least four questions that are equally appropriate for the last answer.)

Weak data

The intellectual flexibility involved in these exercises provides clear evidence of how misleading similarly ambiguous tests can be when they are used to measure IQ or an applicant's suitability for a job, say, or a course of study. This is because excessively literal marking tends to work against creative or original thinkers. They may be overlooked simply because they have come up with answers that the examiners had not previously considered, could not understand, or did not realize were valid. So in any situation, before dismissing other people's opinions, ideas, or solutions as "wrong," it's always a good idea to take a second look at the thinking that may lie behind them. They could have found an answer that improves on the "right" one.

Find the Links

A category of questions commonly found on IQ tests are those designed to measure someone's ability to look at ideas and problems in alternative ways. These often ask you to find similarities between two apparently different things. A typical example might be: How are a cup and a spoon alike? Possible answers are:

1. They both have rims and handles.
2. They both require the use of high temperatures in their manufacturing process.
3. They are both frequently given as christening presents.

The exercise that follows encourages you to explore this idea in reverse: given a list of characteristics, can you think of two (or more) items that share them? For possible answers, turn to "Solutions," on page 141.

1. Name two things that:
   - are made from plant-based material
   - have traditionally been given as romantic gifts
   - are often sold in fancy packaging
2. Name two things that:
   - provide shelter for living things
   - have part of their structure underground
   - benefit from a sunny location
3. Name two things that:
   - are used as teaching aids
   - are made from minerals
   - have five letters in their name
4. Name two things that:
   - are protected by covers
   - are commonly used during relaxation
   - come in a range of different sizes and colors

MATCH GAMES

After centuries of attempts to harness fire so it could be produced quickly, easily, and safely, toward the end of the eighteenth century a solution was found through advances in chemical science—the match. Throughout the years, matches have been found to have many alternative uses, from three-dimensional model making to units of measurement or gambling currency. Many of us will recall some point in our childhood where we emptied a box of matches and used them to create geometrical shapes.

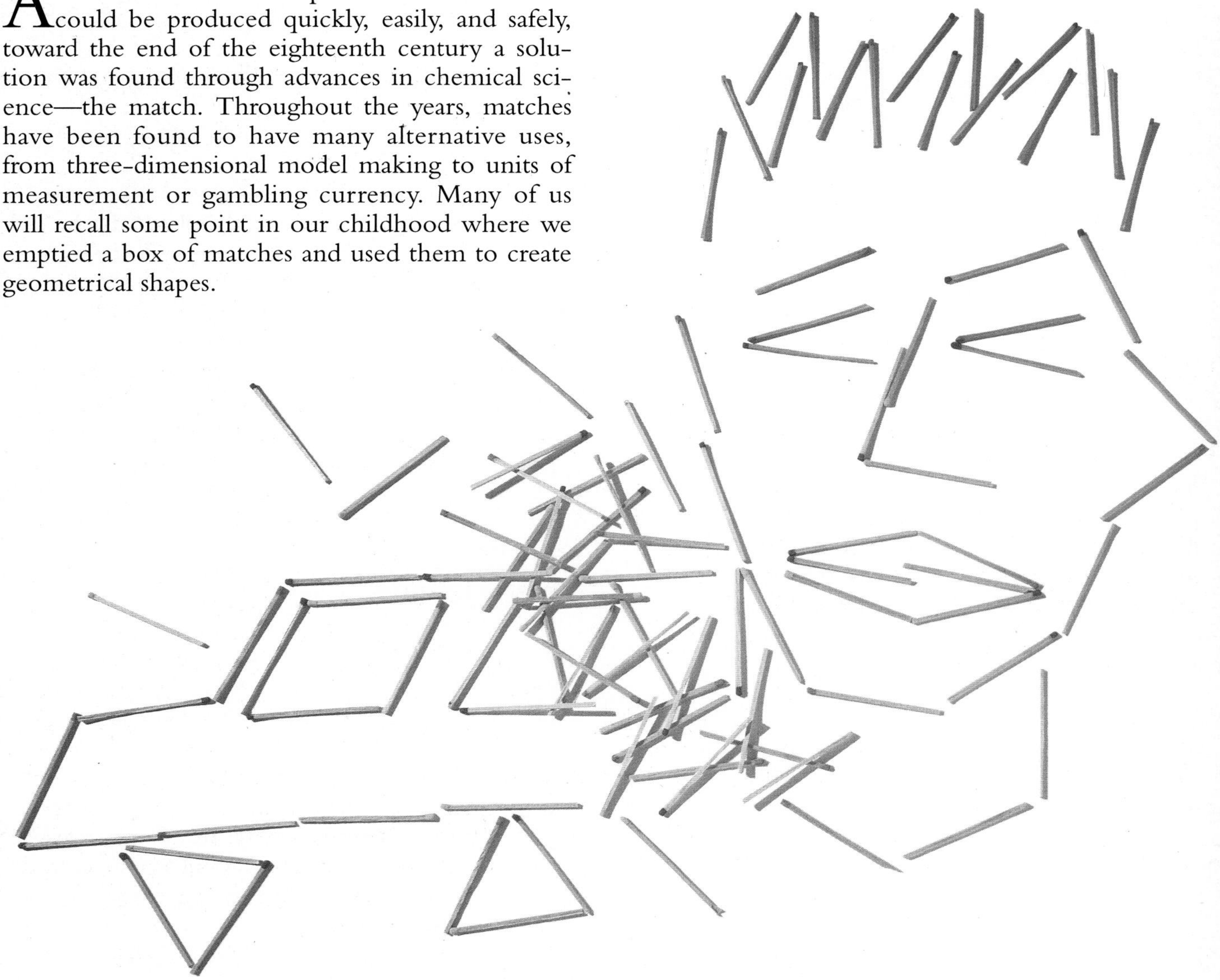

Matches can also help us to develop our creative skills. One simple game that can provide you with amusement and inspiration is to take a small box of matches and empty it onto a table. The game is to look at the random assemblage and try to "see" pictures in the pile. For example, you may just be able to catch the outline of a face, an animal, or a landscape. Obviously, there are no right or wrong answers—just let your imagination run free.

Here you will find a number of other puzzles and games that use matches. All of the puzzles will require you to think laterally to figure them out. The answers are in "Solutions," on page 141.

Counting the squares

This first puzzle may seem hard until you know how to do it. Take 13 matches and arrange them in the following way. Removing one of the matches, can you find a way to rearrange the remaining 12 so that they create five squares in total?

The game of Nim

Here is a simple strategy game for two players using 16 matches. First of all, arrange them on a table in four rows like this:

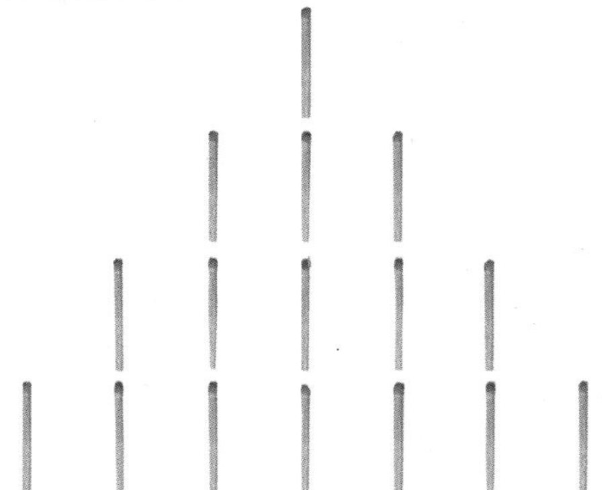

Players take it in turn to remove any number of matches from a single row. The object is to be the player who removes the final match. For example, player 1 begins by removing two matches from the second row. Player 2 responds by taking five matches from the bottom row. Now, the table looks like this:

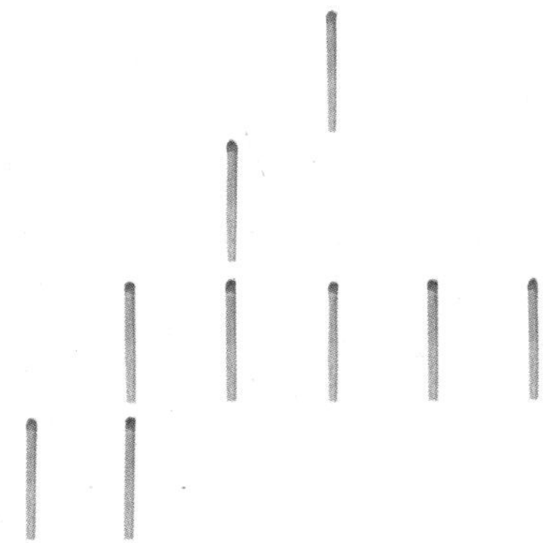

Then, player 1 takes all five matches from the third row. Player 2 takes the final two from the bottom row. The table now looks like this:

As you can see, whichever match player 1 removes, player 2 will still win.

Nim is a deceptively simple game. The early moves are especially critical. The odds are stacked firmly against the player who starts—if the other player is experienced at Nim, it may be impossible for him or her to be beaten.

Increasing the triangles

First of all, make a triangle out of three matches, like the one that is illustrated below. Then, by adding a further three matches to the original shape one at a time (leaving the original shape intact), work out how to produce a shape that is made up of four triangles. Achieving this is not straightforward; however, you may use some sticky substance, like plasticine, to help you.

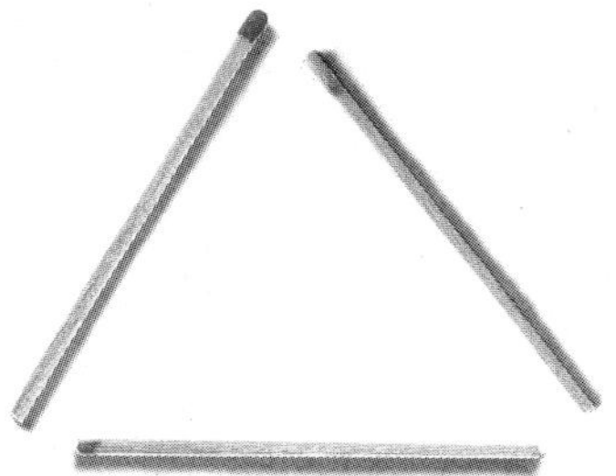

Move the matches

Here are three puzzles based on the Roman numeral system (which is explained on pages 98–99). In each case a simple piece of arithmetic is shown, but the answer is wrong. It may be clear to you what the answer should be, but how can you get to it? The correct solution can be found by moving just one match.

II − I = II

III − II = IV

V × I = IX

Visual Illusion

Over the last few years images such as those illustrated here have become a popular phenomenon. Known as autostereograms or "Magic Eye" pictures, they comprise brightly colored patterns of randomly placed dots that, when studied, can reveal a striking three-dimensional image.

A pattern of dots

The autostereogram was developed in 1959 at the Bell Telephone Research Laboratories. Researcher Bela Julesz created the representation of a square hovering above the surface of the paper by bringing together two slightly different patterns of dots—one for each eye. Research proved that the perception of a third dimension is created after the images from each eye have been fused in the brain. It is the brain that creates these effects, not the retina.

In 1990, Christopher Tyler and Maureen Clarke of the Smith-Kettlewell Eye Research Institute in San Francisco found a way to combine two slightly altered pictures using a computer. Each picture is made up of millions of small dots called "pixels." Because each eye sees each picture from a different perspective, by altering the position of pixels on the horizontal plain, "hidden" images can be created.

How to see the image

The hidden images are revealed when your eyes are focused behind the two-dimensional plane of the picture, and the dots are brought into alignment. To see the images hidden in the pictures on these pages, hold the book upright about 12 ins (30 cm) from your eyes. Make sure the page is not tilted and no light is glaring on it. Imagine that someone is holding an object six ins (15 cm) behind the page, and look through the page to focus on it. You should feel your eyes "defocusing." Resist the urge to look back at the page and the image should slowly materialize.

What can you see?

Using the technique outlined above, look for the hidden images in "Night Sky," right, and "Sea Life," below.

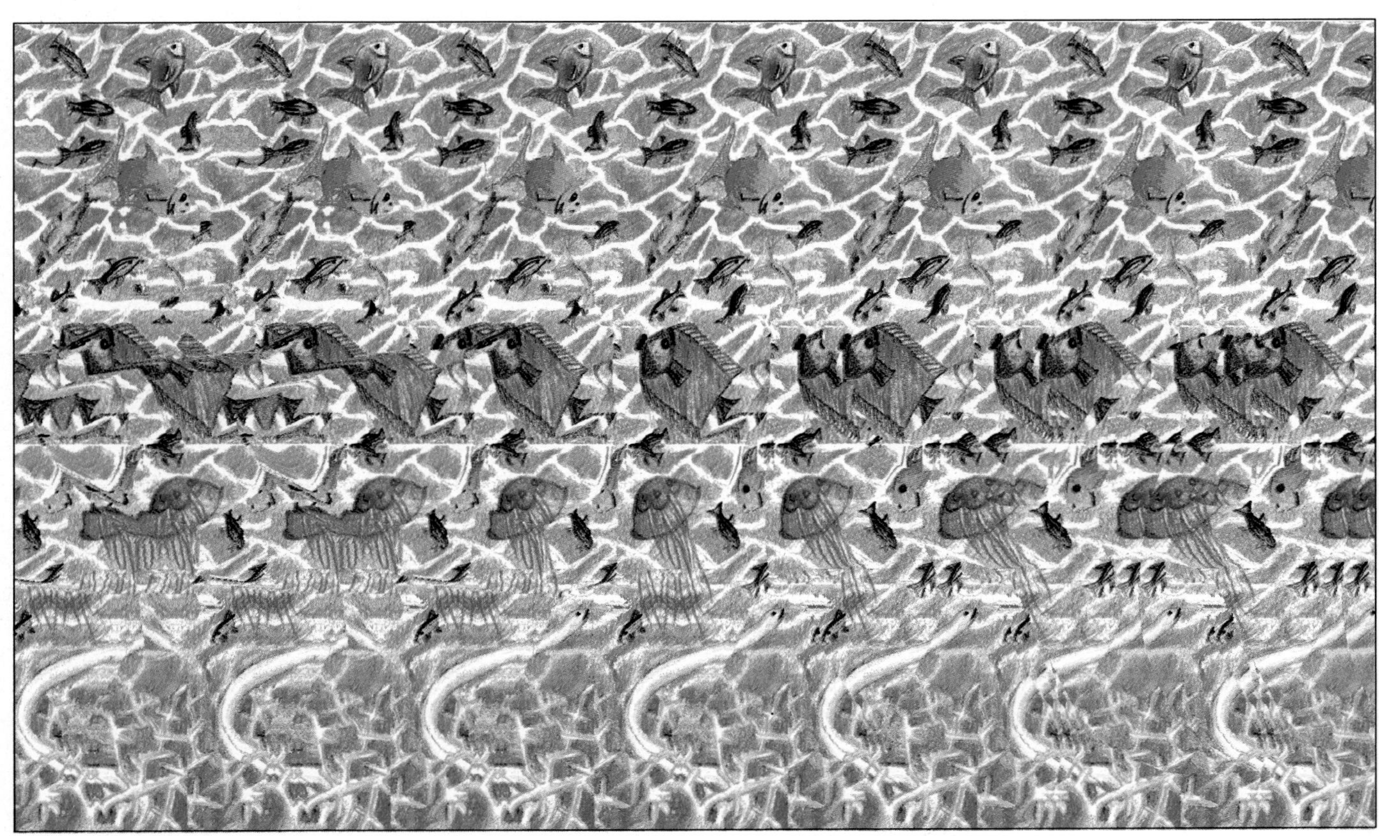

IMPROVE YOUR DEXTERITY

WHEN YOU ARE LOOKING for strategies to improve your mental capacity, juggling is unlikely to be the first one that springs to mind, yet as an activity, it has much to offer. To begin with, juggling can help you become more ambidextrous—able to coordinate the two sides of your body and the two sides of your brain. Just as most human beings tend to have one side of their brain that is dominant, (see "Left or Right?" pp. 20-21), the same is also true of our bodies. Balancing mind and body has been shown to be mutually beneficial—a balanced mind tends to create a balanced body, and a balanced body produces a balanced mind.

Juggling can also produce significant benefits in physical and mental fitness. It can help to tone muscles, sharpen reflexes, refine hand-eye coordination, enhance concentration, and improve balance and poise. Juggling is also known to be an excellent means of relieving stress by helping you to relax.

Get down to it

You will probably have seen highly skilled jugglers effortlessly tossing all kinds of objects in the air, from rings and skittles to more complex items, such as hats, canes, and even flaming torches. Beginners, however, should start with three small balls. Tennis balls, or something similar, will do, but the best balls are soft, specially made juggling balls that don't bounce. The only other major requirement is a largish space, preferably one with a high ceiling. Also, the fewer breakable items there are around the better—because you are certain to make your fair share of mistakes. Many people also find that background music can aid relaxation and concentration.

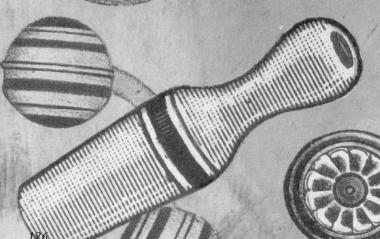

The three exercises shown below take you from simple first steps, like juggling with a single ball, to the standard three-ball technique. Try not to be put off when the early exercises don't allow you to perform gravity-defying feats immediately.

Juggling with one ball

In order to get used to the feel of the ball, take hold of it and move it around in your hand. Get used to the sensation of its weight and texture. Making sure that your posture is upright but relaxed, gently toss the ball up in the air and let it fall into the other hand. If the ball does not land in the required place, don't reach out to make a catch, just let it drop to the floor, and start again. Ideally, the ball should move in a smooth arc, the apex of which lies just slightly above your head. The crucial lesson of this exercise is

that you should never watch the flight path of the ball—you may find this is difficult to achieve at first. Try to concentrate on the top of the arc—looking straight ahead. You are sure to drop the occasional ball, since at this stage you should be more concerned with tossing them in the air correctly than with catching them. This exercise may look simple, but don't be deceived—mastering it is the secret of all juggling. As with any learning process, you should practice little and often, making sure you master each step before going further. You will probably find it most effective to restrict your practice to stints of 10 or 15 minutes, or until your arms begin to ache.

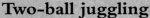

Two-ball juggling

Once you have mastered the first exercise, you are ready to introduce a second ball. Mastery of the two-ball movement comes in three stages. You might find the first exercise rather surprising in that the object is to let the balls drop!

1. Timing the throw. Many right-handed people find it very difficult to throw a ball accurately with the left hand—this is usually less of a problem for left-handed individuals, whose natural biases will already have been compromised, living in a predominantly right-handed world.

Take one ball in each hand. Using the same movement shown above, toss the ball in your right hand. As it reaches its highest point, toss the one in your left hand in the same way. This step is all about timing the toss, so don't attempt to catch either ball—let them fall to the floor. Practice this step until you can throw confidently with either hand.

2. Catching one ball. You are now ready to progress to the second stage—catching one of the balls. Repeat step 1, but this time try to catch the first ball in your left hand; you should still let the second ball fall to the floor. Once again, you shouldn't reach out to make the catch—if the ball doesn't fall close to your left hand, let it drop and start again.

3. Catching both balls. When you have mastered catching a single ball, repeat step 2, but this time try to catch both balls.

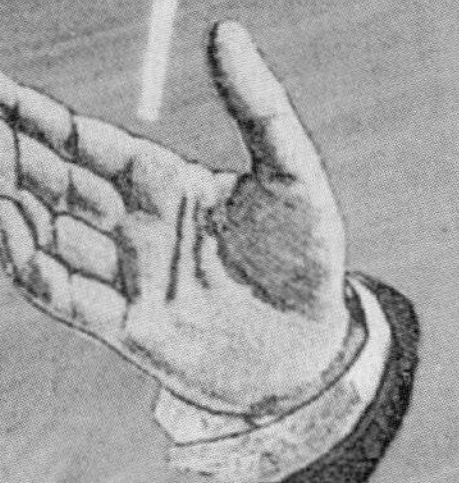

Three-ball juggling

When you can throw and catch two balls you are ready to move onto "real" juggling—manipulating three balls. The technique for three-ball juggling is simply an extension of the previous exercise.

1. Tossing three balls. Pick up your three balls. Place two in your right hand (think of them as balls 1 and 3), and one in your left hand (ball 2). Toss ball 1 from your right hand. As it reaches maximum height, toss ball 2 from your left hand. As that ball reaches its maximum height, toss ball 3 from your right hand. Let all three balls fall to the ground.

2. Catching one ball. Repeat step 1, this time catching ball 1, but letting balls 2 and 3 drop.

3. Catching two balls. Repeat step 2. This time you should attempt to catch balls 1 and 2, but let ball 3 fall to the ground.

4. Catching three balls. Repeat the previous step, this time catching all three balls. Balls 1 and 3 will now be in your left hand, and 2 in your right hand.

5. The cycle. You are now ready to perform a repeating cycle. Going back to the end of step 4, ball 1, having been caught by the left hand, is tossed back just as ball 3 reaches its apex. The sequence continues until a ball is dropped. If you think of the first cycle as being three tosses and three catches, the second cycle is effectively its mirror image—balls 1 and 3 are tossed back in the same way, but this time from the left hand. At any given time, one ball should be at its maximum height as a second is about to land, and a third ball is being launched into the air.

Remember, the more you practice the better you will become. Start off by aiming to complete two cycles—that's six tosses and six catches. When you have mastered that, then you will be entitled to call yourself a juggler!

JUGGLING TRICKS

When you've mastered the basic three-ball technique, there are many other variations that you can learn. Try your hand at the following:

Juggling two balls with one hand

Take the balls in your right hand. Toss the first ball in the air, making a slight clockwise sweep with the hand, creating an inward-pointing circular movement. You can vary the height of the throws, but you will probably find it easiest to start just above your head. When the first ball has reached its maximum height, toss the second ball up in a similar way. The key to mastering this technique is to keep your hand moving in a repeating circular rhythm, so that when the balls are tossed or land, they always do so at the same point in the sequence. To achieve this rhythm, always try to toss the balls to the same height, or as near as possible.

There are a number of alternative one-handed juggling techniques: You can reverse the hand movement of the method described above, making a counterclockwise sweeping motion, forming an

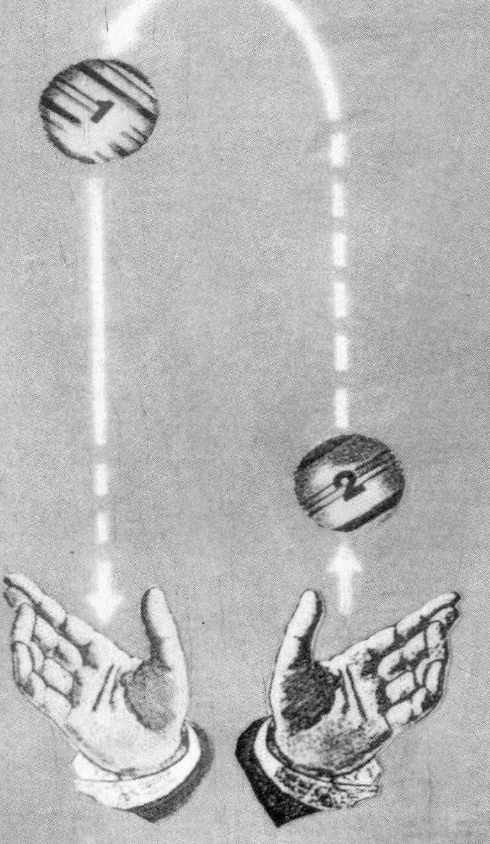

outward-pointing circle. Alternatively, you can simply toss the two balls straight up in the air in a smooth vertical movement.

Juggling two balls in the same hand can be quite physically demanding at first, because you may have to call upon muscles that get little regular use.

Four balls

The ultimate test of the one-handed technique is to perform the exercise above with both hands simultaneously. This requires great dexterity. To begin with, you need to master the two-ball technique using your weaker hand. Unless you can perform to the same standard with both hands, then juggling four balls will be extremely difficult.

While there are numerous possible variations, the main choice you have to make is how to synchronize your hands. You can create a rhythm where both hands perform identical movements, or you can use staggered timing, where the hands start moving at half-cycle gaps. This means that each hand alternates each step in turn.

The shower

Many people who have never been taught the basics of juggling immediately attempt a variation on "the shower," a maneuver that is very simple to perform, but extremely difficult to manage with any fluidity. With this variation, the right hand tosses a ball into the air, the left hand catches it and passes it back to the right hand, usually at waist-height. This passing process is called a "vamp," and the aim behind the "shower" is for the juggler to create a circle where balls sit in each hand while the third is at its peak height.

- Take two balls in the right hand (call them balls 1 and 3), and one in the left hand (ball 2).
- Toss ball 1 up in the air.
- When ball 1 reaches its apex, vamp ball 2 with the left hand, while simultaneously tossing ball 3 with the right hand. Catch ball 1 with the left hand.
- Repeat the sequence.
- As you get better at this and begin to feel more confident, you can try adding more balls.

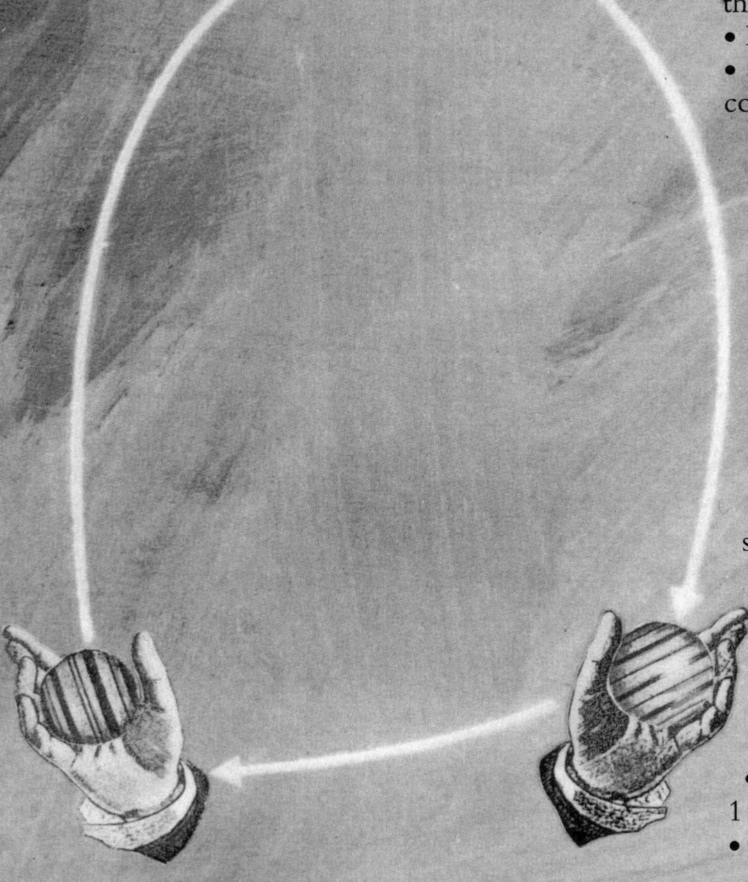

Juggling with a partner

It is also possible to juggle with another person. Beginners can use any of the techniques shown above or on the previous two pages; in every case, one person plays the role of each hand. The following example uses the three-hand juggling movement shown on pages 126–127.

Player A stands to the right of player B. Player A takes two balls (balls 1 and 3) in the right hand, but does not use his left hand at all. Player B takes one ball (ball 2) in the left hand, but, similarly, does not use the right hand.

- Player A tosses ball 1 in the air.
- When it reaches its maximum height, player B tosses ball 2 in the air, and simultaneously prepares to catch ball 1.
- When ball 2 reaches its apex, player A tosses ball 3 into the air, and prepares to catch ball 2.
- When ball 3 reaches its apex, player B tosses ball 1 back into the air, and prepares to catch ball 3.
- Repeat the sequence.

SOLUTIONS

Pages 18–19
How much do you remember?

0–5 This low score does not mean that there is no hope for your memory—it's more likely that your initial approach is wrong in some way. Perhaps you are too tense because you are simply trying too hard or, at the other extreme, you may not be concentrating well enough.

6–10 Not bad, but you need more practice.

11–15 You're doing pretty well, but make sure that you don't get bogged down with one approach—try to mix a reasonable level of concentration with scanning over information in a rapid, relaxed fashion.

16–20 You have excellent all-round recall, and are able to retain both visual and written information with ease. But there is always room to improve, so now try setting yourself even harder tests.

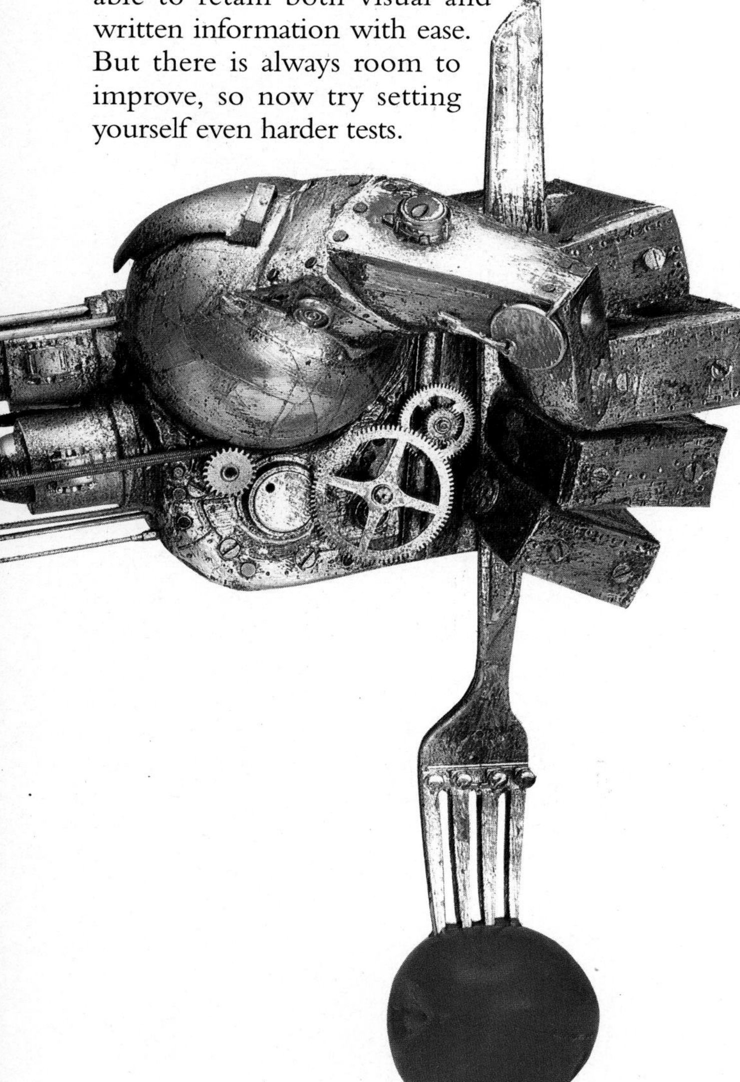

Pages 24–25
Are You Set in Your Ways?

The first three problems test a range of rational thinking methods. What sort of problems did you find easiest? It may be that you have something of a mental block that holds you back from solving math problems, and that you were happier with the questions about words, or those with images, even though they were designed to be the same standard.

So you may have been holding yourself back as a result of "subject-blindness" even before you got to the last two questions. If you had particular problems with the final section, then it could be that you are setting more general self-imposed limitations. This is hardly surprising, since we are all taught to think in a fairly rigid, structured way. The trick is not to get stuck permanently in this mind rut, but to know when to cast your mental net a little wider. Further information on how to do this appears in Chapter Two.

1. Number-crunching

a) The answer is 47. You can see that the numbers get larger, so this means that either adding or multiplying numbers will give you your answer. If you write out your calculations to this puzzle as follows, then you will see instantly how to discover the missing one:

5 7 9 14 19 24 26 28 33 38 43 45 47
+2 +2 +5 +5 +5 +2 +2 +5 +5 +5 +2 +2

b) The missing number is 24. This is worked out as follows:

12 6 24 12 48 24 96 48
÷2 **x4** ÷2 **x4** ÷2 **x4** ÷2

c) The answer is 144.5. All you need to do for this puzzle is to work with the decimal numbers, not the entire numbers. So: .5 + .25 – .25 = .5. There is only one option with .5.

d) 96. Add the numbers outside the bracket and divide the sum by 2.

2. The right word

a) The answer is elephant. This is the only word that doesn't end with an "e."

b) Frank

c) The odd one out is the lemon, because it is the only citrus fruit.

d) Fish : water. Tortoise : shell. Sheep : grass.

3. Seeing for yourself

a) The answer is c), because it is a different height to the other triangles.

b) What you have to do is move just three counters, as shown:

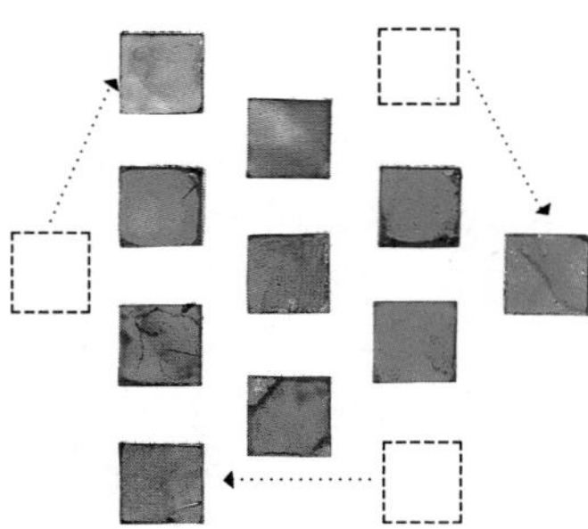

c) There are several different ways of arranging the six matches; this is probably the easiest.

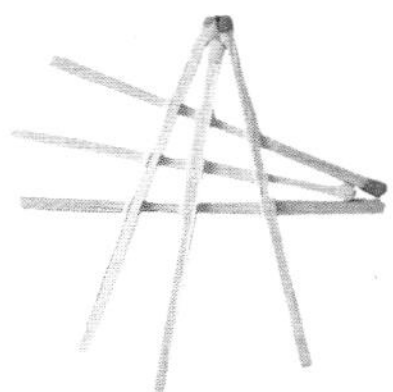

d) The total is 29. Opposite faces of a die add up to seven. Therefore, you can easily figure out what each die should read and add up the figures.

4. The final challenge

a) Empty the inner box and fix it to the wall with the tacks. Now stand the candles on the box.

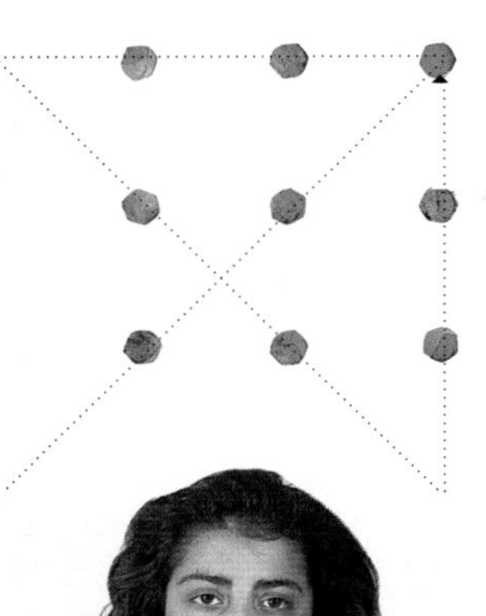

b) Here is one way in which you could solve the puzzle. There was nothing in the question to suggest that your lines couldn't go outside the dot pattern!

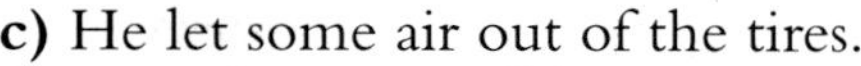

c) He let some air out of the tires.

d) In 36 hours it will be midnight.

What is your style?

Different people are used to thinking in different ways. If you got on fine with **1a)** and **1b)**, but came a little unstuck with **1c)**, then you are happy with simple logic, but find it hard to break out of it. **2a)** doesn't need a real wordsmith to solve it—people with a good visual sense will spot that one word has no "e" at the end. The other questions in **2** require you to rummage around your memory to get on the right thinking track. **3a)** would be picked up instantly by those with a feel for shape, size, and volume, while **3b)** and **3c)** tap into the ability to use a visual imagination to think several moves ahead. Section **4** calls for you to break out of set patterns, and think differently, using your initiative to solve the puzzle. For instance, why do you need to limit your lines to the boundaries of the shape made by the dots?

Pages 28-29
The string problem

Tie a small object such as a key to the end of one string. Now set that swinging backward and forward and you will be able to grab it while holding the second string in your other hand. You probably wasted a great deal of time thinking about how you could get to the string, which is totally impossible, without reformulating the problem in terms of how you could get the string to come to you. Alternatively, you may have come up with another, different solution—remember, there isn't always just one answer to a question.

Pages 34-35

As you can see from the picture below, it is very easy to draw false conclusions if you have no more than partial information.

Pages 40-41
What's Your Thinking Style?
Section 1

1. The circle is the odd one out—the other figures in the line are straight sided.
2. The correct answer is **a)**.
3. a) The balls move clockwise inside the circles.
4. The first pair of drawings is based on a square; inside the second square is a half square at the top and a whole, smaller, one at the bottom. Therefore, the second circle should have a semi-circle at the top, and a whole, smaller, circle at the bottom.

  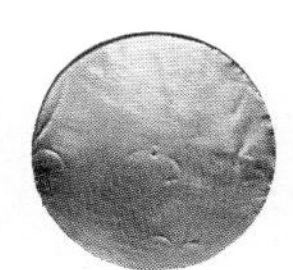 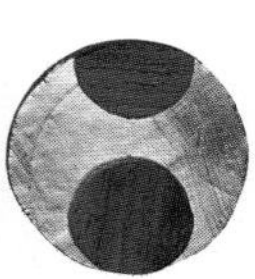

5. c) It is the only design where the central cut-out extends to the edges of its immediate surround.

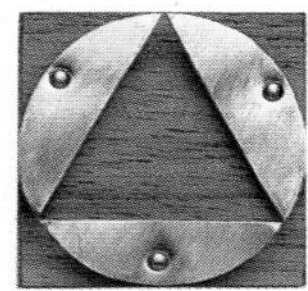

6. (c) Image rotated 180° counterclockwise.
7. (b) Each set of arrows should appear in every row.

8. The correct answer is **(d)**.

Section 2

1. 20
2. 17
3. 41p
4. 2
5. 16
6. 60 mph
7. 60
8. 39 percent of 429
9. 8
10. 79

Section 3

1. Seagull
2. Most dogs have nine legs (obviously this is false!)
3. Spade
4. Drive
5. Hockey stick
6. Barber
7. Sharks can never swim in the water (false)
8. Janet
9. Pace. The words pace and race rhyme, just like fish and dish. Also, the letter D moves two positions along the alphabet to F, as does P to R.
10. Swim

Pages 44-45
Do You Think Straight?
Tinseltown:

Answer: *The character of Pencil Trousers is an agent and Muscle Man is an actor.*
Neither an actor nor an agent can say "I'm an agent," because an actor would not lie and say he was an agent, and an agent would not tell the truth and admit he was an agent. Therefore, Bouffant could not have said she was an agent. But Pencil Trousers did lie when he told our heroine that Bouffant said she was an agent, which consequently must make him an agent. Muscle Man said that Pencil Trousers was lying when actually Pencil Trousers *was* lying. This means that Muscle Man told the truth, so he must be an actor. From the information given, it is impossible to know which of these categories Bouffant would fall into.

On to Rerun Pass:

Answer: *They are both directors.*
The short-order cook cannot be a lying agent, because as a result his wife would have to be an actor, and so his statement would have been true. For the same reason, the bartender cannot be an agent. Therefore, neither one of them could be an actor or an agent. They both have to be directors, and both of them are lying.

Stopover in San Smarto:
Answer: *The correct day of the week is Thursday.*
Mondays and Thursdays are the only days the producer can make the statement "I lied yesterday." This is so because on Monday he can lie, and say he lied on Sunday (one of his truth-telling days) and on Thursday (one of his truth-telling days) he can honestly say he lied on Wednesday (one of his lying days). Thursdays and Sundays are the only days the casting agent can say she lied yesterday. (On Thursday she will be lying when she says it, and on Sunday, she will be telling the truth.) The only day they can both say they lied yesterday is Thursday.

Pages 52-53
A tale of two cities

Since we know that the dolphin is worth 3 carrots, working out the values of the remaining currencies can be made easier by using a combination of the matrix and some simple mathematics. Start by subtracting the amounts of each column where a dolphin appears. The middle horizontal column: 10 (the total carrot value) - 3 (the value of the one dolphin) = 7 carrots (which represents one shell and one ships' wheel.)

Now move on to the bottom horizontal column: 9 (the total carrot value) - 3 (the value of the one dolphin) = 6 carrots (which represents one shell and one fish). Finally subtract the amounts of the middle vertical column: 12 (the total carrot value) - 3 (the value of the one dolphin) = 9 carrots (representing one fish and one ships' wheel).

Next, look at all three results together:
7 = a shell + a ships' wheel
6 = a shell + a fish
9 = a fish + a ships' wheel

By logical process of elimination we can work out that a shell is worth two carrots, a fish is worth four carrots, a dolphin three carrots and a ships' wheel equals five carrots. When translated into numbers, the matrix can be seen as follows:

4	4	2	= 10
2	5	3	= 10
2	3	4	= 9
= 8	= 12	= 9	

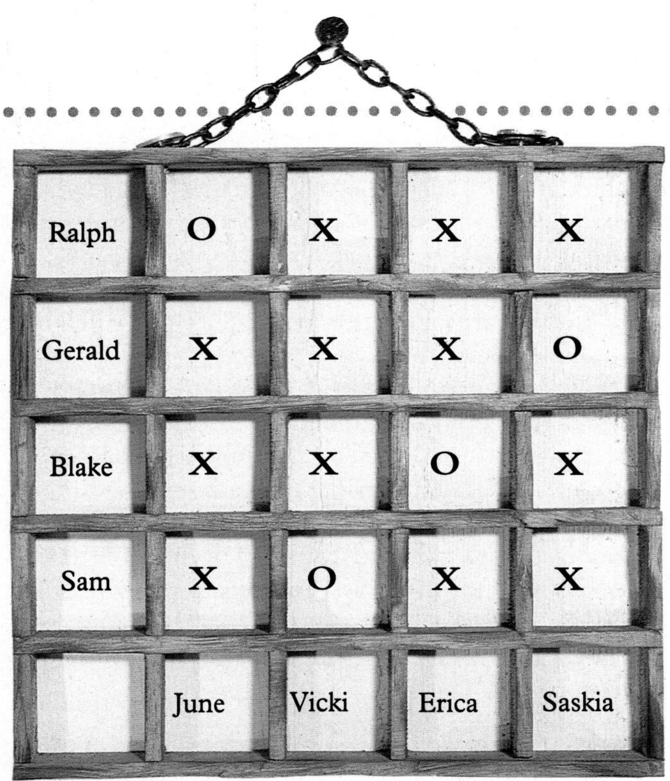

Ralph	O	X	X	X
Gerald	X	X	X	O
Blake	X	X	O	X
Sam	X	O	X	X
	June	Vicki	Erica	Saskia

Does love conquer all?

Above is a completed matrix that shows you who is married to whom. If an X appears in the box it means the man whose name appears at the left of that row and the woman whose name appears at the bottom of that column cannot be married. An O denotes a married couple.

Pages 64-67 Who Done It?

It appeared that this was a straightforward burglary. The guard testified that no one had entered and left, so the robbers must have come through the window. But the guard had assumed that Moody was working alone, when his murderer was already in the room. The glass from the smashed window lay outside the building, showing that it had been broken from the inside. The office door had also been locked from the inside, and Moody would have had no reason to lock it himself. This suggested to me that the culprit was one of his colleagues.

On the surface, three of them had motives. I discounted Lee Mullard, even though in many ways he was the most obvious suspect. He was nowhere near as tough as he looked, but turned out to be a church-going teetotaller. Never judge a book by its cover. Jennifer Arthur, whom Alison Thurston accused, certainly did not like Moody—she admitted it herself. And her drinking tied her with the bottle at the scene. But I've had experience with alcoholics before. They tend to be lonely people. I felt safe generalizing that Jennifer hung round the office late with a man she did not like only because she craved company. Her story about

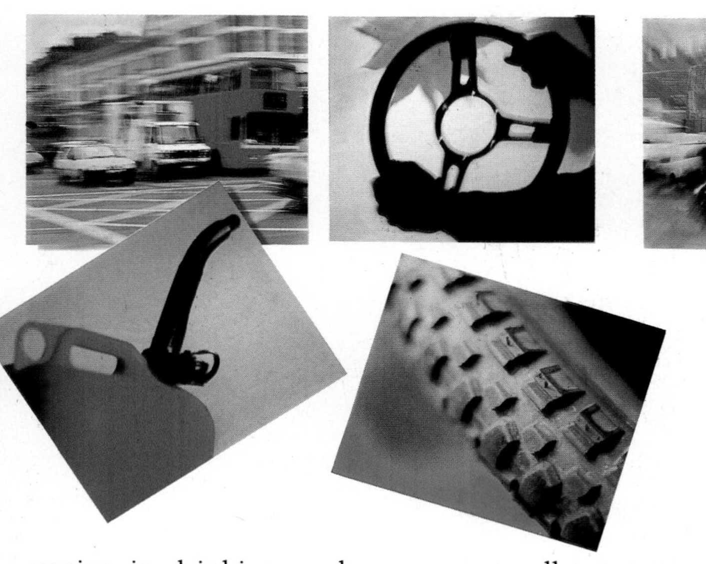

staying in drinking on her own rang all too true with me. Alison Thurston seemed a suspect on the strength of two things: her tempestuous affair with Moody and the fact that she called in late. But many lovers argue and very few come to blows, let alone murder. Besides, this didn't look like a crime of passion. The late arrival could just have been coincidence. Of all of them, she was the only one who showed any kind of emotion at the discovery that Moody was dead.

That left Alan Preston. Preston had a motive: he made it clear that he wanted Moody's job. He knew that the safe had been opened and that it seemed like a burglary. He was the only one to give me an alibi for the precise time that Moody died—everyone else told me what they were doing all evening, but his alibi began at 10:00. And, if he had seen the weather forecast as he claimed, then he would never have been surprised by the rain in the morning and come in without a raincoat. I figured that he had worked late with Moody, shot him, locked the door, faked the burglary, and smashed out the window to leave. Alan Preston was the murderer.

Pages 74-75
The car accident

The incidents took place in the following order:
2, **5**, **12**, **15**, **4**, **9**, **6**, **17**, **3**, **1**, **8**, **18**, **19**, **14**, **11**, **13**, **7**.
Superfluous information:
10, **16**, and **20**.

Salary raise

The important points are: **5**, **6**, **3**, **7** (the order will differ from person to person).
Points **4** and **9** may or may not be important, depending on the situation.
Points **1**, **2**, and **8** are irrelevant to your case.

Pages 84-85
Brain teasers

A penny saved is a penny earned.

Pages 86-87
Decipher these!

1. Can you understand this cryptogram? (Written backward and respaced.)
2. Mindpower (where A = 1, B = 2 and so on).
3. Well done you have worked this out (where A = 1, B = 2 and so on).
4. A miss is as good as a mile (where letters A = j, B = k and so on).
5. Beauty and the beast. (Where a symbol stands for each letter. The examples given provide all the letters except "l," "n" and "d"; you have to use intelligent guesswork to work these out.)
hand ➼ ✈ ✣ ▲
fatty ✔ ✈ ☞ ☞ ◆
table ☞ ✈ ✂ ★ ☎
dainty ▲ ✈ ✏ ✣ ☞ ◆
sane ❄ ✈ ✣ ☎
6. Improve the way you think (changed as above).

Find the missing letter

ex**e**rcis**e**s
lan**g**ua**ge**s
interpretat**i**o**n**
bibl**io**graphy
crypto**g**ram

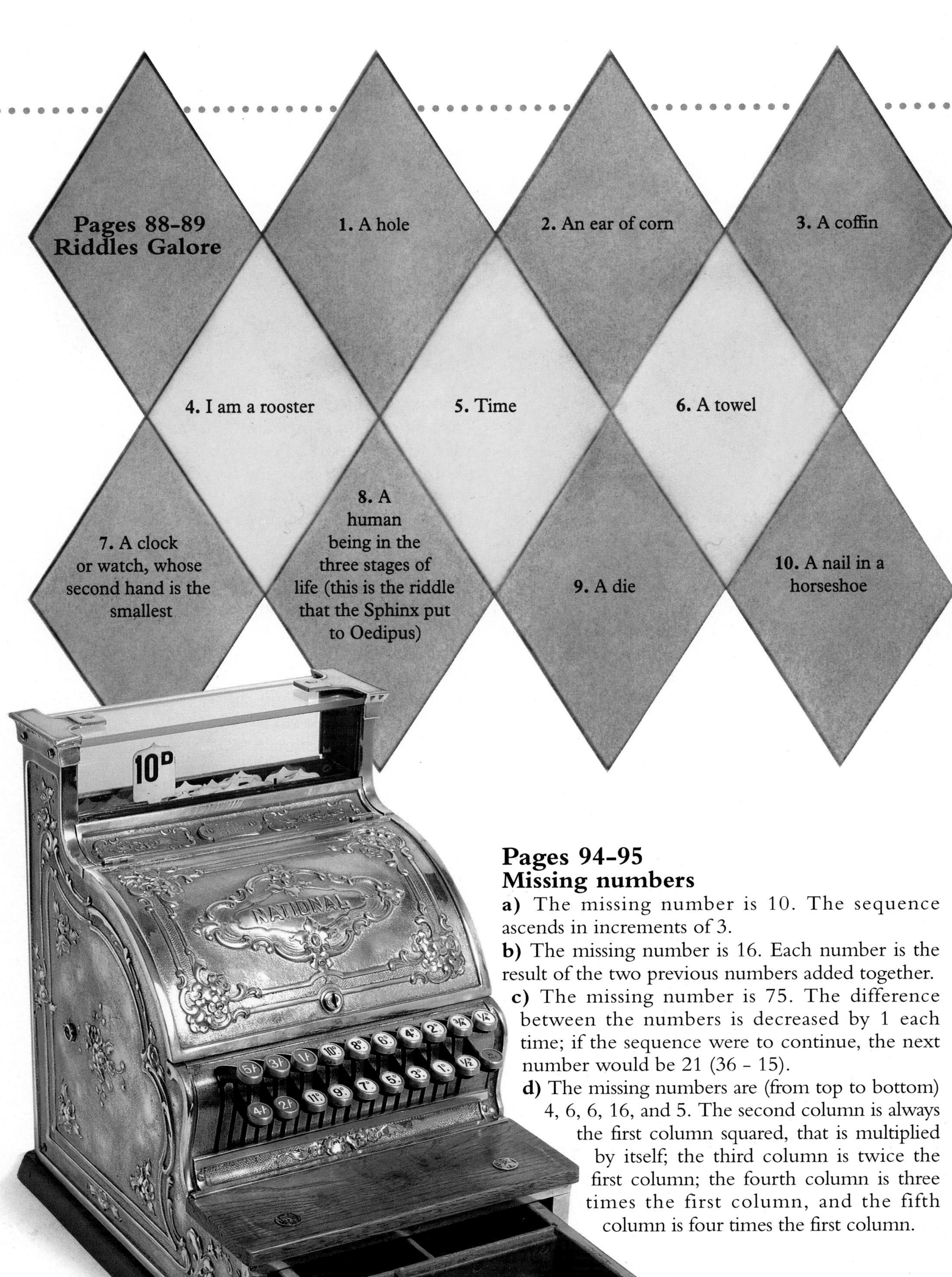

Pages 88-89 Riddles Galore

1. A hole

2. An ear of corn

3. A coffin

4. I am a rooster

5. Time

6. A towel

7. A clock or watch, whose second hand is the smallest

8. A human being in the three stages of life (this is the riddle that the Sphinx put to Oedipus)

9. A die

10. A nail in a horseshoe

Pages 94-95 Missing numbers

a) The missing number is 10. The sequence ascends in increments of 3.

b) The missing number is 16. Each number is the result of the two previous numbers added together.

c) The missing number is 75. The difference between the numbers is decreased by 1 each time; if the sequence were to continue, the next number would be 21 (36 - 15).

d) The missing numbers are (from top to bottom) 4, 6, 6, 16, and 5. The second column is always the first column squared, that is multiplied by itself; the third column is twice the first column; the fourth column is three times the first column, and the fifth column is four times the first column.

Making connections

a) The second column is half of the first; the third column has two subtracted from the second; the fourth column multiplies the third by two; the fifth column adds two to the fourth. The second row is incorrect as it doesn't obey these rules (the third number in the second row should be 2).

b) You can see that the lists are identical except that 8 appears in one list and 9 in the other. If you divide each string into pairs of numbers going from left to right, you will see that they make groups of 30 and 31. The difference between 28 and 29 should give you the answer: the first line shows the number of days in each month in a regular year, the second line shows the days in a leap year.

Complements

5	95
4	96
41	59
42	58
33	67
19	81
14	86
36	64
21	79
65	35
73	27
61	39
18	82
37	63
29	71
16	84

Logic

a) Yes, he should arrive at 12:00 pm. The journey is 100 miles (200 ÷ 2) and takes two hours (100 ÷ 50).

b) If they work for five hours Janet will fill 40 boxes (5 x 8), her son Mark will fill 20 (5 x 4), and her daughter Wendy will fill ten (5 x 2). Therefore the total is 70.

Probability

a) 1 ÷ 6 (0.167). There are six possible outcomes—the number six is one of them.

b) The likelihood of shaking a four is exactly the same as shaking a six, i.e. 1 ÷ 6.

c) The probability of shaking either a six or a four works out at 2 ÷ 6 (0.33).

d) Here you have three possibilities out of a possible six, i.e. 3 ÷ 6 (0.5).

Pages 96-97
Test yourself

1. 4424
2. 127
3. 10000
4. 1000111
5. 110011
6. 1000
7. They are the same.
8. 10212110

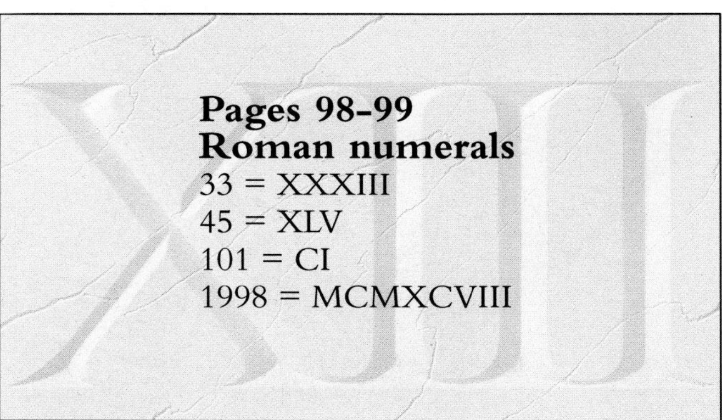

Pages 98-99
Roman numerals

33 = XXXIII
45 = XLV
101 = CI
1998 = MCMXCVIII

Pages 100-101
Sweet sales

1. False.
2. False, they sold the same amount.
3. True, it was 21.53 percent.
4. False, it was 11.28 percent.
5. True, Humbugs will sell 24,368; Smarties will sell 24,318.

Bill and Ted's money adventure

1. True.
2. False, it was $280.
3. True.
4. False, Bill has $60.
5. True.

The match makers

1. True.
2. False, it was $5,000,000.
3. True.
4. False, there is not enough information to tell.
5. True.

This problem was very complicated, and in order to help you figure out how it was done, look at the following table and notes:

	Total	U.S. sales	Exports	U.S. price	Exp. price
SureFire	120m	110m	10m	20c	30c
SuperStrike	40m	20m	20m	10c	15c
SuperFire	40m	20m	20m	n/a	n/a

- If 120m is 60 percent of all matches produced, then there were 200m matches produced in all.
- A quarter of this total is exported, so the rest of the matches (150m) are for the U.S.
- We can work out the share of the export market (SuperStrike and SuperFire have the same share, which is double that of SureFire).
- Working backwards, we can figure out U.S. sales and totals for all companies.
- We know how much SureFire and SuperStrike are paid for each box of matches, but we do not have enough information to work out the cost for Superfire matches.

Pages 104–105 Math or magic?

The only mental arithmetic required was the ability to work out how many letters were in the chosen name. It didn't matter how many cards were dealt as a result of the initial calculation. The card shown to the audience is dealt when the first letter of the chosen name is spoken. It therefore becomes the bottom card of the second pile. The first pile of cards is irrelevant. The second pile is placed on top, so however many letters were in the chosen name, the card shown to the audience must be that number of cards away from the top of the deck.

Naming the day

1. Sunday 2. Thursday 3. Monday 4. Sunday

Pages 106–107 Think and draw

If you followed the instructions correctly, your drawing should look like this:

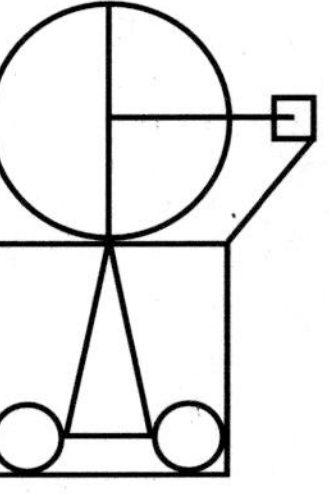

Pages 108-109
Where are you going?

If you followed the instructions correctly, you will end up at village entrance B.

Straight ahead

If you look closely at the picture, you will see quite a few potential hazards. For instance, a pedestrian is about to step in the road on the left. A dog next to him seems to be about to run out into the road. Further down, a motorcycle seems to be jutting into the road, and it is hard to tell whether the rider is leaving his bike, or going back to it. A small boy on the right of the windscreen has thrown his ball into the road: Is he going to dash out after it? Just past him, a man is carrying a ladder—which may swing round into the road. At the end of the road, there are road works that seem to block the way. In the mirror, you can see an ambulance coming up behind the car; drops of water on the windscreen indicate that it is starting to rain, and a leaf flying through the air may distract you momentarily. On another part of the car, the gauges show that the fuel tank is almost empty.

Pages 116-117
Pairs of tens

A. 4 5 1 9 3 6 4 2 2 8 4 5 9 8 2 7 3 8 4 9
B. 9 2 6 9 6 5 4 7 8 3 9 1 7 4 9 8 0 9 8 7
C. 4 7 9 4 6 3 5 1 4 6 8 0 7 9 8 3 1 9 8 1
D. 5 3 4 7 6 5 2 3 9 8 7 6 5 4 8 6 7 4 5 6
E. 9 6 7 4 5 3 7 6 7 4 6 2 8 4 6 3 4 3 5 5
F. 9 7 5 3 4 2 1 9 4 7 2 6 9 1 7 3 5 1 9 7
G. 1 0 6 8 5 4 3 8 6 7 4 9 7 8 5 7 6 4 3 6
H. 7 3 4 6 5 8 7 9 6 8 5 5 3 5 2 4 3 7 5 8

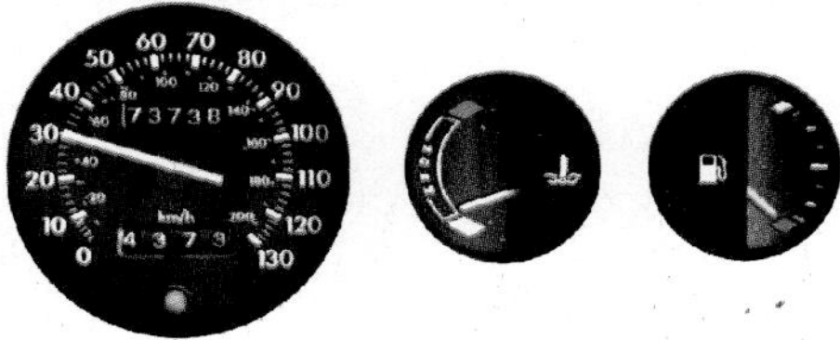

I. 9 9 9 2 9 1 1 9 5 7 6 3 4 2 9 9 8 0 6 7
J. 2 8 6 7 0 8 9 6 7 3 4 2 9 4 6 8 4 3 2 1

Adding triplets

A. 2 7 2 1 6 3 8 1 4 5 5 3 4 2 6 2 3 4 8 7
B. 2 5 4 3 1 4 2 3 5 4 6 3 4 2 4 6 5 3 2 4
C. 8 1 1 7 5 9 8 7 6 4 5 9 7 8 3 2 5 5 3 4
D. 8 7 5 6 3 9 8 6 7 1 9 1 1 7 9 8 7 8 2 4
E. 1 9 6 7 5 4 3 2 4 3 3 1 2 2 2 1 2 1 2 7

Checking nonsense

1. aitry hdter nshuf uergf jnvgc wertr otyug fgdsd khoty bgcfd sdfs
2. qtyre oiuhg nbvfg lmkye qpokj nyvte dtrwe nvygt nkbuy huftr qtire mtire
3. fkyre gusbh guygh jhgju guyhg gkhjg ghjgf gkhjg gfjhg bknjk bolorog molog

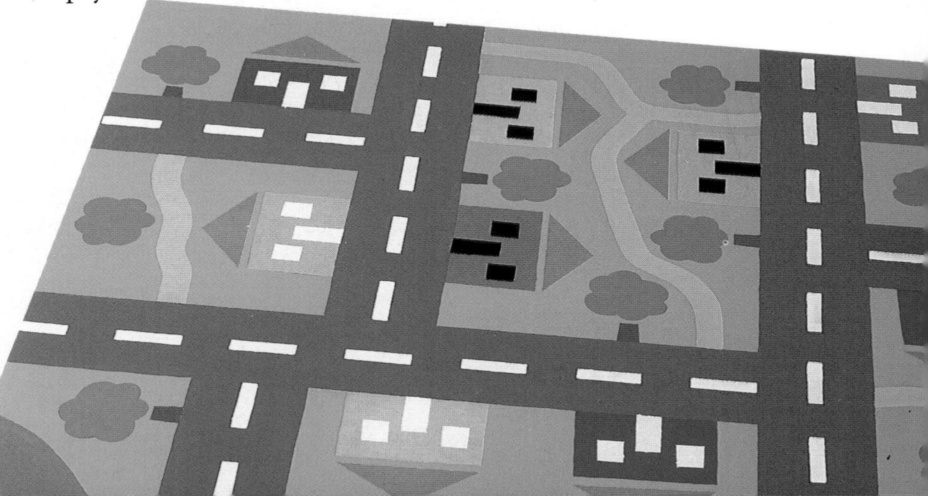

Symbols

A.

❄ u ✌ f ✌ ✌ r h h f ▼ g u ❄ ✌ i k o e t 6 r
❄ u ✌ y ✌ ❄ r h y f ▼ g V ❄ ❄ i k O e q 6 r

B.

❄ ✖ × ✖ ❄ ❄ ✖ × ✖ ❄ ✖ × ❄ ✖
❄ × × ❄ ❄ ❄ ✖ × ✖ ❄ × × × ❄

C.

d ❄ l ✱ ❄ i r y u 8 y ❄ ✱ y t ❄ e p 0 8 y
d ❄ P ✱ ❄ l r y u y 8 ❄ ❄ y t ✱ e p . 8 y

D.

❍ p o p ❏ p p o p p o o ❙ ❐ ❏ ❐ p o p
❍ p ❍ p ❏ p p ❍ p o o p ❙ ❐ ❐ ❏ o p p

Proof-reading

There are three sets of differences between A and B. Appear and appeal have been reversed; apparition has an extra "r."; approbation is omitted.

Pages 120–121
Turning the tables

1. How many days are there in a leap year?
2. Which delicacy is made from a sturgeon's eggs?
3. What is the capital city of Colombia?
4. Who was the first president of the U.S.?
5. On what date did World War I begin?
6. When was the "hundred years war" fought?
7. Who was the first man in space?
8. What is the numerical value of pi?
9. Who are the only Americans to have won motor racing's Formula One title?
10. Which three elements start the periodic table?
11. Name a star of the film *The Wizard of Oz.*
12. Which central European country shares a border with seven other countries?

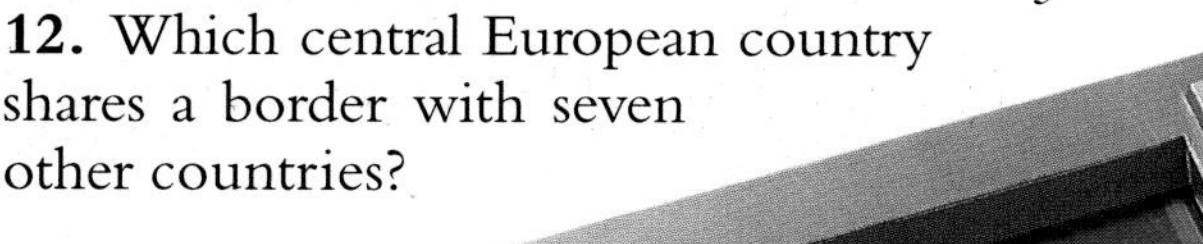

Double jeopardy

1. What are the colors of the Japanese flag? What are the two main categories of wine?
2. Which country is situated at the base of the Black Sea? Which bird is eaten at Christmas ?
3. What is the square root of 144? How many cakes are in a dozen?
4. On which animal did Walt Disney base his first and most famous character? What do you call a computer's manual control pad ?
5. What is 8 multiplied by 3? What are the two missing numbers in this sequence: 1_ _ 8 32?
6. In which Italian city would you find Michelangelo's statue of David? What was the first name of the nurse who gave her name to the Nightingale style of hospital ward?
7. Spades, hearts, and clubs are three card suits. What is the fourth? Which stones are often chosen as engagement rings?
8. What number Pennsylvania Avenue is the White House? Name the first year of the seventeenth century.
9. What is the name of the fruity, often

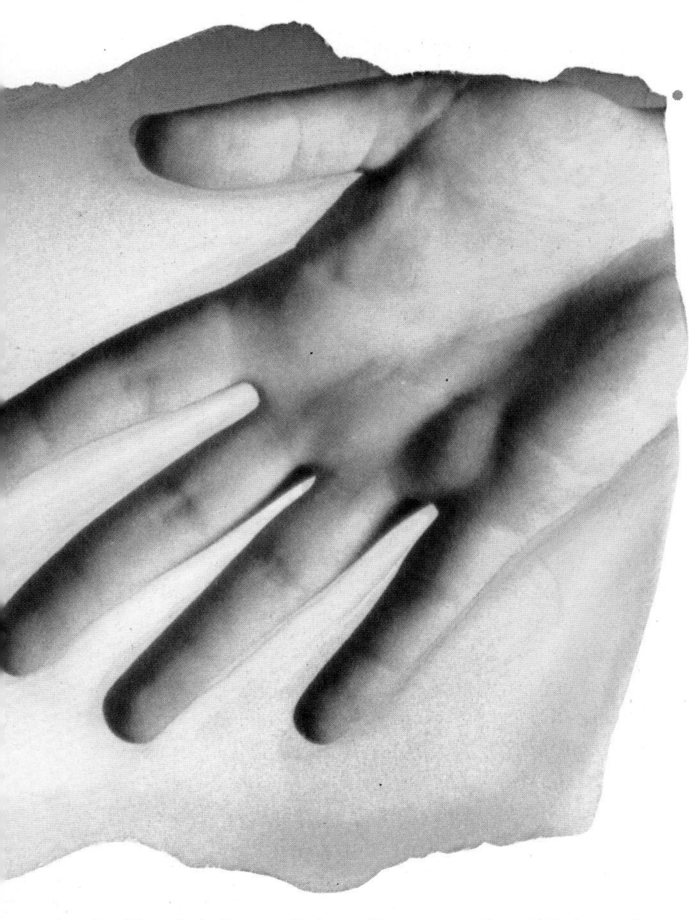

alcoholic drink traditionally served cold in a large bowl? Which puppet figure is the partner of Judy?
10. What are you as fit as? What is an informal name for a violin?
11. What do most vertebrates have in their jaws? Which part of a comb goes through your hair?
12. Marrons glacées are made from which nut? How do you describe brownish-red?
13. How many degrees are in a circle? What does 18 times 20 equal?
14. What lights cigarettes and fires? How do you describe clothes that look well together?
15. What do you call the structure that runs above valleys, roads, rivers and streams, rail lines etc? Which card game for four players was originally devised from whist? What is the upper part of the nose called? In music, what do you call a transitional passage between main themes? What is the name for a small partial denture?

Find the links

1. perfume and chocolates
2. a house and a tree
3. chalk and slate
4. a sofa and a book

Pages 122-123
Counting the squares

You can use the twelve matches to make four squares where each one shares two of its sides. Where is the fifth square? It is a large square that contains the four smaller squares.

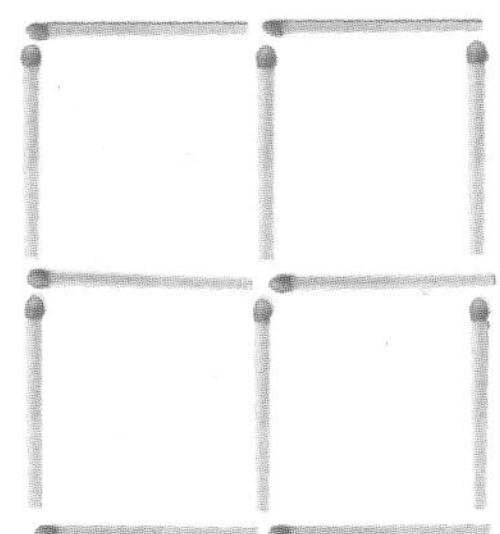

Increasing the triangles

This puzzle has quite a tricky solution. With one end of the new matches resting on each corner the other ends should rest together forming a three-dimensional pyramid shape.

Move the matches

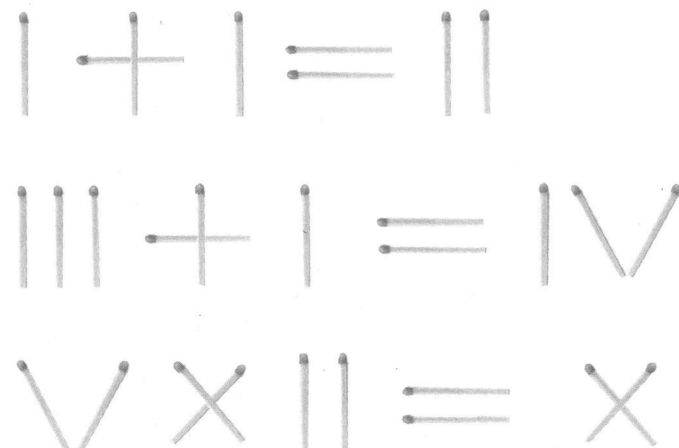

INDEX

Page numbers in *italics* refer to illustrations; page numbers in **bold** refer to self-assessment and problem-solving exercises.

BIBLIOGRAPHY

James L. Adams, *Conceptual Blockbusting: A Guide to Better Ideas;* Penguin Books, London, U.K., 1987

Franco Agostini and Nicola Alberto de Carlo, *Intelligence Games;* Simon & Schuster, New York, U.S., 1987

Ludy T. Benjamin, Jr., J. Roy Hopkins, Jack R. Nation, *Psychology;* Macmillan, New York, U.S., 1987

William Bernard and Jules Leopold, *Test Yourself: IQ;* Corgi, London, U.K., 1989

Colin Blakemore, *The Mind Machine;* BBC Books, London, U.K., 1988

Richard J. Block and Harold E. Yuker, *Can You Believe Your Eyes?;* Robson Books, London, U.K., 1991

Eamonn Butler and Madsen Pirie, *Boost Your IQ;* Pan Books, London, U.K., 1988

Tony Buzan, *Make the Most of Your Mind;* Pan Books, London, U.K., 1988

Tony Buzan with Barry Buzan, *The Mind Map Book;* BBC Books, London, U.K., 1995

Tony Buzan and Raymond Keene, *Buzan's Book of Genius and How to Unleash Your Own;* Stanley Paul, London, U.K., 1994

Philip Carter and Ken Russell, *The Mensa Puzzle Book 3*; Sphere Books Limited, London, U.K., 1991

John S. Dacey, *Fundamentals of Creative Thinking;* Lexington Books, Lexington MA, U.S., 1989

Shakuntala Devi, *Figuring;* Penguin Books, London, U.K., 1990

Hans Eysenck and Michael Eysenck, *Mindwatching;* Multimedia Books, London, U.K., 1989

Martin Gardner, *Mathematical Puzzles and Diversions;* Penguin Books, London, U.K., 1959

Daniel Goleman, *Emotional Intelligence;* Bloomsbury, London, U.K., 1995

James Greene and David Lewis, *Know Your Own Mind;* Penguin Books, London, U.K., 1983

Richard Gregory, *The Intelligent Eye;* Weidenfeld & Nicolson, London, U.K., 1977

Keith Harary and Pamela Weintraub, *Right Brain Learning in 30 Days;* The Aquarian Press, Harper Collins, London U.K., 1992

Marvin Levine, *Effective Problem Solving;* Prentice Hall, Englewood Cliffs, NJ, U.S., 1988

Derek Rowntree, *Learn How to Study;* Sphere Books Limited, London, U.K., 1991

Peter Russell, *The Brain Book;* Routledge, London, U.K., 1980

Oliver Sacks, *The Man Who Mistook His Wife for a Hat;* Picador, Pan Books, London, U.K., 1985

Marilyn vos Savant and Leonore Fleischer, *Brain Power;* Judy Piatkus, London, U.K., 1992

Paul Sloane, *Lateral Thinking Puzzles;* Sterling Publishing Company Inc., New York, NY, U.S., 1991

Raymond Smullyan, *What is the Name of This Book?;* Penguin Books, London, U.K., 1990

Norman Sullivan, *Test Your Intelligence;* Blandford Press, London, U.K., 1988

CREDITS

Illustrators
Altered States, Maria Beddoes, Melvyn Evans, Roy Flooks, Romy O'Driscoll, Emma Parker, Martin Ridgewell

Model Makers
Gail Armstrong, Mark Gaskin, Mark Jamieson, Justin Illusions, Mike Shephard

Photographers
Simon Battensby, David Glick, Paul Grant, Mark Hamilton, Neil Phillips, Jonny Thompson, Alex Wilson

Props suppliers
Sacha Shoes, The Hat Shop: Covent Garden

Picture sources
The publishers are grateful to the following individuals and picture libraries for permission to reproduce their photographs:

Bruce Coleman Ltd./*Kim Taylor* 106b; *Steven C. Kaufman* 107t; *John Shaw* 86bc, 87bl; *Uwe Walz* 107br
The National Gallery, London 18-19
Science Photo Library/*Biophoto Associates* 22-23
Every effort has been made to trace copyright holders. If there are any unintentional omissions, we would be pleased to insert appropriate acknowledgments in any subsequent editions of this publication.

c=center; t=top; b=bottom; r=right; l=left